Programmer's Python: Async
Threads, processes, asyncio & more

Something Completely Different

First Edition

Mike James

I/O Press
I Programmer Library

Mike James Programmer's Python Async:
                    Something Completely Different
1st Edition
ISBN Paperback: 978-1871962765
ISBN Hardback: 978-1871962772

First Printing, 2022
Revision 0

Published by IO Press   www.iopress.info
In association with I Programmer   www.i-programmer.info

The publisher recognizes and respects all marks used by companies and manufacturers as a means to distinguish their products. All brand names and product names mentioned in this book are trade marks or service marks of their respective companies and our omission of trade marks is not an attempt to infringe on the property of others.

Extracts from Programmer's Python are available as parts of an ongoing series on the I Programmer website, **www.i-programmer.info**.

To keep informed about forthcoming titles in the series visit the publisher's website, **www.iopress.info**. This is also where you will also find errata and any additional material. You can also provide feedback to help improve future editions.

Preface

Asynchronous programming is hard to get right, but it is well worth the trouble. An application that doesn't make use of async code is wasting a huge amount of the machine's potential. Whenever the program interacts with the outside world it has to wait for very, very, slow humans or even very slow communications to do something. If your code isn't asynchronous then it just waits for what might seem like years from the processor's point of view – remember a processor can execute around 10 million instructions in a second. If your program has to wait for even a fraction of a second that's thousands of instructions wasted.

The solution is to give the machine something else to do with all that free time and this is one of the objectives of creating asynchronous code. A second objective, that is often more important, is to make a program go faster by taking advantage of the multiple cores offered by a modern processor. In this case we need to divide our code into separate units of execution that can run on different cores. This is still asynchronous programming, but now more than one part of the program is running at the same time. This is usually called concurrency and it encounters the same problems as asynchronous programs running on a single core.

What this means is that the same set of programming skills help you write efficient correct programs when running on a single core or on multiple cores and this is what this book is all about.

Python has some remarkably good facilities for asynchronous programming. The latest is the asyncio module which is receiving a lot of attention at the moment, but the story started earlier. Python has modules that let you work with threads and processes in sophisticated ways and these are the foundation on which asyncio is built.

This book starts off looking at the basics of asynchronous programming and then looks at processes followed by threads. The reason for dealing with processes first, the opposite way to normal, is that Python has a problem with threads by way of the GIL, Global Interpreter Lock. This restricts Python programs to one thread at a time and it means that you cannot use threads to increase the speed of a program no matter how many cores your machine has. The same is not true of processes, which is why we'll begin there.

After threads we go on to consider the problems of asynchronous code – sharing data, communicating and race conditions – together with some of the solutions – locks, pools, managers, futures and so on. Then we move on to asyncio and the problem of working with single-threaded asynchronous code. For many applications the best solution will be asyncio integrated with thread and process pools and controlled using locks. In short, to make sense of the latest technology, asyncio, you need to master the earlier foundations on which it is built.

This is a fairly advanced book in the sense that you are expected to know basic Python. However, it tries to explain the ideas using the simplest examples possible and as long as you can write a Python program, and reason about what it does, you should have no problems.

This is not a cookbook and there are no complete examples of real programs – that's your assignment. In fact, the examples are deliberately as short as possible to make sure that you can see what the ideas are. Large, real-world examples aren't good at focusing the mind on how the smaller things work – this is an example of not being able to see the tree for the wood. The small examples are also not necessarily written in the best way or in "Pythonic" style. It is important that the examples show how things work rather than impress the reader with cleverness. If you really know Python then by all means improve the examples, but ask yourself, "is this really more understandable?"

The version of the language used is Python 3.10, but the descriptions hold for nearly all of Python 3 with minor additions as the version number increases. There is no reason to consider Python 2. Most of the techniques described would not work on Python 2 and it should now be consigned to history.

Thanks are due to my editors at I/O Press, Kay Ewbank and Sue Gee for their aggressive proof reading and attention to structure and detail. If you spot any errors that have been overlooked we'll be happy to correct them.

Mike James
September 2022

Table of Contents

Chapter 10
Subprocesses **179**

Chapter 11
Futures **193**

Chapter 12
Basic Asyncio **211**

Chapter 13
Using asyncio   **237**

Chapter 14
The Low-Level API   **267**

Appendix I
Python in Visual Studio Code   **285**

Chapter 1

A Lightning Tour of Python

Python is a phenomenon of modern programming. It is an interpreted, object-oriented language that started out being simple and easy to use, and has slowly collected such a wide range of sophisticated features that it is now the language of choice for almost every area of programming, from web development to data science, which are the two top spheres in which it is deployed, with all other conceivable uses met along the way. Python manages to be an all-embracing tool thanks not only to its core features but also to a huge number of libraries that have bolstered its inbuilt capabilities.

This book is the third to date in the "Programmer's Python, Something Completely Different" series, which aims to show how Python compares to and diverges from its competitor languages such as Java and C++. The first one, with the subtitle "Everything Is An Object" focuses on how Python handles object and the second, subtitled "Everything Is Data", which is perhaps a stretch, looks at Python's approach to data handling. Now we turn our attention to asynchronous and concurrent programming in Python and will discover, yet again, that it has a distinctive way of going about the problems that every programming language has to solve, justifying again the use of "Something Completely Different.

Before we consider async, this chapter is a brief introduction to Python for the beginning to intermediate programmer who is already comfortable with ideas such as variables, constants, loops and conditionals. It isn't a complete overview of Python, more a guide to the things that an experienced programmer coming from another language would notice, or would need to notice in order to make full use of Python's unique style. If you have read either of the other volumes in the series you can skip ahead to Chapter 2.

Python's Origins

Because of the way Python has risen to prominence over the past decade it comes as a bit of a shock that it dates from 1990 when it started as a hobby project by a single individual, Guido van Rossum. Many of the characteristics of Python and the overall direction of the project are down to decisions made by van Rossum who only relinquished the title of Benevolent Dictator For Life or BDFL for short, given to him by the Python community, in 2018. Python is now overseen by the Python Software Foundation, a non-profit corporation that aims to promote, protect, and advance the language and own its intellectual property rights and it is also officially sponsored by Microsoft where van Rossum now works as a Distinguished Engineer in the Developer Division with the stated aim of making Python better.

Python's logo depicts two intertwined snake-like heads, which suggests van Rossum named his language project after a huge serpent but the name is a tribute to Monty Python's Flying Circus, a classic satirical television series with a quirky sense of humor of which he was an enthusiastic fan at the time. If you've never encountered the TV show you may by puzzled by some of the pythonesque references used in the Python ecosystem, such as the IDE being called IDLE in tribute to cast member Eric Idle and my frequent use of "spam". And of course the reference to "Something Completely Different" was a catchphrase for the original TV series and was also the title of the first of its spin-off films.

Python went through a rough patch in its transition from Python 2, a very usable version of the language but which offered room for improvement, to Python 3 which uses a more logical and better organized approach to classes and objects, but at the expense of not being backward compatible. Python has now recovered from this divisive episode and its popularity has soared recently, partly because it offers something to programmers at every level.

As it is an easy language to get started with it is now widely encountered in educational settings. Although you can write Python as if it was a scripting language, it has added the full panoply of objected-oriented features and has a depth that you can make use of as your programming skills progress. It is also dynamically typed. This is something that pleases many open-minded programmers and infuriates the more strongly-typed – you can guess which side of the argument I'm on.

Python is an open-source language and you can use it and distribute it without charge, even for commercial use. You can download a version for Windows, Linux or Mac complete with a visual development environment, and the good news is that your Python application will often run irrespective of which platform you developed it on, i.e. Python is largely platform-independent. Python 3.10, released in October 2021, is the version of the language used under Windows in this book and Python 3.7 is the version used with Linux.

Basic Python

Now we have a lightning tour of Python for the beginning to intermediate programmer who is already familiar with some fundamental programming ideas. You can also consider it as a statement of the minimum you are expected to already know.

Python is an interpreted language and whatever you type in is obeyed at once. Python is dynamic and variables can be assigned to without any need to declare them first.

Built-in types include floating point, complex numbers, unlimited precision integers and strings.

Notice that already we are moving into some unusual areas – most languages don't bother providing complex numbers or integers with as many digits as you like. What is more, Python decides the type of variable needed according to what you try to store in it. For example:

```
x=2+3j
```

is complex, and:

```
x=123456578901234567891234567890123456789
```

is a long integer.

Notice that this is the first example that Python is not strongly typed. Every Python object has a type, but the variables that reference those objects do not in the sense that a variable can reference any object at any time.

The fundamental way of working with text in Python is to use a string. Strings work much like they used to in Basic in that there is no equivalent to a fundamental character type – if you want to work with a single character just use a one-character string. Strings are immutable – once defined they cannot be changed. When you appear to change a string you are in fact creating a new string from the old one.

Strings support concatenation and slicing. For example:

```
s = "Spam" + "Spam"
```

gives SpamSpam and:

```
s[i:j]
```

is a slice of the string from offset i up to but not including offset j. The first character of a string is at offset 0 so:

```
s[0,1]
```

gives S and:

```
s[0,2]
```

gives Sp and so on.

Slices are also a general feature of Python data types and the `slice` is a special object which can be used in your own custom data objects.

You can also use a repeat operator. For example:

```
s="Spam"
s=s*3
```

is three times the amount of `Spam`, i.e. `SpamSpamSpam`.

Data Structures

After discovering the basic types, the next thing you should be interested in are the data structures that are available.

In Python there are no arrays but this doesn't matter because it has the list which can be used as if it was a simple array. Lists are in general more powerful and easier to use than arrays. You can create a list simply by writing constants within square brackets. For example:

```
x = [1,2,3,4]
```

is a list of numbers. You can access list members using an index notation and you can insert and delete items in the same way. For example, if:

```
x = ["spam","brian","grail"]
```

then `x[0]` is `"spam"` and:

```
x[2] = "holy grail"
```

replaces the last item, `"grail"`, by `"holy grail"`.

Notice that, unlike other fundamental Python data types, the list is a mutable object, i.e. it can be changed without making a new copy. In this mode of use lists look like arrays but they can be used in more sophisticated ways. The real power of a list is that it can contain any type of data including any Python objects and other lists. The items within a list can be of mixed type.

Even more sophisticated is the dictionary, which you can think of as an associative array – that is, you can look things up using non-numeric keys. For example:

```
x = {"meat":"spam",0:"brian","holy":6}
```

Something appears to be missing here and `x[0]` is `"brian"` and `x["meat"]` is `"spam"`. Both keys and values can be strings or numeric values. The dictionary is in many ways the most important data structure in Python and is used internally to implement many sophisticated features.

Control Structures – Loops

Next we'll take a brief look at the control structures that are available in Python. As you would expect, there are `for` and `while` loops and a full block structured `if` statement. The only slight surprise is that the `for` loop enumerates through a list rather than numeric values. There is no C- or Java-style `for` loop with *start expression*, *end expression* and an increment. Instead, `for` loops iterate though the elements in a sequence. So, for example:

```
x = ["spam","brian","grail"]
for z in x:
    print(z)
```

steps through each value stored in the list x.

To create a more traditional numeric `for` loop, you can make use of the `range(n)` function which returns a list which runs from 0 to n-1. For example:

```
for z in range(10):
```

repeats for values of z from 0 to 9.

Note that Python tends towards the idea of iterating through collections rather than the classic enumeration loop that varies an index from a start to a final value using a specified step size. If you are more familiar with enumeration loops then you might find this a difficult change to get used to, but if you find you are writing things like:

```
for i in range(0,3):
    print(x[i])
```

then it is time to get used to using sequences and iterators.

A well as the `for` loop, Python offers the `while` loop:

```
while condition:
    code block
```

the code block is repeatedly executed as long as the condition is true. For example:

```
i = 0
while i < 10:
    print(i)
    i += 1
```

prints 0 to 9. The `while` loop is the only conditional loop that Python supports – there is no until loop, for example.

You can also use `break` to jump out of a loop and `continue` to bring the current iteration to an end and start the next. Note that they work with `for` and `while` loops.

For example:
```
i = 0
while i < 10:
    print(i)
    if i == 5:
        break
    i += 1
```

In this case the loop ends when i is 5 – you can think of the break as breaking out of the loop.

Another difference between Python and other languages is that else can be paired with for and while as well as being used in if statements, see later. When used in a loop the else is executed if the loop is exited normally, i.e. a break isn't used to end it. For example:
```
for z in x:
    if z == "brian":
        break
else:
    print("not found")
```

In this case the not found is only printed if the loop ends normally and the break isn't taken. The break causes a jump out of the loop, including the else clause. There has been much debate about how appropriate the use of the term "else" is in a loop – it might have been better named "then", but if you read it as "not-break" or something similar it makes more sense. Whatever you call it, it is useful.

Space Matters

The for loop is a compound statement header and this brings us to the subject of multi-line statements and blocks. You need to pay special attention here because this is something that Python does differently from most other languages.

Other languages use curly brackets { } to group instructions into a block that is treated as one entity. Often these entities are also indented in control structures to show where they start and end. For example in C/Java-like languages you would write something like:
```
for(z=0;z<10;z++){
    print("z=");
    print(z);
}
```

In this case the curly brackets indicate the repeated block of statements includes both print commands, i.e. they form the body of the loop. Notice that the statements in the body of the loop have been indented and this is good programming practice but not mandatory.

In Python indentation is used to identify the block and it isn't optional. For example, in:

```
x = ["spam","brian","grail"]
for z in x:
    print(z)
```

which produces:

```
spam
brian
grail
```

the body of the loop is just the print statement and the indent is supplied automatically when you enter the colon : and press return. In general, a colon at the end of an instruction means the start of an indented block.

It is important to realize that in Python layout can change the meaning of a program. If you manually enter indents using tabs or spaces then you determine the block that a statement belongs to. For example, if you type in:

```
for z in x:
print(z)
```

without an indent, then the result is an error message as the `for` loop doesn't have a block to execute and the `print(z)` is the next instruction. This is clearer to see in:

```
for z in x:
    print("z = ")
    print(z)
print("loop finished")
```

In this case the body of the loop consists of the first two print statements and the third is outside of the loop and is executed when the loop ends.

The use of indents to give meaning to code is one of Python's most controversial features.

To make things slightly more complicated you can write a single instruction following the colon. For example:

```
for z in x: print(z)
```

works perfectly.

Using indents has the advantage that good layout is essential to the working of the program. But if you need to change the structure of the program it can be more difficult than using curly brackets to mark blocks. For example, to include the for loop in another for loop you have to increase the indent of every line by one. This is made easier by the right tools, but the fact still remains that sometimes you have to take the global structure of a program's text into account.

This brings us to the universal question – do you create an indent using tabs or spaces? You might be surprised to discover that Python prefers spaces. You can use tabs if you want to, but you cannot mix using tabs and spaces even if they produce the same indent.

Conditionals and Indenting

Where indents often become an issue is in conditionals such as `if` statements. Consider, for example:

```python
if x == 1:
  print("block 1")
  y = 2
  if y == 2:
    print("block2")
  print ("block 1")
print("Ifs complete")
```

You can see that this way of entering blocks of code seems strange at first, but you very quickly get used to it and it has many advantages. Notice the use of the `if` statement and the symbol for a logical test of equality, `==`.

Which "if" an "else" statement pairs with is controlled by indenting, for example:

```python
if x == 1:
   print("block 1")
   y = 2
   if y == 2:
      print("block 2")
   else:
      print("block 3")
   print("block 1")
```

In this case the `else` pairs with the inner `if` statement. Now consider:

```python
if x == 1:
   print("block 1")
   y = 2
   if y == 2:
      print("block 2")
else:
   print("block 3")
   print("block 3")
```

In this snippet the `else` pairs with the outer `if` and both print statements are in the else block. Always remember that it is the number of indents that define which block a line belongs to. Any set of consecutive lines with the same indent forms a single block.

Python ifs also have the `elif` clause to test another condition. For example:

```python
if x == 0:
    print("case 0")
elif x == 1:
    print("case 1")
elif x == 2:
    print("case 2")
else:
    print("case other")
```

The first `elif` will only be executed if the first `if` is false, the second only if the first `elif` is false and so on. As soon as one of the if, elif or else clauses is true the if statement is complete.

Pattern Matching

Until recently Python didn't have a multi-case selection statement – usually called a select or a case in other languages. The introduction of pattern matching has made up for this deficiency and more. At its most basic pattern matching provides just a simple multi-case select:

```
myValue=4
match myValue:
    case 1:
        print("one")
    case 2:
        print("two")
    case 3:
        print("three")
    case _:
        print("more than three")
```

This selects the case that matches the current value of `myValue`. The final case uses _, a wildcard, to match any thing and so implement a default case.

Pattern matching can be much more complicated than this simple example. You can make use of unpacking to match the structure of data. For example:

```
myPoint=(0,2)

match myPoint:
    case (0,0):
        print("0  0")
    case (0,y):
        print(y)
```

The first case matches exactly the tuple `(0,0)` and the second matches all tuples that have zero as the first element. You can make use of any variables introduced in the pattern within the implementation of the case.

Everything Is An Object – References

At the very start of this introduction to Python I said that it was an object-oriented language and you might well be wondering when the objects are going to make their appearance. Well, in a sense they already have. Python calls just about everything an object and this reflects the way the Python system treats everything equally. This *"everything is an object"* idea has one very big consequence that you need to be aware of as early as possible. Whereas in most programming languages you store values in variables, in Python variables store references to objects. You can think of a reference as a pointer to an object which exists independently of the variable. For example, consider:

```
x = 1
y = x
y = 2
```

In this case you might read this as "store 1 in x, copy what is stored in x to y, now store 2 in y." At the end we have 1 in x and 2 in y.

Everything works as you would expect, but this is not what is happening. The correct interpretation is that x is set to reference the object 1, then y is set to reference the same object, and finally y is set to reference the new object 2.

In this case the result is the same as if the values had been stored in the variables, but this isn't always the case. Consider the same process, but now with a list:

```
x = [1,2,3]
y = x
y[0] = "spam"
```

If you read this as the list [1,2,3] is stored in x, then the contents of x are stored in y and the first element of the list in y is changed to "spam" then you have to conclude the x[0] is still 1. This is not the case as x is set to reference the object [1,2,3], then y is set to reference the same object, i.e. no copy is made, and finally y[0] is changed to "spam".

I hope now you can see that the first element of the object that x and y reference has been changed and that this means that in Python variables hold references to objects. This is also a motivation for the fact that Python variables are not **typed.**

In other languages variables are typed in the sense that they can only reference objects of a specific type or their derived types. For example, once a variable has been created to reference a list it can only be used to reference a list or a subclass of list. In Python a variable is a reference to an object and the object may have a type, but the variable certainly doesn't. It can be used to reference any object of any type at any time. Also notice that in Python all variables are local to the object that they are declared in.

Functions

In Python a function is a valid example of an object. To define a function you use the def command, complete with parameters if needed, and a return statement to return a value, for example:

```
def add(x,y):
    return x+y
print(add(2,3))
```

As always, the body of the function is determined by the indent. Notice that parameters are untyped and this is both a convenience and a possible problem. For example, with the above definition of add, the following works perfectly:

```
print(add("lumber","jack"))
```

and displays:

```
lumberjack
```

If you find this strange and worrying then it is perhaps because you have been in the grip of strongly-typed languages for too long! There are many advantages of strong typing but there are also many complexities that only arise because of it.

When you write the add function you are thinking about "adding" together two objects and it is up to the system to work out what you mean by "+" for any two objects you care to pass.

Adding works for lists as well, so:

```
print(add([1,2],[3,4]))
```
prints:
```
[1, 2, 3, 4]
```

With untyped parameters you can pass anything you like to a function and what it does with the objects you pass depends on what they are. If you know about generics in other languages you can express this as "in Python, every function is generic".

One more complication is that we need to know the scope of a function or a variable definition. The basic idea is that a name belongs to the name space that is appropriate to where it is first used and this can be local, global or built-in. So if a variable's first use is in a function then it is local to that function. More generally, a variable first used in an object is local to that object as functions are just special cases of objects. Variables first used in a block are local to that block and you cannot use a variable's value until it has been initialized.

In Python variables are local unless you declare them to be global. If you want to make a variable name global from within a function or object you have to declare it as such using global, but this is generally not a good idea. Notice that this is the opposite of the way most other languages handle the problem.

Arguments are also influenced by 'the everything is an object' idea and the fact that variables hold references and not values. What this means is that when you pass something in a parameter it is a reference to an object that is passed. In short, all parameters are passed by value, but what is passed is a reference to an object. This is usually called pass by reference. This results in a behavior which many programmers will regard as strange. For example, suppose you write:

```
def test(a):
    a = 1
```

then when you use this function with a call like:

```
x = 2
test(x)
print(x)
```

you will see 2 printed. The value of x is unchanged by the assignment within the function.

Ah, you might say, this is pass by value, but this isn't accurate. What is happening is that when the function is called, the local variable a is set to "point" to, or to reference, the same object that x is "pointing" at. Thus, when a is accessed it returns 2. When the 1 is assigned to the variable a it is treated as an object and a is simply set to point or reference the new object i.e. 1. The original variable is still pointing at, or referencing, the original object, i.e. "x" is still pointing at the object 2.

When you work with simple objects like numbers then this does look like pass by value, but as soon as you pass a more complex object it becomes clear that it is passing a reference by value or is more properly a **pass by object reference.** If you try:

```
def test(a):
    a[0]= "spam"
```

and use:

```
x=[1,2,3]
test(x)
print(x)
```

you will discover that the list in the calling program has its first item changed to "spam". The reason for the difference is that you have changed part of the object that both variables are pointing at. There are also facilities for passing arguments by name, variable numbers of parameters and parameter defaults.

Python also has a lambda expression facility, which allows any expression to be treated essentially as a data object and passed as a parameter to another function. The Python lambda is more like an anonymous function object than a true lambda.

Objects and Classes

Python implements objects using the traditional mechanism of defining a class and then creating instances of the class. However, it isn't quite the tradition that you find in C++, Java or C#. It is more like the way objects work in JavaScript. The idea of a class in Python is once again influenced by the *'everything is an object'* idea. Yes, a class is just an object, but with some special features that enable you to use it to create a clone of the object – an instance.

You can define a class complete with instance properties and methods and use it by simply calling the class as if it was a function. In Python properties are generally called attributes – property is reserved for something slightly more advanced which roughly corresponds to an attribute with get/set accessors.

One minor complication is that you have to use an additional variable, usually chosen to be self, as a reference to the particular instance of the class within attribute and method declarations. You also need to create instance attributes within a function called __init__ which has a double underscore on each side.

Functions with two prefixed and two trailing underscores are an essential part of Python and are usually called "magic" or "dunder", from double underscore, methods. Far from being strange or magic, they are methods that the system uses or expects to be used for various standard purposes. In general, you should not define your own methods with double underscores unless you have a very good reason. What you can do is provide your own implementations of the magic methods that the system uses.

If this all seems like an arbitrary set of rules then the good news is that it is very logical and understanding the deeper way it all works is well worth the effort. Consider, for example:

```
class point:
    def __init__(self):
        self.position=(0,0)
    def setpos(self,x,y):
        self.position=(x,y)
    def display(self):
        print(self.position)
```

This defines a class called point which has one instance attribute, position, and two instance methods, setpos and display.

Each of these has self as its first parameter. This is automatically set to reference the instance which is calling the method. You can now create an instance of the class using:

```
a=point()
```

Notice that the brackets are all-important – without them you create a variable referencing the class, not an instance of the class. This is a big difference between Python and other object-oriented languages – the class is actually an object that is created on an almost equal footing with its instances.

You can refer to methods or attributes using the usual dot a.*method*() notation. For example:

```
a.setpos(1,2)
```

and:

```
a.display()
```

When you call a method such as:

```
a.setpos(1,2)
```

the self parameter is automatically set to the instance, a in this case. Thus the method call is transformed into:

```
setpos(a,1,2)
```

In fact, all method calls are translated from:

instance.*method*(*parameters*)

to:

class.*method*(*instance*,*parameters*)

and the first parameter is the self you include in every method definition.

You can even call instance methods directly using this form. For example:

```
point.setpos(x,1,2)
```

is entirely equivalent to:

```
x.setpos(1,2)
```

It is, of course, this trick that Python uses to implement object instances. Any method call on an instance is converted into a call to the function hosted by the corresponding class object.

The __init__ method is the object's initializer and if you supply parameters for it it you can define what looks like a non-default constructor – the parameters you use correspond to those that __init__ needs. For example, if you include:

```
def __init(self,x=0,y=0):
  self.position=(x,y)
```

in the definition of point you can now initialize it using:

```
x = point(1,2)
```

and if you don't specify a value then a (0,0) point is constructed by default. There is also a destructor method.

Inheritance

You might imagine that an interpreted system couldn't handle inheritance at all well. However, Python can and it is all done interactively. If you use a class definition of the form:

```
class name(superclass):
```

then the new class inherits all of the methods defined in *superclass*. For example:

```
class complexpoint(point)
```

defines a new class called `complexpoint` and inherits all of the methods defined in `point`. You can, of course, define new methods and override existing methods. If a method cannot be found in the class's definition, the superclass's definition is searched. If the method cannot be found in the superclass then any super-superclass that might exist is searched and so on until a definition is found or an error is generated. You can also arrange to call the inherited method directly using the class name as the first parameter of the call, i.e. explicitly setting the `self` parameter.

Finally, it is worth knowing that operator overloading is supported using a range of standard method names. For example, if you want to define an addition for `point` then you need the following method:

```
def __add__(self,other):
    self.ans = (self.pos[0]+other.pos[0],self.pos[1]+other.pos[1])
    return self.ans
```

Notice that this is another magic method. Now you can write:

```
z = x+y
```

where x and y are point objects. Notice that z isn't a point object but a tuple and this can be a problem if you want to use the overloaded plus operator a second time.

In general, operators should return results of the same type. If you want to return a point object you have to use:

```
ans=point()
ans.setpos(self.pos[0]+other.pos[0],self.pos[1]+other.pos[1])
return ans
```

Overriding operators might not seem like something you want to do, but after using Python for a while I can assure you that you will.

Main and Modules

When you write a program any commands in the script are obeyed and any output goes to the terminal window that you have been using to try out Python. Although it isn't necessary, it is fairly common to give the script a main function, i.e. a function which is executed first, using the single line:

```
if __name__ == "__main__":
    main()
```

When Python runs a module it sets __name__ to main and this can be used to select the function to start the script off. Scripts can be stored and used as modules within other scripts. To load a script as a module you use the command:

```
import modulename
```

In this case the script is loaded but __name__ isn't set to "__main__" and this can be used to suppress the startup routine in the script.

If you only want to import a subset of the names in a module you can use the:

```
from module import name
```

command instead and make use of wildcard characters to express patterns that the name has to match.

Using predefined modules is one of the strong points of Python and you will find that using import is one of the quickest ways to build a program.

IDEs for Python

You can get started with Python using IDLE or the command line, but to be productive you need an IDE – Integrated Development Environment. An IDE makes it easy to enter and edit programs. The editor usually offers syntax coloration and completion of possible keywords and variables. You can run a program with a single click and create projects which have multiple files. More importantly, an IDE generally has a visual debugging option where you can run your program and have it stop at breakpoints so you can examine what it stored in variables.

If you haven't already used an IDE then once you get used to it the increase in productivity will come as a surprise. There are many who will advise you that you need to work using the command line and use a simple editor, Emacs or Vim say, but this is a hard way to work. You should know how to use these basic tools to craft a program, but using them for everyday programming is like trying to code without a computer. Smart programmers make use of every tool they can get and an IDE makes things easy.

Picking an IDE is a matter of personal taste. My own choice is Visual Code Studio, VS Code. While it isn't as powerful as Microsoft's subscription-based Visual Studio, which also has strong support for Python, VS Code is free and supports Python and several other languages. It is an active open source project that delivers frequent improvements. You can find out more about using VS Code with Python in Appendix I.

For a Python-specific IDE you could opt for JetBrains Pycharm, which is available in both an open source community edition and a professional paid-for edition. If you already use Eclipse, then the PyDev plugin is worth considering. Another choice is Jupyter, which is particularly popular in data science. It provides the ability to interweave Python code, graphics and text to create an interactive notebook, but it is probably not a good place to start for general-purpose computing.

Pythonic – The Meta Philosophy

There are many programming philosophies inside the Python community – object-oriented, aspect-oriented, functional programming and so on – and you can't expect everyone to agree on the best way to do something. However, as well as general approaches to programming, there is also a meta philosophy that is attached to Python, which is both good and bad. The idea is often expressed as *code should be "Pythonic"*.

Pythonic is usually taken to mean writing code that works in a way that is idiomatic Python, that is, using the facilities in Python and not writing Python as if it was Java or C++ or any other language. This is a good idea, but often it is used as a criticism - *"Your code may work but it isn't very Pythonic"* or *"Your code is unPythonic"*. When leveled against a beginner, or a new convert from another language, this can seem like a statement that the newbie isn't *"one of us"*. If you are going to criticize a Python newbie's code, don't. Instead point out how Python has a better way and leave the "unPythonic" unspoken.

There are occasionally good reasons for writing code which looks unPythonic – clarity is in the eye of the beholder – and good Pythonic code is never compact obfuscated code.

There is also a well-known set of principles expounded in "The Zen of Python". You can see this by typing at the command line:

```
import this
```

It starts:

```
Beautiful is better than ugly.
Explicit is better than implicit.
Simple is better than complex.
Complex is better than complicated.
Flat is better than nested.
...
```

All wonderful statements, but they are often used to justify some approach or other without really thinking things through. One programmer's beautiful is sometimes another's ugly. What is simple depends on what you know – I think tensor calculus is easy, but I have to admit that I seem to be in a minority. It is important not to justify a particular approach by simply quoting one of the Zen sayings. You have to take the whole thing into account and make an informed judgment, which is a very Zen thing to do.

There is also a broader philosophy that Python is designed never to be "surprising". That is, if you can guess how it should work then that is how it should work. Things should work as a reasonable programmer would expect them to. This is a good philosophy and one that has guided much Python development, especially the move from Python 2 to 3. However, "surprising" is another relative term. When you start to dig into Python, things become increasingly more sophisticated and it is arguable that many a reasonable programmer would not have an expectation of what might or might not be surprising. The Zen of Python sums it up a related principle nicely:

```
There should be one – and preferably only one
                      --obvious way to do it.
Although that way may not be obvious at first unless you're Dutch.
```

When working in Python it is common to implement something using a set of code constructs and then step back and look at it and realize that you could simplify it by using some Python feature that you forgo when working on the initial code. This is great and it often results in code that works better and is more Pythonic. The danger is that you will Pythonic-ise your code into something dense and unreadable. Come back later and your mind will no longer be attuned to the problem or the expression of the solution. It won't have had the benefit of the easy steps through which your solution evolved. Keep in mind at all times that the objective isn't to be Pythonic; it is to write clear code.

In the examples in this book I have tried not to reduce them to the smallest possible statement. Indeed, some of them are broken into steps that would often be rolled up into a single, but less obvious, operation. Pythonic code is often not the best for showing how things work. In particular, I have chosen to import modules so that references to the resources they contain have to be written as qualified names.

For example, if `myModule` contains `myClass`:

`import myModule`

means you have to write:

`myModule.myClass`

The reason for this verbose choice is precisely to make clear which objects in an example have come from the module. Similarly I tried to use only one new idea per example and to not use Python idioms that make it more difficult to see the new element in the example.

Where Next

This lightning tour of Python has attempted to give you the flavor of the language and point out the features that confuse the programmer used to other object-oriented languages like C or Java. Now we can move on to the topic of this book – asynchronous code and how to create it.

Summary

- Python initially looks like other languages you might know, but this is deceptive. Python often takes a unique and idiosyncratic approach.

- In Python everything is an object. Objects do carry an indication of type, but variables are untyped. Variables store references to objects, not values.

- Integers in Python have an unlimited number of digits. Strings are immutable and support slicing, like many other Python collection objects.

- There is a range of sophisticated data types. The list does the work of the array in other languages. The dictionary is essentially an associative array. The tuple is a lightweight immutable list.

- Python is different from other languages in that code indentation alters the meaning. A block of code consists of a set of consecutive statements at the same indent level.

- The `for` loop is a general iteration loop, i.e. it iterates over a collection of objects rather than a numerical start, stop, step range. To construct a numeric loop you would use the `range()` function. The only other loop provided is `while`.

- Conditionals `if`, `elif` and `else` are used to structure complex conditions.

- Pattern matching is provided for the most complex conditional structures.

- Functions are objects but beginners can ignore this and write ad-hoc scripts as if they were functions in any other language. Classes are objects, but beginners can also ignore this and pretend they are using a classical class-based language. Objects have attributes, some of which can be functions. Inheritance works much like other languages, but class objects are directly involved in retrieving attributes. Modules are how Python code is packaged into larger units.

- Select a full IDE to make your work easier. Do not believe the assertions that the command line and a "simple" editor is best – programmers need all the help they can get. Programming is hard enough without making it harder by refusing what help there is.

- Never use "unPythonic" as term of abuse and understand that The Zen of Python is always in the eye of the beholder. Good Python is a clear expression of what the code is doing.

Chapter 2

Asynchronous Explained

The term asynchronous or async is often used without realizing what a wide range of situations it covers. Asynchronous code is a very general term and it is important to identify the different possibilities in order to understand why there are so many ways of approaching the problem. If you think that there is only one good approach to asynchronous code then the chances are you have only imagined a small range of possible interpretations.

So before we find out about the different ways that Python provides facilities for async code we need to find out the different ways that it occurs and is present in modern systems.

The ideas in this chapter are introduced in a very general way and the focus is on the concepts rather than their implementation. In later chapters we will encounter many of the same ideas, but as implemented in Python.

If you just want to "get on with the code" jump to the next chapter as this one describes the general principles. However, knowing the general principles will help you understand why the modules that you will encounter later are as they are and why you might need something slightly different to solve your problem.

It also works the other way round. If you find the following discussion too abstract then you will benefit from finding out how Python does the job and then returning to the general principles.

A Single Thread

For simplicity we start off with the idea that there is a single processor within the machine running our programs. This used to be the norm, but today most processor chips contain multiple "cores" each one capable of executing code. It is still easier to ignore these multiple cores when writing programs and it is only later do you start to wonder if all this power can be used to make your programs work better.

When you first start programming you have to absorb the idea that what you are doing is writing instructions that are obeyed by the computer one after another – this is the default "flow of control". You can modify this flow of control by writing if statements and loops and so you build a program that does something useful. For most programmers this is enough – controlling a single thread of execution is relatively easy and there is little that is not obvious about how things work. Generally a program starts executing and the single thread of execution follows your instruction through to the end of the program without doing anything unexpected.

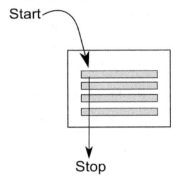

Of course, in the real world the flow of control would include branches and loops and in principle the program might never end due to an infinite loop.

From the point of view of simplicity a single thread of execution is ideal and if you can stay with that model for your program then do. However, modern computers have to work with the external world. Data arrives over communication channels, users click buttons and menu options and generally there is an expectation that when something important happens it will be dealt with. What this means is that the single thread of execution has to be interruptible. It has to be able to stop what it is doing, move to running another program and then return to what it was doing, as if nothing had happened.

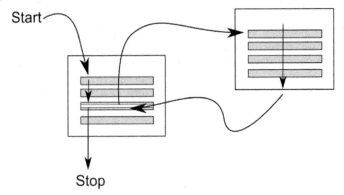

Dealing with urgent actions is one reason for making programs interruptible, another is simply the need to wait for the outside world. If a program needs to read some data then it could be many seconds before it is available. In that time the program simply has to wait for the data. This is a huge waste of processor power. A modern processor can execute millions of instructions in a second and even having to suspend a program for a fraction of a second can waste thousands of potential instruction executions. What should we do about this huge inefficiency? You cannot ask the waiting program to move on because it can't do anything until its data arrives. What you can do is ask the processor to run another part of the program that doesn't need the data. This is another example of asynchronous programming as the waiting program doesn't know when it will restart or what other programs have run while it was waiting.

In the asynchronous world many of the things that we take for granted about our programs are no longer true. For example, we generally suppose that the value in a variable will not change if we do not explicitly change it. This is not true in asynchronous code as another program could change a variable while your program is doing something else. Not only this, but it could change a variable while you are in the middle of using it – this is a race condition as the outcome depends on which program gets to change the variable first. The first program's update is lost because the final update overwrites it.

Asynchronous code is simply where the thread of execution can be interrupted, used to run a different block of code and then resume the code it was originally running. It is asynchronous because exactly when the jump from your code to some other code isn't under your control. It can happen anywhere within your program and as such it isn't synchronized with what your program is doing. We usually say that single-threaded code that is written without any allowance for this sort of interruption is synchronous and code that is aware of this sort of interruption is asynchronous.

This idea of the running of code being interrupted to run some other code is just the start. Things get complicated very quickly and exactly how you can best think about it depends on the nature of the interruption. This is what we need to look at next.

Processes

Operating systems interrupt the running of code all the time. The idea is that you have multiple active programs in memory. At any given time one of them has the current thread of execution and is running. The others are not being obeyed and they are said to be suspended. The operating system allows each program to run for a short period of time and then interrupts it and starts running one of the suspended programs. This all happens so fast that to the user it looks as if all of the programs are running at the same time.

This is generally referred to as multitasking, or more exactly preemptive multitasking, as the operating system uses its power to suspend the running program as opposed to cooperative multitasking when the operating system passively waits for the running program to yield and suspend itself.

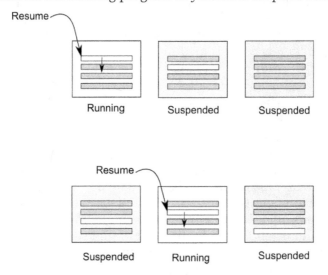

The key idea here is that each of the programs is isolated from the others and stopping and starting them is safe because there is no interaction between them. Indeed it is what allows a naive user or programmer to run multiple applications on a single processor without having to think about the complexities of asynchronous programming.

When the operating system stops a running program it saves the program's state which is restored when the program is restarted. In this way the interrupted program isn't affected by the interruption. Even so, there are times when interactions between programs are unavoidable due to changes to the global environment, for example when one program deletes a file that another program wants to use. Code run in this way is generally called a process and in practice a single application may be made up of multiple processes each doing a specific job with minimal communication.

Processes are isolated from each other as much as the hardware allows. For example, most modern machines processes do not share memory. Each process is mapped into its own area of memory and there is no chance of one accidentally changing the data that belongs to another. Most operating systems do provide facilities to allow processes to communicate, but these are very controlled to limit unwanted interactions.

Switching between processes, which involves suspending the running process, swapping memory, storing any volatile data and starting one of the suspended processes, is usually referred to as a context switch. As you can imagine, the overhead is relatively time consuming and context switching is best minimized. There is also the problem of selecting which of the processes to wake up and this is generally called scheduling. Given a set of suspended processes, a good scheduler will make sure they all get a fair share of runtime while allowing some processes to claim higher priority. In practice this isn't an easy problem to solve and schedulers generally work sub-optimally for any given situation. One thing that all schedulers are good at, however, is avoiding running processes that waiting for some external event to occur – waiting for data for example.

I/O-Bound and CPU-Bound

Processes, and code in general, is often classified into two types – CPU-bound and I/O-bound. An I/O-bound process wouldn't run any faster if you increased the speed of the CPU because it spends most of its time waiting for data to be sent or received via other parts of the system. CPU-bound processes, on the other hand, spend little time waiting for I/O and if you increase the speed of the CPU they would complete their task sooner. Operating systems allocate more processor time to CPU-bound processes and keep I/O-bound processes suspended while they wait for data transfers to be complete.

Notice that there are two distinct reasons for a running process to be suspended. The first is just that its allocated time has run out. To keep the system responsive, the operating system has to stop the running process and start another. The second is when some piece of hardware needs attention and this can happen at an arbitrary time. In this case the hardware generates an interrupt, which is a signal that the processor has to stop the current process and switch to running code that deals with the hardware. This is generally called a hardware interrupt or just an interrupt and the code that is run is an interrupt handler.

Threads

Processes are one way to divide up a program into asynchronous tasks but switching between them is, as already mentioned, an expensive operation. Most operating systems also implement a less demanding form of multitasking in the form of threads. A thread is unit of execution within a process. That is threads share the same memory and hence the same data. They can interact freely with one another as long as they are within the same process. A single process can have lots of different threads each running a different portion of the code.

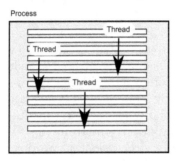

Notice that in principle different threads can run exactly the same code, however, it is usually much simpler to write the program so that each thread has its own code i.e. its own job to do.

In a single CPU system only one of the threads can be running at any particular time – the others are suspended. Most operating systems schedule threads within processes and prefer to swap between threads in the same process so as to avoid the larger cost of a process swap. Even so creating and changing which thread is running is costly and there are various practical approaches to minimizing this overhead.

Threads share the same memory and this means they have access to all of the variables in the process. As already mentioned, they also share the same code and this can be a problem. Code that can be shared between threads without problems is generally referred to as "thread-safe" and most code isn't thread-safe. For example, consider a function which creates a form for a user to enter data. This isn't likely to be thread-safe by default as if it is started on a new thread then the data entered while running on the old thread will be overwritten. To make code thread-safe you have to do some work to make sure that the code is re-enterable, i.e. can be interrupted in mid-execution and restarted with a new thread. In the case of the form function the solution to making it thread-safe is to allow each thread to have its own copy of the form object so that it can initialize it without changing any other forms being used.

36

To answer the question "is this code thread-safe" you simply have to work out what happens if the code is part way through executing and it is started again with a new thread. Is the original thread's state unchanged by this? If the answer is "yes" the code is probably thread-safe.

Locking

Many other details about how we use threads have to be taken into account, but the most important is the lock. Given that threads share memory, there is a potential for two or more threads to use the same memory in such a way that none of them achieve the intended outcome and this is the pitfall that locks protect against.

The standard example is adding one to a variable. If thread1 reads myVariable and discovers it contains 41 it can add one to it to get 42, which it stores back in the variable. If thread2 reads myVariable before thread1 has stored its new value then it too reads 41. It then adds one to get 42 and stores this back in the variable. The variable now holds 42 whereas if both updates had completed without interfering with each other the answer would have been 43. This is called a "race condition" because the outcome depends on whether the first thread stores its result before the second thread reads the value.

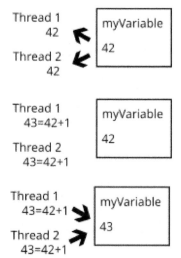

The solution to race conditions, and other problems that arise in making code thread-safe, is to use locks. A lock restricts access to a resource so that only one thread, or more generally a maximum number of threads, can access the resource at the same time. For example, our race condition described above can be avoided by insisting that a lock is acquired before any thread can access myVariable. That is, thread1 locks myVariable, reads its value, adds one and stores the result back in myVariable and only then releases the lock. If thread2 tries to access myVariable while thread1 is updating it then it will not be able to acquire the lock and it will have to wait until thread1 is finished with the update. In this way no race condition can make the result anything but 43. The only downside is that thread2 has to wait while thread1 completes its update. This slows things down, but at least the result is correct. A general principle is that threads should hold locks for the shortest possible time so as not to hold up other threads for longer than necessary.

An alternative to locking is to make the access to myVariable atomic. An atomic operation cannot be interrupted. This has the same effect as locking, but in many cases it is more efficient as it can be implemented in hardware.

Deadlock

The biggest potential problem with locking is deadlock. Imagine that thread1 needs resources A and B and locks A. If thread2 also needs A and B but locks B before thread1 can acquire the lock then we have a problem. thread1 cannot progress because it needs resource B which thread2 has locked. thread2 cannot progress because it needs resource A which thread1 has locked. Neither can release the locks they have because they are waiting to acquire other locks before moving on so they both just stay suspended potentially forever.

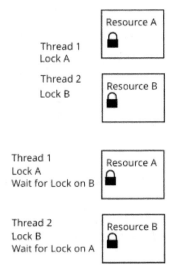

This is deadlock and it can arise in ways that are much more complicated then this simple illustration. Deadlock is a possibility whenever a set of threads needs to lock a set of resources. To avoid deadlock any set of resources needs to be locked as a single operation, which is easier said than done.

Processes with Multiple Threads

Once we have introduced the idea of a thread we have to modify our view of processes – just slightly. Now each process can be running more than one thread:

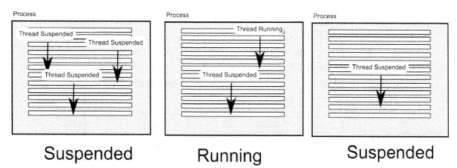

On a single-core machine just one of the threads will be running at any given time and the operating system now schedules threads to run within processes. As before, switching between threads in the same process is less costly than switching threads between processes. Also threads within processes find communication easy, but threads between processes are isolated by default and need to use special methods to communicate. Locking is usually applied between threads in a single process as process isolation automatically protects local resources.

Modern operating systems usually regard a process as being a "container" for at least one thread. In this view the process simply determines the common environment for threads that are running within it and the threads are the basic unit of execution and scheduling.

Single-Threaded Async

Even though threads have been available for some time the majority of applications don't make use of them. The single-threaded process is the default in nearly all languages. You might think that if you need to take advantage of asynchronous operation then the thing to do is to add some threads so that work can continue when your program is waiting for something. This is a reasonable assumption but it doesn't take into account how difficult managing threads is – so much so that many languages have the built in assumption that additional threads are to be avoided where possible.

There is also the simple fact that so far no one has built a successful multi-threaded UI. It seems that the task is too difficult because the interaction with the user has to occur in the order that that user thinks it happened. As a result, single-threaded processes are very common and languages introduce additional constructs to make asynchronous programming easier with a single thread. This is what the `asyncio` module in Python is all about.

The first commonly encountered single-threaded async mechanism is the callback. If you program in almost any language you can't avoid using callbacks because they are commonly used as part of the operating system interface. Suppose that you want to open a remote file then the operating system call to do the job will often provide a callback parameter which accepts a callback function. The idea is simple, instead of waiting until the remote file is loaded, something that could take minutes, the thread is allowed to carry on running. When the file is available the operating system runs the callback and the processing of the file can continue.

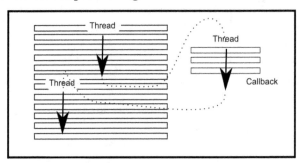

In the diagram the callback is shown as somehow separate from the rest of the code. Of course it isn't, but we tend to think of it as something special and removed from the usual flow of control.

This sounds easy – call the callback when the resource is ready – but it is very subtle. The first thing to realize is that as there is just one thread it is the thread that runs all of the code in the process, including the callback. This means that any idea that you might have of the callback running as soon as the resource is ready is nonsense. The callback has to wait until the thread has nothing else to do. In essence what happens is that the thread does some work and then suspends itself waiting for the callback. If the resource loads before the thread is suspended then nothing happens until the thread is free. Using a single thread with a callback means you can be sure that things happen in a predictable way.

At this point you might realize that the only advantage of this approach is if the thread has something else to do while waiting for the resource to be ready. If the thread doesn't have anything to do then it might as well just wait for the resource and continue with the code that has been separated into the callback. When you think of specific cases it can often be difficult to see what the thread might be doing. For example, if you are downloading an image file then the program is probably going to be waiting for the download so that it can get on with processing the image. What is a thread to do while waiting?

There is a very general and common answer to this question. Today many processes have an interface with the user via a GUI and the thread is responsible for keeping this GUI active – this is why the single thread is often called the UI thread. That is, when the user clicks a button the thread has to respond to the click, animate the button and do whatever the button is supposed to do. In an ideal world the thread would respond at once to a button press and to anything else the user is doing. A good UI minimizes the time it takes for the thread to respond to the user – it minimizes the latency.

Events

If the UI thread is dealing with a button push it cannot instantly respond to something else that the user initiates. More generally, the UI thread cannot respond to anything the user does if it is executing code. What this means is that ideally the UI thread should do nothing but wait for something to happen and when it does it should deal with the matter and get back to waiting for the next thing to happen as quickly as possible. In other words, the ideal UI thread does close to nothing at all.

There is also the problem of avoiding the UI thread missing a user action while it is busy doing something else – no matter how short the something else is.

To deal with this strange situation the idea of an event together with an event queue and an event handler was invented. User actions on the UI are formalized as events, a click on a button say. Each event can have a number of event handlers, such as onClick, associated with it. The UI thread is associated with a queue that events are stored in when they happen. The UI thread takes the first event in the queue and runs the event handler. When the UI thread has finished processing the current event it looks at the queue to see if there is another event. If there is it processes it and so on until the queue is empty when it loops waiting for the next event to arrive in the queue.

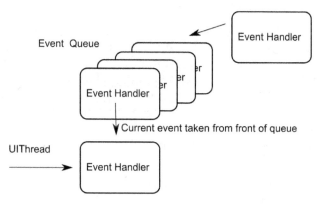

This may sound a complicated way to implement a UI, but it has many advantages. The first is that user events aren't lost as they are stored in the queue as they occur and wait until the UI is free to process them. The user events are also processed in the order in which they occur as the queue preserves the order. Finally each event waits for the minimum possible time and overall latency is reduced.

The event queue can also accommodate async mechanisms other than events associated with the UI. For example, callbacks can be added to the queue after a resource is loaded. The callback can either be given priority or just handled after any events in the queue. You can arrange for timed actions by allowing timing events to be included in the queue. Basically you can use the event queue for any code that needs to be executed – your only problem is finding a way to present it so that it looks reasonable.

The key characteristic of a single-thread event queue system is that at any given time only one block of code is being executed. Other blocks of code are either dormant or in the queue waiting for the UI thread to come free to execute them. Once a block of code starts it runs to completion and only then does the UI thread become free to run another item from the front of the queue. That is, execution of an event handler is never preempted by another event.

At this point we need to step back for a moment and think about the overall context that the event queue is running in. The UI thread is a thread in a process and as such the operating system will preempt it and give another thread in another process a chance to run. This is usually not something that the event-oriented programmer would notice or need to worry about. The only effect it has is to slow things down and potentially increase the latency in unpredictable ways. Even so it is reasonable to see the event handling system as a cooperative multitasking system running underneath the preemptive multitasking system provided by the operating system.

Events or Threads?

An alternative to an event queue is to simply assign a thread to each of the tasks and let the operating system handle the scheduling. This is the option adopted by most web servers, for example Apache. When a request for a web page comes in the web server starts a new thread and starts it running code to handle the request. In this way each web page request is handled by its own thread and each thread is scheduled by the operating system so that if the thread has to wait for a resource, other threads get to run. This is theoretically a good way to ensure that each web page request gets the best service time.

The alternative is use an event queue. Each request for a web page is added to the event queue and a single thread deals with them in a first come first served order. Once again, if the request has to wait for a resource the thread moves on to process another event and so web page requests progress together. This is the approach used by Node.js and it is claimed that it is much faster. In tests Node.js starts out working at roughly the same speed as Apache, but when the number of concurrent requests is 200 or more Node.js is roughly five times faster at completing requests. However, the comparison is not a simple one and you can argue that when correctly configured Apache and threading is much faster than the event queue.

Notice that, as already explained, using threads to speed up a UI isn't a practical proposition mainly because of the need to make sure that the order of user actions is preserved. When serving web pages it doesn't matter which order the pages are delivered, when responding to button clicks it matters which button event handler is run first.

Callback Hell

This all seems reasonable but callbacks are a problem. Events aren't so much of a problem because event handlers are usually single units of execution that are called do a quick job and release the UI thread. Callbacks are a different matter because they usually occur inside code that needs their results. For example, if you write some code that loads an image over a network then usually you want to do something before the load and something afterwards:

```
set up image
download image
process image
```

Ideally you would want your code to wait until the download image step was completed, but in a synchronous system this would mean that the single thread was blocked and unable to keep the UI responsive.

The basic async solution is to use a callback:

```
set up image
download image(process_image)
```

where process_image is now a call to a function that will occur at some time in the future. Notice that now what happens after the image has been loaded has been moved from its natural position, after the load step, to a function that is somewhere else in the code. In fact, everything after the download step has to be moved to the function and the code has effectively been split into two parts – before the load and after the load.

This doesn't seem so terrible when you first meet it in simple situation such as this, but it quickly gets very messy. For example, suppose you want to download two images and use the first image before the second:

```
set up images
download image1(process_image)
download image2(process_image)
```

This does start both image downloads running and one of them will finish, but how can you make sure that image1 is used before image2?

One solution is to put the download of image2 in the process_image function:

```
set up images
download image1(process_image1)

process_image1()
        download image2(process_image2)
        process image1
process_image2()
        process image2
```

In this case image1 finishes downloading before image2 starts and we have lost any advantage of having them download concurrently.

There are lots of other examples where callbacks complicate the logic of a program and very quickly become unmanageable, hence the common use of the term "callback hell". The problem mostly stems from the way the use of a callback divides the code into before and after. It is much better to keep the code together. Compare the previous example with the synchronous code to do the same job:

```
set up image1
download image1
process image1
download image2
process image2
```

Now the program waits while image1 downloads and processes it before downloading image2. Notice that this clearly easier-to-understand code has the disadvantage that the download of image2 doesn't save time by overlapping with the download of image1. Even so the synchronous code is much easier to reason about. Consider changing it so that if image1 downloads correctly then image2 isn't required:

```
set up image1
download image1
if image1 is not ok
        download image2
process image
```

Try your hand at converting this into callbacks to see how unnatural callbacks make the code. In general, dealing with errors that occur in a chain of callbacks is difficult and not easy to understand.

Modern approaches to single-threaded async code does away with callbacks using promises or the more sophisticated async/await and this is exactly what Python does with the `asyncio` module. Even so, you will encounter existing libraries that have not been updated to include these newer mechanisms. The good news is that most of the time it is easy to create your own interfaces to update them.

More Than One CPU – Concurrency

Until comparatively recently having more than one CPU in a machine was a rare occurrence. Hardware was expensive enough to make one CPU all that was available for most tasks. With the increasing number of transistors available on a chip and with the limit being reached on CPU clock rates, the only way manufacturers could make use of the extra circuitry was to integrate more than one CPU, or core, per chip. Today even the least powerful processor has two cores and four and eight cores are fairly common. This means that a single-processor chip can be running multiple programs at the same time. This is usually referred to as concurrency or true parallelism.

Before the advent of multiple cores multitasking, threads and so on were just ways of sharing the processing power of a single core. In this sense they were, and still are, basically a software-based simulation of true parallelism. What this means is that transitioning to true parallelism doesn't add that much to the situation, except of course the potential for increased speed.

There is nothing new in moving from one core with threads to multicore with threads. You still have the same problems of isolation and interaction between threads and the need for locks on shared resources. You might think that the important difference was that now two threads can attempt to modify the same resource at exactly the same time. This cannot happen with single-core threading where only one thread is actually running at any given time. In this case the two threads are swapped very fast, but they never run at the same time.

This distinction seems important until you realize that what matters in any access to a shared resource is which thread "wins" in a simultaneous access. Real hardware generally doesn't allow exact simultaneous access. If two threads try to change a memory location "at the same time" only one of them will succeed in making the change. If we have two threads, one trying to write 42 to a memory location and the other trying to write 43, then only one will succeed and when the memory location is read it will hold either 42 or 43 depending on which thread "won", i.e. was the last to change the memory location. This is same situation as if the two threads were running on a single core – one of the threads writes to the memory location last and hence the memory location holds either 42 or 43.

This means that true parallelism doesn't introduce anything new that we have to deal with over and above multitasking with a single core.

In the following chapters the term asynchronous will be used to mean multithreading with one or more processors. The term concurrency will be used to emphasize the fact that more than one core is possibly in use.

Summary

- Most programs are single-threaded because this is much simpler, but multi-threading can make a program faster and more responsive.

- A process is an isolated block of code which runs as a single application or as an identifiable part of a large application. Processes don't generally interact with one another except via special facilities, provided by the operating system.

- On a single-CPU machine, at any one moment one process will be running and the rest will be suspended. Every so often the operating system changes which process is running – a context switch – so as to make it look as if all processes are running simultaneously.

- Processes or programs are often I/O-bound or CPU-bound. An I/O-bound program spends most of its time waiting for external hardware. A CPU-bound program spends most of its time using the CPU.

- A thread is a lightweight process and differs in that threads are not isolated from one another and share memory and code.

- As threads and processes can share resources, there is always the possibility of a race condition occurring where the outcome depends on the order that the resource is accessed.

- Locks are the standard way of solving the problem of race conditions by demanding that a thread or process acquires a lock before accessing the resource.

- Locks slow things down and introduce the possibility of deadlock where threads compete for locks in such a way that none of them can acquire all of the locks they need to proceed.

- A more modern view of a process is that each process can have multiple threads. The threads within a process share resources, but processes are still isolated from one another.

- For I/O-bound programs a single thread is often sufficient. An event loop is used along with a queue of code waiting to run. The main thread runs tasks from the event queue as they become ready. Most of the tasks in the queue are suspended, waiting for I/O to complete.

- Single-threaded asynchronous execution uses callbacks which are run when I/O completes or an event occurs. Callbacks are a problem because they distort the logic of a program.

- Having multiple cores allow threads to actually run at the same time – true parallelism or concurrency. Concurrency adds little that is new to asynchronous programming.

Chapter 3

Processed-Based Parallelism

Most books on asynchronous programming start by looking at threads as these are generally regarded as the building blocks of execution. However, for Python there are advantages in starting with processes, which come with a default single thread of execution. The reasons are both general and specific. Processes are isolated from one another and this makes locking less of an issue.

There is also the fact that Python suffers from a restriction on the way threads are run called the Global Interpreter Lock or GIL which only allows one thread to run the Python system at any specific time. This means that, without a lot of effort, multiple threads cannot make use of multiple cores and so do not provide a way of speeding things up. There is much more on threads and the GIL in the next chapter, but for the moment all you need to know is that processes can speed up your program by using multiple cores. Using Python threads you cannot get true parallelism, but using processes you can.

What this means is that if you have an I/O-bound task then using threads will speed things up as the processor can get on with another thread when the I/O bound thread is stalled. If you have CPU-bound tasks then nothing but process parallelism will help.

The Process Class

The key idea in working with processes is that your initial Python program starts out in its own process and you can use the `Process` class from the `multiprocessing` module to create sub-processes. A child process, in Python terminology, is created and controlled by its parent process. Let's look at the simplest possible example:

```python
import multiprocessing
def myProcess():
    print("Hello Process World")

if __name__ == '__main__':
    p1=multiprocessing.Process(target=myProcess)
    p1.start()
```

In this case all we do is create a `Process` object with its `target` set to the `myProcess` function object. Calling the `start` method creates the new process and starts the code running by calling `myProcess`. You simply see `Hello Process World` displayed.

There seems to be little that is new here, but a lot is going on that isn't obvious. When you call the `start` method a whole new process is created, complete with a new copy of the Python interpreter and the Python program. Exactly how the Python program is provided to the new process depends on the system you are running it on and this is a subtle point that is discussed later.

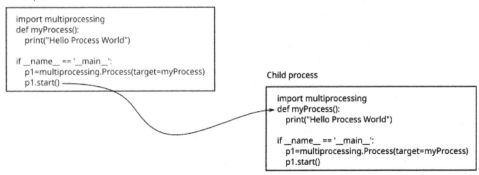

For the moment you need to follow the three simple rules:

1. Always use if `__name__ == '__main__':` to ensure that the setup code doesn't get run in the child process.

2. Do not define or modify any global resources in the setup code as these will not always be available in the child process.

3. Prefer to use parameters to pass initial data to the child process rather than global constants.

The reasons for these rules are explained in detail later.

In general to create and run a new process you have to create a `Process` object using:

```
class multiprocessing.Process(group=None, target=None,
                    name=None, args=(), kwargs={}, daemon=None)
```

You can ignore the `group` parameter as it is just included to make the call the same as the one that creates `threads` in the next chapter. The `target` is the callable you want the new process to run and `name` is that applied to the new process. If you don't supply a name then a unique name is constructed for you. The most important parameters are `args` and `kwargs` which specify the positional and keyword parameters to pass to the callable.

For example:

```
p1=multiprocessing.Process(target=myProcess,(42,43),
                                         {"myParam1":44})
```

will call the `target` as:

```
myProcess(42,43,myParam1=44)
```

The `Process` object has a number of useful methods and attributes in addition to the `start` method. The simplest of these are `name` and `pid`.

The `name` attribute can be used to find the assigned name of the child process. It has no larger meaning in the sense that the operating system knows nothing about it. The `pid` attribute, on the other hand, is the process identity number which is assigned by the operating system and it is the `pid` that you use to deal with child processes via operating system commands such as `kill`.

Both the `name` and `pid` attributes help identify a process, but for security purposes you need to use the `authkey` attribute. This is set to a random number when the `multiprocessing` module is loaded and it is intended to act as a secure identifier for child processes. Each `Process` object is given the `authkey` value of the parent process and this can be used to prove the process is indeed a child process of the parent, more about this later.

The multiprocessing module also contains some methods that can be used to find out about the environment in which the child processes are running.

- ◆ `multiprocessing.cpu_count()` gives the number of CPUs i.e. cores in the system. This is the theoretical maximum number of processes that can run in parallel. In practice the maximum number available is usually lower.

- ◆ `multiprocessing.cpu_set_executable()` gives the location of the Python interpreter to use for child processes.

A Python process isn't a basic native process. It has a Python interpreter loaded along with the Python code defined in the parent process and it is ready to run the function that has been passed as the `target`.

Daemon

Processes are independent of one another and this means that it is possible for a process to create a child process and then end leaving the child process running. In practice this isn't a good idea as the parent process should be in control of any processes it creates. By default child processes do not end when their parent terminates. This is slightly dangerous in the sense that you can create orphaned processes that just carry on running until the user notices and stops them manually.

If you want a child process to terminate automatically when its parent process terminates you have to set the `daemon` attribute to `True`. If you know what a Linux/Unix daemon process is this will seem to be the wrong way round. A Linux/Unix daemon process runs in the background with no user interaction and has no parent process. In contrast, a Python `daemon=True` process is totally dependent on its parent to keep it running. To see this in action try:

```python
import multiprocessing

def myProcess():
    while True:
        pass
if __name__ == '__main__':
    p0=multiprocessing.current_process()
    p1=multiprocessing.Process(target=myProcess,daemon=True)
    p2=multiprocessing.Process(target=myProcess,daemon=False)
    p1.start()
    p2.start()
    print(p0.pid)
    print(p1.pid)
    print(p2.pid)
    print("ending")
```

You can see that this starts two processes – one daemon and one non-daemon. The parent process comes to an end and you will see the ending message displayed. If you examine the process that are running after the program has ended you will discover that the process with the `pid` non-daemon process is still running. You can check which processes are running under Linux using the `ps` command and under Windows using the task manager. Under Windows the main program, i.e. the parent process, is listed as running whereas under Linux it is shown as suspended. In either case the process consumes no CPU time and waits for its non-daemon child process to end.

If you run this program under a debugger then the results you see will be contaminated by the action of the debugger. To see the true behavior you have to run the program from the command line. If you are using VS Code run the program with the command `Python: Run Python File In Terminal`. This runs the program without the IDE or debugger getting in the way.

To summarize:

- A non-daemon process (`daemon=False`) continues running even if its parent terminates.

- A daemon process (`daemon=True`) terminates if its parent terminates.

As already mentioned, this seems to be the wrong way round compared to the usual Linux/Unix definition of a daemon process. You can test to see if a thread is a daemon using:

```
Thread.daemon
```

which is `True` if the thread is a daemon.

Waiting for Processes

Sometimes it is necessary to wait until a child process has completed its allotted task. Any process can wait on another using the `join` method:

```
Process.join(timeout)
```

will put the calling process into a suspended state until the `Process` terminates or until the specified timeout is up. The timeout is specified in seconds and if it is `None`, the default, the `join` waits forever.

You can discover what state the `Process` is in using `Process.exitcode` which gives you `None` if the sub-process is still running and its exit code otherwise. Usually an exit code of zero is used to signal that everything was OK. You can set the exit code to n using `sys.exit(n)`. Another way is to use `Process.is_alive()` which returns `True` if the sub-process is still running and `False` otherwise.

There are two methods that will terminate a process. `Process.terminate()` stops the process running by sending a `SIGTERM` signal under Linux or calling `TerminateProcess` under Windows. The result should be the same – the process stops running without completing any exit handlers and `finally` clauses. Any child processes of the process you stop will be orphaned. Clearly it is a good idea only to terminate processes that don't have child processes. In most cases terminating a process should be a last resort and you should arrange for processes to run to completion.

Alternatively you can use `Process.kill()` which is a more aggressive way to stop a process, as it uses the `SIGKILL` signal under Linux, which in theory always succeeds in terminating a process. If it doesn't it is an operating system bug.

You need to know that `Process.Close()` doesn't stop the process. Instead it raises a `ValueError` if it is still running. What it does is to release the resources still owned by the `Process` object associated with the process.

The `join` method is very flexible in that you can join a process that has already terminated and it will return immediately, but it is an error to try to join a process that hasn't started. You can join a process multiple times and you can join multiple processes.

For example:

```
p1.join(1)
print("Possibly not finished")
p1.join(1)
```

will pause the process waiting for p1 to complete. If it doesn't finish after
one second then the join returns and we see Possibly not finished
displayed. Then the program waits for the process to finish for another
second. You can continue this until the process completes. The advantage of
this approach is that join suspends the calling process allowing the CPU to
run other processes. If you simply poll on the state of the child process the
CPU is kept occupied doing nothing. That is:

```
while p1.is_alive():
    p1.join(1)
    print("not finished")
```

frees the CPU while looping every second to check that the process has
finished whereas using:

```
while p1.is_alive():
    print("not finished")
```

the loop finishes when the child process finished – but in this case it keeps
the CPU occupied.

You can use join to wait for multiple processes to end:

```
p1.join()
p2.join()
p3.join()
```

This will only continue when all three processes have completed. Notice
that the order of completion doesn't matter.

Waiting for the First to Complete

The above example waits on p1 and p2 and p3 to finish. What is more
difficult is to wait until one of the processes is complete, i.e. wait for p1 or
p2 or p3, whichever completes first. The easiest way to do this is to make use
of the Connection object which is introduced later as a way of
communicating between processes. The technique relies on the sentinel
attribute to return a handle to a system object that becomes "ready" when
the process is complete. This is a low-level feature that changes how it is
implemented depending on the operating system. The good news is that at
the Python level it works in the same way under Linux and Windows.

The `multiprocessing.connection.wait` function will wait on a list of sentinel handles until one of them becomes "ready". It returns a list of sentinel handles that have become ready, for example:

```
import multiprocessing
import multiprocessing.connection
import random
import time

def myProcess():
    time.sleep(random.randrange(1,4))
if __name__ == '__main__':
    p1=multiprocessing.Process(target=myProcess)
    p2=multiprocessing.Process(target=myProcess)
    p3=multiprocessing.Process(target=myProcess)
    p1.start()
    p2.start()
    p3.start()

    waitList= [p1.sentinel,p2.sentinel,p3.sentinel]
    res=multiprocessing.connection.wait(waitList)
    print(res)
    print(waitList.index(res[0])+1)
```

The first part of the program simply creates three processes which wait for random times to use as an example of waiting for the first process to complete. The final part of the program builds a list of sentinel values, one per process. Then we use the `wait` function to suspend the parent thread until one of the child processes completes. The return value is a list of sentinel values that are "ready" and these values are easily converted into the numbers of the processes that have finished. Notice that the program only takes the first sentinel value in the list. In practice you might want to process them all. Also, as all the processes in this example are non-daemon, they all run to completion after the main process ends.

As the set of sentinel values only has to be an iterable, refer to ***Programmer's Python: Everything Is An Object***, ISBN: 978-1871962741 if you are not familiar with this distinction, you could write it as:

```
waitDict= {p1.sentinel:p1, p2.sentinel:p2, p3.sentinel:p3}
res=multiprocessing.connection.wait(waitDict)
print(waitDict[res[0]])
```

This has the advantage of making the `Process` object corresponding to the process that finished first easier to find, i.e. `waitDict[res[0]]` is the process object.

Computing Pi

As a simple example, suppose you want to compute the mathematical constant pi to a few digits using the well-known formula:

```
pi=4*(1-1/3+1/5-1/7 ... )
```

This is very easy to implement, we just need to generate the odd integers, but to get pi to a reasonable number of digits you have to compute a lot of terms. In other words, this series is very slow to converge. The simple-minded synchronous approach is to write something like:

```
def myPi(m,n):
    pi=0
    for k in range(m,n+1):
        s= 1 if k%2 else -1
        pi += s / (2 * k - 1)
    print(4*pi)
```

This computes the series from the mth to the nth term. The reason for this elaboration is that it allows us to compute different parts of the series in different processes. Of course,

```
myPi(1,N)
```

computes the full series up to the Nth term.

If you try this out:

```
if __name__ == '__main__':
    N=10000000
    t1=time.perf_counter()
    myPi(1,N)
    t2=time.perf_counter()
    print((t2-t1)*1000)
```

You will find that it takes about 1700 ms to compute Pi to five digits on a medium speed Windows PC and 4500 ms on a four-core Raspberry Pi 4.

We can easily modify the calculation by splitting the sum into two portions and using a separate process for one half of the sum:

```
if __name__ == '__main__':
    N=10000000
    p1=multiprocessing.Process(target=myPi,args=(N//2+1,N))
    t1=time.perf_counter()
    p1.start()
    myPi(1,N//2)
    p1.join()
    t2=time.perf_counter()
    print((t2-t1)*1000)
```

Running this reduces the time to 1200 ms on the PC and 2500 ms the Pi 4.

If you try these programs out using an IDE or a debugger than you may well discover that there is no significant speed gain. As before, this is because of the way programs are run under the debugger – again, to appreciate the speed increase try running them from the command line.

Notice that the computation is performed using Python's unlimited precision arithmetic, Bignum arithmetic, so you could continue to use this very slowly converging series to compute any number of decimal places. To know more about Python's novel approach to large numbers see Chapter 2 of **Programmer's Python: Everything Is Data,** ISBN: 978-1871962598.

Thus far we haven't explored any way that data can be exchanged between processes, so our only option is to print the results from each one. The subject of sharing data between isolated process is a complicated one and is postponed until Chapter 7. Processes may be isolated from one another, but they do share a single Terminal instance and so the print sends data to the same output.

Increasing the number of processes to four on the Pi decreases the time to 1600ms, which demonstrates some decreasing returns on using parallelism. The complete program is:

```
import time
import multiprocessing

def myPi(m,n):
    pi=0
    for k in range(m,n+1):
        s= 1 if k%2 else -1
        pi += s / (2 * k - 1)
    print(4*pi)

if __name__ == '__main__':
    N=10000000
    p1=multiprocessing.Process(target=myPi,args=(N//4+1,N//4*2))
    p2=multiprocessing.Process(target=myPi,args=(N//4*2+1,N//4*3))
    p3=multiprocessing.Process(target=myPi,args=(N//4*3+1,N))

    t1=time.perf_counter()
    p1.start()
    p2.start()
    p3.start()
    myPi(1,N//4)
    p1.join()
    p2.join()
    p3.join()
    t2=time.perf_counter()
    print((t2-t1)*1000)
```

However, if you increase N to 100000000 the single-process version takes 45 s and the four-process version takes just 12 s. For longer running processes the initial overheads matter less.

Fork v Spawn

The final part of this chapter examines a subtle complexity of the way that processes are started on different systems. If you use the rules given earlier then you probably can ignore this section, but if you want to know exactly how things are working you need to read on.

The standard Linux/Unix way of creating a child process is the fork operation. When you first meet it the fork doesn't seem a very sensible way to create a new process, but it has many advantages once you start to make use of it. A fork operation makes a complete copy of the current process as the new process and execution continues from the point that the fork occurred. That is, the child process is an exact clone of the parent process.

This seems pointless until you know that there is a very simple test that the process can use to discover which one is the original and which is the new child process. Both processes make the test and one continues on as before and the other calls code that makes it different:

```
fork
if child-process:
        target()
rest of program
```

This code works in the parent and the child process and this is one of the fork's advantages – just one source code module to run in both processes. It also means that the child process has exactly the same environment, global variables etc, as the parent process had at the point the fork was executed. This is how the child process gets definitions of the functions and classes it might use. They are not passed as parameters to the child process – they are present because of the fork operation. That is when you use:

```
p1=multiprocessing.Process(target=myPi,args=(N//4+1,N//4*2))
```

the function myPi exists in the child process because it is a clone of the parent process. Only the reference to myPi is passed as a parameter. The same is true of the arguments passed to the child if they are functions or objects. That is a reference is passed but the functions and objects are already present in the child as it is a clone of the parent process.

The Python `multiprocessing` module is designed to work under any operating system, but when it runs under Linux/Unix it makes use of the fork method and when it runs under Windows it simulates the fork method by starting a new process, loading in the Python interpreter and then loading and running the Python program. This simulation is called the spawn start method and it is the default for Windows.

Python uses fork as its default start method under Linux/Unix. To be clear what this means is that the child process is a complete copy of the parent, including the Python interpreter and any global resources that have already been created by running the parent.

It really is as if the entire program had been cloned and carries on running by calling the target function. Notice, however, that the global resources in the child process really are copies. Any changes to them are not passed back to the parent process.

Parent process

```
Python Interpreter

Global resources created by the pogram

import multiprocessing
def myProcess():
    print("Hello Process World")

if __name__ == '__main__':
    p1=multiprocessing.Process(target=myProcess)
    p1.start()
```

Child process

```
Python Interpreter

Global resources created by the program

import multiprocessing
def myProcess():
    print("Hello Process World")

if __name__ == '__main__':
    p1=multiprocessing.Process(target=myProcess)
    p1.start()
```

Windows doesn't support a fork operation and hence the need to simulate one using the spawn start method. The big difference is that the spawn start method starts a new process, loads the Python interpreter and loads and runs the Python program, i.e. this is not a clone of the original process but a reconstruction. The Python program has to be run from scratch to create the global resources and to read in the definitions of all of the objects, including functions, defined in the program. When this is complete the target function is called.

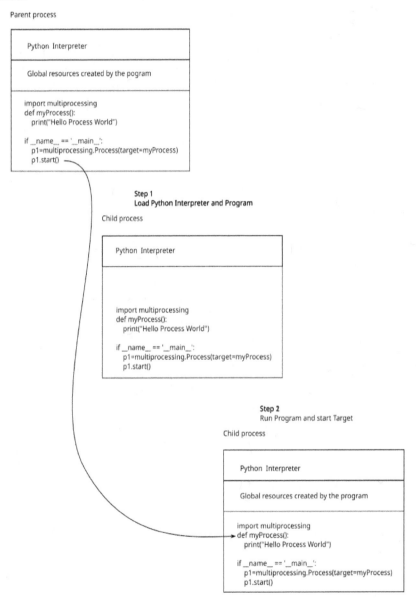

The program has to be run to recreate the state just before the start method was called so that target can be run. This means that you have to be careful how you create the child process. For example, if you simply create the child process in the code that is rerun in the child then another child process will be created and so on. This is sometimes called a "fork bomb", even though in this case it is the lack of a true fork that causes the problem. Contrast this behavior with the fork method which doesn't run the Python code again in the child process as it is cloned and simply carries on running from where it left off, i.e. you don't get a fork bomb if you use a fork.

For example, under Linux, or more generally using the fork start method, you can write:

```
import multiprocessing
def myProcess():
    print("Hello Process World")


p1 = multiprocessing.Process(target = myProcess)
p1.start()
print("finished")
```

Notice that we now don't have an if __name__ == '__main__': instruction, but everything works perfectly. The program that is passed to the child process is identical, but the execution point is within the start method which sets the target running rather than continuing the program. So you will see just one finished printed as the child process continues the progress with the target not the remainder of the program. It is as if the program was:

```
p1.start()
if(child process):
        target()
        exit subprocess
print("Finished")
```

The print("Finished") is only executed on the parent process.

If you try the same program on Windows, or more generally using the spawn start method, you will simply see an exception:

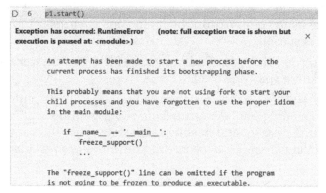

As the error message suggests, the solution is to use the if __name__ == '__main__' construct to avoid running the part of the program that creates the child process. The point is that __name__ is only set to main in the parent and hence the main program isn't run in the child process.

That is if you use:

```
import multiprocessing
def myProcess():
    print("Hello Process World")

if __name__ == '__main__':
    p1=multiprocessing.Process(target=myProcess)
    p1.start()
    print("Finished")
```

then it will run correctly on Linux/Unix or Windows even though it isn't necessary when using the fork start method.

This is easy enough to understand and in both cases, fork or spawn, the main program isn't run a second time in the child process. This said, there are still differences between the two start methods that you need to be aware of as early as possible to avoid subtle errors.

The fork method doesn't re-run the Python program at all, but the spawn method does. With this in mind consider the following program:

```
import multiprocessing

def myProcess():
    global count
    print("child process",count)

count=42
print("main1",count)
if __name__ == '__main__':
    p1=multiprocessing.Process(target=myProcess)
    count=43
    print("main2",count)
    p1.start()
```

Notice that myProcess now uses a global variable which is set to 42 before the start of the main code. Within the main code count is set to 43 before the child process is started.

What value do you think the child process prints? The answer depends on whether a fork or a spawn is used.

If a fork is used under Linux/Unix then the program in the child process calls target. The program isn't rerun from the beginning as it is a clone of the program in the parent and has the same state. That is, count is currently set to 43 as in the parent. This means that the child process displays 43.

Also, as the program isn't re-run from the start you see:

```
main1 42
main2 43
child process 43
```

The first two lines are printed by the parent process and the final line is printed by the child process.

On the other hand, if a spawn is used under Windows then the entire program is restarted in the child process which means that count is set to 42 and the main code isn't run so it doesn't get set to 43. So what you see is:

```
main1 42
main2 43
main1 42
child process 42
```

and count is 42 in the child process. Also notice that the first print instruction is also obeyed in the child process as it is outside of the main code and hence you see main1 42 printed twice, not just once.

This might seem complicated but you can reduce it to the two simple rules given earlier:

1. Always use if __name__ == '__main__': to ensure that the setup code doesn't get run in the child process.

2. Do not define any global resources in the main code as these will not be available in the child process if a spawn is used.

To illustrate what goes wrong if you don't follow the second rule, consider:

```
import multiprocessing

def myProcess():
    global count
    print("child process",count)

if __name__ == '__main__':
    p1=multiprocessing.Process(target=myProcess)
    count=43
    print("main2",count)
    p1.start()
```

If you try this out using a fork it works perfectly because the running program is cloned and when the child process starts running the target there is a global count variable. If you try this using a spawn the program is run from the start but now the main code is skipped and hence there is no global count and you see an exception.

In practice, you should try to avoid providing global resources to the child process – use parameters passed to the target instead:

```
import multiprocessing

def myProcess(count):
    print("subprocess",count)

if __name__ == '__main__':
    p1=multiprocessing.Process(target=myProcess,
                                    kwargs={"count":42})
    p1.start()
```

A point that is often overlooked is that when using the spawn method you need to import the modules that your child process uses outside of the main program. That is, if there is a module that the parent process uses but the child processes do not, include the import in the main program not in the code that the child process executes. For example, the previous example to compute pi could be written:

```
import time
import multiprocessing

def myPi(m,n):
    pi=0
    s=-1
    for k in range(m,n):
        s= -1*s
        pi += s / (2 * k - 1)
    print(4*pi)

if __name__ == '__main__':
    import multiprocessing
    import multiprocessing.connection
    import time
    N=1000000
    p1=multiprocessing.Process(target=myPi,args=(N//2+1,N))
    t1=time.perf_counter()
    p1.start()
    myPi(1,N//2)
    p1.join()
    t2=time.perf_counter()
    print((t2-t1)*1000)
```

This avoids loading the unused modules into the child processes when a spawn is used as the start method. This also works with a fork, but in this case the modules are loaded in the child processes as the fork duplicates the parent.

If you include

```
print(multiprocessing.cpu_count())
```

as the last line of myPi then you will discover that running under Linux/Unix you don't see an error as multiprocessing is imported, but under Windows you do as the spawn doesn't load the module.

Forkserver

There is a third start method – forkserver. It is generally thought that the fork method of creating a new process is fragile and a spawn is preferable. On Linux/Unix, however, the natural way to create a new process is to use a fork, but you can use a spawn. The downside is that a spawn is slower as the program's state has to be reconstructed by being run.

A compromise is to use a forkserver. This can be thought of as using a fork operation to implement a spawn. What happens is that a simple server process is created, complete with the Python interpreter, and it is used thereafter to create any new processes needed. When asked to create a new child process, the server forks itself creating a minimal new Python process. It then loads and runs the Python program from the start, just like the spawn process.

Parent process

```
Python Interpreter

Global resources created by the pogram

import multiprocessing
def myProcess():
    print("Hello Process World")

if __name__ == '__main__':
    p1=multiprocessing.Process(target=myProcess)
    p1.start()
```

Step 1
Create a Server

Forkserver

```
Python Interpreter
Preloaded modules
```

Step 2
Load Program and start Target

Child process

Fork

```
Python Interpreter
Preloaded modules

Global resources created by the program

import multiprocessing
def myProcess():
    print("Hello Process World")

if __name__ == '__main__':
    p1=multiprocessing.Process(target=myProcess)
    p1.start()
```

What this means is that your program, apart from the code after the `if __name__=='main'`, is run. This is just like the case of a spawn.

Forkserver supports a relatively undocumented optimization that can be used to avoid the repeated loading of modules into child processes. Notice that when the Python program in the child process is run any imports are performed from scratch. To avoid this overhead you can preload the modules into the server image. That is, the Python server that is forked can already have the required modules loaded and it is provided to the child processes by the fork rather than by being reloaded and hence re-executed. To do this you use the method:

```
context.set_forkserver_preload([list of modules])
```

The context object is introduced in the next section, but this method is only available for the forkserver `start` method. For example:

```
import random
def myProc():
    global random
    print(random.randint(1,6))

if __name__ == '__main__':
    import multiprocessing
    ctx = multiprocessing.get_context('forkserver')
    ctx.set_forkserver_preload(['random'])
    p1=ctx.Process(target=myProc)
    p1.start()
    p1.join()
```

The `random` module is preloaded into the server and this means that it is automatically provided in a child process without having to be imported. It is necessary to include the `import random`, however, to allow the interpreter to work out what is happening – a module isn't loaded if it is already present. It is doubtful that this is a useful optimization unless the child process is loading a large module and is subject to a tight time limit.

Controlling Start Method

If you don't want to use the default start method you can set a choice using:

```
multiprocessing.set_start_method("method")
```

where *method* is one of spawn, fork or forkserver. You can only set the start method once, hence it is best placed in the main section and it applies to all child processes.

You can discover what start methods are supported using:

```
multiprocessing.get_all_start_methods()
```

which returns a list of supported methods on the current system.

To find out the current start method use:

```
multiprocessing.get_start_method()
```

If you need to set the start method for individual processes, which is not a good idea, then you can use a context object:

```
multiprocessing.get_context(method = start method)
```

This returns a context object which you can use in place of `Process` to create child processes. You can customize the `context` object as it has all of the attributes of the `Process` class. For example:

```
ctx = multiprocessing.get_context('forkserver')
p1=ctx.Process(target=myProc)
```

starts `p1` using a forkserver. Any customization only affects child processes created using the context object.

Summary

- A process runs as a program in its own right, isolated from other processes.

- Using multiple processes running on multiple cores can speed up a program.

- The `Process` class can be used to create a child process and run a target function.

- It is best practice to follow the three rules:

    1. Always use if `__name__` == `'__main__'`: to ensure that the setup code doesn't get run in the child process.

    2. Do not define or modify any global resources in the setup code as these will not always be available in the child process.

    3. Prefer to use parameters to pass initial data to the child process rather than global constants.

- Daemon processes, i.e. `daemon=True`, stop running when their parent ends. Non-daemon processes, the default, continue to run until they complete.

- You can use `Join` to wait for a process to finish.

- `multiprocessing.connection.wait` can be used to wait for the first process to finish.

- Python uses three different ways to start new processes – fork, spawn and forkserver.

- Fork is the default on Linux and works by cloning the parent process and starting the target function running.

- Spawn is the default on Windows and works by recreating the parent process by creating a new process, loading Python, loading and running the parent program before starting the target.

- Forkserver creates a server loaded with Python and any modules that the child process needs. When a child process is created the server is forked and then the parent program is loaded and run before the target is started.

- You can set the start method to be used to one of the supported methods on a particular operating system.

Threads are often described as lightweight processes, but while they are a lot like processes there are some important differences. In this chapter we discover how to create and control threads within a single process.

As the `multiprocessing` module is based on the `threading` module you will find much of this chapter similar to the previous chapter, but there are important differences even at this level.

The Thread Class

When you start running a Python program you have a single thread, usually referred to as main thread. This just runs the Python interpreter, which in turns runs your Python program. You can create additional threads using the Thread class:

```
class threading.Thread(group=None, target=None,
                       name=None, args=(), kwargs={}, *, daemon=None)
```

where for the moment, `group` isn't used, `target` specifies the callable to start the thread running, `name` is an optional identifier for the thread and `args` and `kwargs` are the positional and keyword arguments passed to the target. Discussion of the `daemon` parameter is best left until later.

Once you have a `Thread` object you can start the callable running in a new thread using the `start` method:

```
import threading
def myThread():
    print("Hello Thread World")

t1=threading.Thread(target=myThread)
t1.start()
```

You will see `Hello Thread World` displayed by the new thread before the program comes to an end. The thread that runs the target is in the same process as the main thread and all of the global variables that are accessible to the main thread are accessible to it – both threads share the same memory space. This has some important consequences which we will explore in detail later.

The `name` attribute of the thread is purely for you to use to identify the thread – it is of no importance to the system. The two attributes `ident` and `native_id` are more useful in that they are unique across the system at the time the thread is running. The `ident` attribute is an integer that is assigned by the system. It is the system identifier of the thread and can be used in other system calls that need a thread id. Both are globally unique across the entire system, but only while the thread is running. When the thread ends the assigned `ident` and `thread_id` may be reused. Notice that `native_id` isn't available on all systems and is only available from Python 3.8 onwards.

Threads and the GIL

Threads are very different from processes in that they share the runtime environment. That is, they have access to the same set of variables and objects as they run within the same process. Processes, on the other hand, each have their own copies of all of the variables within the program and there is no interaction between them. This sharing of resources seems to make things simpler, but in many ways it creates additional problems.

At the time of writing another major issue is the GIL – Global Interpreter Lock. The current implementation of CPython, and some other implementations like PyPy, allow only one thread to use the Python interpreter code at any one time. This isn't very important on a system that has only a single CPU or core as only one thread is active at any given time anyway, but it does stop programs from running faster on multicore machines.

Although other implementations of Python, Jython for example, do not use the GIL they may in fact be slower than CPython or lack support for all of the modules that CPython does. There are attempts both to remove the GIL from CPython and to improve its performance. The main reasons for the continued existence of the GIL is that it allows Python to work with C-based libraries that are not thread-safe and it keeps single-threaded programs fast.

If you have a set of CPU-bound Python threads then the GIL determines that only one thread is running at any given time and there is no potential speedup. If you want to speed up a program using multiple cores then you need to use processes rather than threads. However, all is not lost. A multi-threaded program can be faster than a single-threaded program if the threads are mostly I/O-bound. When a thread does any I/O it generally has to wait for the operation to complete and it releases the GIL, allowing another thread to start execution. This means that a set of I/O-bound threads will run faster even with the GIL

As the GIL is a lock on the Python interpreter it is also freed if a thread calls C code to do something. That is, a thread usually releases the GIL if it isn't running Python code. The "usually" is because the Python code has to explicitly release the GIL and it can be difficult to work out which Python instructions actually free the GIL. For example, if you compute x=sin(t) then the GIL is released while the C function that performs the computation gets on with its job. This means that the execution of sin(t) can make use of additional cores if available.

A Python CPU-bound thread also gives up the GIL every so often to give other threads a chance to run. This aspect of the GIL was changed in Python 3.9 to make it work better. Originally a thread holding the GIL was allowed to execute a fixed number of Python byte codes. Now it runs for a maximum time before relinquishing the GIL and allowing another thread to run. The operating system decides which of the waiting threads gets to run.

You can find out what this time interval is and set it using:

```
sys.getswitchinterval()
sys.setswitchinterval(value)
```

Currently the default is 0.005 s, i.e. 5 ms. Given that switching threads is an expensive operation the value should be set high, but you can improve the response time of a program by lowering it. Notice that the system may not set the exact value you specify – it could be longer. Also the default of 5 ms is very long by comparison with the execution times of many threads and so it is often possible for a thread to run to completion without being interrupted by another thread.

To summarize:

- Only one thread has the GIL and hence is running Python code at any given time, no matter how many cores the machine has.

- A thread that starts to execute non-Python code, usually C code, should give up the GIL and allow another thread to run Python code.

- A thread gives up the GIL and allows another thread to run if it starts an I/O or other operation that causes it to have to wait.

- A thread also gives up the GIL after switchinterval seconds and allows another thread to acquire the GIL and run.

The GIL is a confusing factor when you are trying to reason about the behavior of a threaded program. Things don't always work as you would expect from a consideration of the way the operating system handles threading. In this sense the GIL gets in the way of the OS scheduler and stops it from doing its job.

Threading Utilities

The threading module provides some general purpose functions for finding out about threads:

threading.active_count()   the number of active threads

threading.enumerate()   a list of currently active threads

threading.current_thread() the Thread object of the current thread

threading.main_thread()   a Thread object for the main thread

threading.get_ident()   the 'thread id' of the current thread

threading.get_native_id() the native id of the current thread

Daemon Threads

Like processes, threads can be daemon or non-daemon. The default is daemon = False, i.e. a non-daemon thread. A non-daemon thread will keep the process alive until all non-daemon threads have ended. As remarked in the chapter on processes this is counter to the usual Linux/Unix daemon which runs in the background, independent of any other process or user interaction. Consider for example:

```
import threading

def myThread():
    while True:
        pass

t0=threading.main_thread()
t1=threading.Thread(target=myThread,daemon=True)
t2=threading.Thread(target=myThread,daemon=False)
t1.start()
t2.start()
print(t0.native_id)
print(t1.native_id)
print(t2.native_id)
print("ending")
```

If you run this you will see the native_id of each thread printed followed by ending, but the process will not end. If you check you will find that all three threads are still running. The idea of a daemon thread is subtle in that any non-daemon threads that are running will stop the main thread from exiting and hence it will not automatically stop any other threads from running, daemon or non-daemon. When all of the non-daemon threads end the main thread can end and this brings any daemon threads that are still running to an end.

Under Windows you need to download and install Process Explorer to view threads. Under Linux use ps with the -t option. Also you cannot always stop a thread using the keyboard break Ctrl- c. Use the Process Explorer or the Kill command under Linux. If you run this program under an IDE and debugger then you are likely to see a more complicated result than just three threads running as described.

Waiting for a Thread

All of the threads that a program creates run within a single process. You can arrange for one thread to wait on another to complete using the Thread object's join method:

```
Thread.join(timeout)
```

This waits for the thread to finish or for the specified timeout. Notice that you have to use Thread.is_alive() to discover if a thread terminated or simply timed out. If you don't specify a timeout the join waits until the thread terminates.

Unlike a process there is no easy and consistent way that one thread can terminate another. That is, there is no thread equivalent of process.kill or process.terminate. The only easy way to stop a thread is via programmed cooperation. That is, the thread has to monitor a shared resource and stop itself when asked to do so by another thread. This is explained in the context of events in Chapter 6.

If you want to wait for multiple threads to finish their tasks then you can simply use multiple joins:

```
t1.join()
t2.join()
t3.join()
print("all finished")
```

The print is only executed when all three threads are complete.

There is no easy way to wait for the first of a set of threads to complete. This is a surprise for many programmers used to other languages. There are ways to do it, but there is no single method that will wait for the first thread of a set to complete. Notice that the simple-minded approach of repeatedly checking is_alive() for each thread isn't a good method as it keeps the waiting thread busy, so tying up the CPU, while waiting for a thread to complete. This is particularly bad given that the GIL means that only one thread can be running at any given time.

So you should not use constructs like:

```
for t in threading.enumerate():
    if not t.is_alive():
        print(t.native_id)
        break
```

to repeatedly check for a completed thread unless you need to keep the waiting thread doing something. Possible solutions to this problem are given in Chapter 6 using a semaphore and in Chapter 11 using Futures.

Local Variables

The idea that threads run in the same process and share the same memory is something that makes them different from using multiprocessing, even though they seem to provide a similar facility. The idea that threads share storage is much more subtle than you might expect and is rarely discussed. Some variables and the objects that they reference are unique to the thread that is using them. - they are "thread local".

A thread starts running the code in any callable object, most usually a function object. Consider the following function and its use by two threads:

```
import threading

def myThread(sym):
    temp=sym
    while True:
        print(temp)

t1=threading.Thread(target=myThread,args=("A",))
t2=threading.Thread(target=myThread,args=("B",))
t1.start()
t2.start()
t1.join()
```

The function simply repeatedly prints whatever is passed to it as the first parameter. Thread t1 prints A and t2 prints B – but how is this possible? If threads share the same memory how is it that t1 gets a copy of the local variable temp and t2 gets a different copy of the variable temp? The answer is that when a function is called all of the local variables, including any parameters, are created and they exist for the time that the function is executing. To be exact, they are created on the stack and the stack is popped when the function finishes. Normally you cannot call the same function more than once "at the same time" but when you use a thread you can. Each time a thread starts executing a function all of its local variables are created on the stack and are only accessible by that thread.

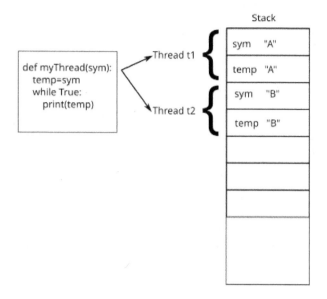

In other words, each thread gets its own copy of any local variables. Putting this another way, local variables are thread local. Compare this to the behavior of an attribute of the function object or indeed any object:

```
import threading

def myThread(sym):
    myThread.temp=sym
    while True:
        print(myThread.temp)

myThread.temp=""

t1=threading.Thread(target=myThread,args=("A",))
t2=threading.Thread(target=myThread,args=("B",))
t1.start()
t2.start()
t1.join()
```

In this case we create an attribute, temp, of the myThread function object. If you aren't sure about this see **Programmer's Python: Everything Is An Object**, ISBN: 978-1871962741. Attributes exist as long as the object that "hosts" them exists and a function object exists even when its code is not being executed.

This means that function object attributes have a longer lifetime than local variables and they are not created when the function is called and destroyed when it ends. Because of this when the function object is accessed via different threads there is only one function object which they share and only

75

one set of attributes which they can work with. As a result what you see if you run the program is a few "A"s and then nothing but "B"s because once t2 starts to run it changes the attribute to B and it isn't changed back to A when t1 runs again.

To summarize:

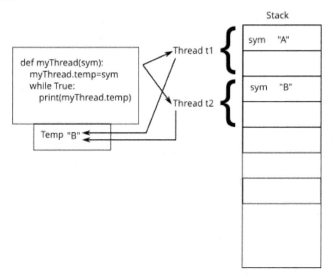

♦ Threads have their own copies of local variables but share global variables and attributes of objects that they do not create.

This last phrase, "objects that they do not create" deserves some clarification. All objects are global, but within a function it is possible for a local variable to reference a newly created object. If such a function is run using a thread then a new object will be created and the local variable will reference the thread's own version of the object, for example:

```
import threading

class MyClass():
    temp=""

def myThread(sym):
    myObject=MyClass()
    myObject.temp=sym
    while True:
        print(myObject.temp)

t1=threading.Thread(target=myThread,args=("A",))
t2=threading.Thread(target=myThread,args=("B",))
t1.start()
t2.start()
t1.join()
```

Notice that the function now creates an instance of `MyClass` and stores the value of its parameter in its `temp` attribute. When `t1` starts to run the function it creates an instance and a local variable `myObject` to reference it. When `t2` starts, it creates another instance of `MyClass` and a new local variable called `myObject` to reference it. Hence both threads have their own objects and their own local variables which reference them. This means that `t1` prints `A` and `t2` prints `B` as before.

When the threads end the local variables are destroyed and the two objects are garbage-collected. If the instance was created in the main program then both threads would reference the same object and its `temp` attribute could only store an `A` or a `B` and so after seeing a few `A`s printed you would see just `B`s.

If all of this seems obvious then well done. A good grasp of what is shared between threads and what is local to a thread is essential to avoiding subtle errors.

Thread Local Storage

It is obvious that global variable are always shared and in most cases this isn't a problem. However, suppose you have some existing code that makes use of a global variable to store its state and we want to make it thread-safe. To do this we have to create a global variable that is thread-local. The `threading` module provides the `local` class which is a global object with thread-local attributes. That is, when you create an instance of `threading.local` any attributes that a thread creates are thread-local, for example:

```
import threading

myObject=threading.local()

def myThread(sym):
    myObject.temp=sym
    while True:
        print(myObject.temp)

t1=threading.Thread(target=myThread,args=("A",))
t2=threading.Thread(target=myThread,args=("B",))
t1.start()
t2.start()
t1.join()
```

This repeatedly prints runs of `A`s and `B`s. The `local` class is used to create a thread-local object, myObject, and `t1` and `t2` use this to create their own thread-local `temp` attributes. If myObject was just a general object, i.e. not thread-local, then `t1` and `t2` would share a single copy of the attribute.

At this point you should be wondering why anyone would want to use threading.local? Notice that a local object cannot be used to persist the state of a function that is repeatedly run using a thread simply because it really is thread-local and different for each thread. For example, you cannot use it to write a function that counts the number of times it has been called irrespective of the thread that calls it. For that you need a simple global variable that is the same for all threads.

There really is no point in using threading.local if you are writing the code from scratch. If you need anything that is local to a thread then create it within the thread and it will automatically be thread-local. To see that this is true compare this example with the previous example – they achieve the same result, but the first one doesn't use threading.local.

To summarize:

- local variables are automatically thread-local
- function parameters are automatically thread-local
- objects created within a thread are thread-local
- the threading.local class creates global thread-local objects which aren't needed in well written thread-safe code.

Computing Pi with Multiple Threads

It is informative to compare the multi-process computation of pi given in the previous chapter with a multi-threaded computation:

```
import threading
import time

def myPi(m,n):
    pi = 0
    for k in range(m,n+1):
        s = 1 if k%2 else -1
        pi += s / (2 * k - 1)
    print(4*pi)

N=10000000
thread1=threading.Thread(target=myPi,args=(N//2+1,N))
t1=time.perf_counter()
thread1.start()
myPi(1,N//2)
thread1.join()
t2=time.perf_counter()
print((t2-t1)*1000)
```

You can see that this is virtually the same program, but using equivalent thread methods. If you try this out you will discover that, compared to the single-threaded version, the computation is slower. For example, on a dual-core Windows machine the time increased from 1700 ms to 1800 ms and on a Pi 4 from 4500 ms to 5000 ms.

This increase in time lag shouldn't come as a surprise. The GIL means that the threads cannot run at the same time and hence they cannot make use of the additional cores. The multi-threaded program takes longer simply because of the overhead in switching between threads.

The computation of Pi is a CPU-bound task and so there is no hope that using multiple threads can speed it up while the GIL is in force. However, when it comes to I/O-bound threads, the story is very different.

I/O-Bound Threads

The only problem with demonstrating I/O-bound threads is to find a simple I/O operation that doesn't require a lot of explanation. The `urllib.request` module is very simple and will download an HTML page of your choice using HTTP:

```
import urllib.request
with urllib.request.urlopen('http://www.example.com/') as f:
    html = f.read().decode('utf-8')
```

This is an I/O operation that frees the GIL while waiting for the file download to complete. If you want to download two HTML pages then the simplest non-threading approach is:

```
import urllib.request
import time

def download():
    with urllib.request.urlopen('http://www.example.com/') as f:
        html = f.read().decode('utf-8')

t1=time.perf_counter()
download()
download()
t2=time.perf_counter()
print((t2-t1)*1000)
```

When this runs, the first download blocks the second download from starting until it is complete and hence there is no overlap in operations. On a medium speed PC and on a Raspberry Pi 4 the operation takes around 340 ms on a broadband connection.

Changing this to a threaded program is easy:

```
import urllib.request
import threading
import time

def download():
    with urllib.request.urlopen('http://www.example.com/') as f:
        html = f.read().decode('utf-8')

thread1=threading.Thread(target=download)
t1=time.perf_counter()
thread1.start()
download()
thread1.join()
t2=time.perf_counter()
print((t2-t1)*1000)
```

Now thread1 starts the download and very quickly suspends its operation, so freeing the GIL and allowing the main thread to continue. The result is that now the time taken is around 200 ms with the Pi 4 being about 10% faster.

If you download four files using a single thread the time for the Pi 4 increases to about 500 ms and using four threads the time is still about 180 ms with similar results for the PC. It seems that you can almost download any number of files without it costing any extra time! This is only true as long as the communications channel and its associated server aren't overloaded by requests.

Sleep(0)

The time.sleep method can be used to suspend a thread for a specific amount of time. This has the side effect of allowing the system to schedule another thread to run in its place. In addition, the time.sleep method also releases the GIL when it starts the suspension and reacquires it when the time is up. What this means is that a thread that uses time.sleep allows the system to schedule other threads.

A common idiom is to use `time.sleep(0)` to give other threads a chance to run, for example:

```
import threading
import time

def test():
    while(True):
        time.sleep(0)
        pass

thread1=threading.Thread(target=test)
thread2=threading.Thread(target=test)
thread1.start()
thread2.start()
thread1.join()
```

This just runs two threads that simply keep the CPU busy running a loop. With the `time.sleep(0)` in the loop Windows Performance Monitor reports 120,000 context swaps per second and with it commented out it reports 800 per second. You can see that the sleep command does suspend the thread. Of course, which thread runs next is up to the operating system which schedules the thread most deserving of CPU time and this might not be a Python thread at all or it could be the thread that just used `time.sleep`. Also notice that the context swaps can occur more frequently than the GIL is released as these are independent actions.

Timer Object

The `Timer` object is described in the documentation as a synchronization primitive. It is better described as an example of how to subclass the `Thread` class. It simply delays the start of the thread for the given interval.

A `Timer` object is created using its constructor:

```
threading.Timer(interval,function,args=None,kwargs=None)
```

This looks a lot like the `Thread` constructor and indeed `Timer` is a sub-class of `Thread` and it creates a new thread as part of the `Timer` object. The `interval` you specify is the delay, in seconds, before the thread is started, running function with the specified arguments.

The `Timer` thread is started using the usual start method and it can be canceled using the `cancel()` method. Notice that this cannot stop the function running once the it is started – it simply cancels the delay.

For example:

```
import threading
def hello():
    print("A delayed hello")

tim=threading.Timer(1,hello)
tim.start()
```

prints A delayed hello after 1 second. Notice that as Timer is a sub-class of Thread you can use join and other Thread methods.

The Timer works by waiting on an Event that is never set, see Chapter 6, and exiting on a timeout:

```
def run(self):
    self.finished.wait(self.interval)
    if not self.finished.is_set():
        self.function(*self.args, **self.kwargs)
    self.finished.set()
```

The run method of the Thread object is called to actually start the thread and it's the one to override to customize the starting of threads. In this case we first wait on a self.finished, which is initialized to be an Event object. As the Event object is usually not set, it simply causes the wait for the specified timeout in self.interval. Once the timeout is up self.function is set running on the new thread. The cancel function simply sets the Event to terminate the wait and the next if statement checks to see if the function has been canceled or should be run.

When you first meet the Timer there is a tendency to think that it is a good idea in need of extending to a repeating timer by reusing Timer. This is possible, but it isn't a good idea. The problem is that when the Timer ends so does the thread, so you can't simply call start again without recreating the thread and this is time-consuming in itself.

A better idea is to override the run function with something like:

```
import threading

class IntervalTimer(threading.Thread):
    def __init__(self, interval, function, args=None, kwargs=None):
        threading.Thread.__init__(self)
        self.interval = interval
        self.function = function
        self.args = args if args is not None else []
        self.kwargs = kwargs if kwargs is not None else {}
        self.finished = threading.Event()

    def cancel(self):
        self.finished.set()

    def run(self):
        while(True):
            self.finished.wait(self.interval)
            if self.finished.is_set():
                break
            else:
                self.function(*self.args, **self.kwargs)
        self.finished.set()
```

You can see now that the run method repeatedly puts the thread to sleep by waiting on the Event for a timeout. Notice that the cancel method works and cancels the next repeat.

Summary

- The `Threading` module is very similar to the `Process` module.
- Threads cannot be used to speed up a Python program because of the GIL – Global Interpreter Lock. This only allows a single thread to be using the Python Interpreter at any given time.
- The current Python thread will give up the GIL to another thread if it is waiting for I/O, running another language, or after it has run for a specific time.
- When a thread releases the GIL the operating system selects the next thread to run, which might even be a thread in another process.
- A non-daemon thread, `daemon = False,` will keep the main thread alive until it is finished. A daemon thread will allow it to end before it has finished.
- You can wait for a thread using `join`. If you specify a timeout you have to test to see why the join ended.
- A function can be used by more than one thread. When this happens all its local variables are unique to the thread – they are thread-local. Global variables and objects are shared between threads and so are locally created objects.
- Global variables can be converted to `threading.local` objects which makes them local to each thread. This is usually only needed if you are using code that you cannot modify to work in more sensible ways.
- Using threads speeds up I/O-bound programs but not CPU-bound programs.
- The function `time.sleep` can be used to suspend a Python thread.
- The `Timer` object isn't as useful for running delayed programs as it seems because it creates and destroys a thread, which means it cannot be used as a repeating timer.

Chapter 5

Locks and Deadlock

The key issue in multi-processing and multi-threading is how to communicate data. For processes things are both simplified and complicated by the fact that there is almost total isolation between different processes. That is, each process has its own set of variables and there are no automatically shared resources. With processes the problem is establishing communication.

With threads, on the other hand, all threads in a single process share the same memory and in particular they all have access to the same global variables. As a result you don't have to do anything much to establish communication between threads. The only thing you have to do is to ensure that access to shared resources is controlled so that updates by more than one thread do not compete and invalidate data. Essentially, you have to synchronize actions between threads and the most common way of achieving this is to use a lock.

In this chapter we look at the Lock class, the simplest and most common of the many types of lock that are available. Processes also have the problem of synchronization and so locks are relevant to them as well. We first look at the nature of the problem and then examine how locking solved it, but creates another problem in its wake – deadlock.

Race Conditions

A race condition occurs when the outcome of two or more operations isn't completely determined because the order in which they could be executed isn't fixed. It is called a race condition because you can think of the outcome as depending on which operation reaches the finishing line first. The actual jargon associated with race conditions is obscure and I'm not going to enumerate all of the possible types of race condition, or indeed what exactly qualifies as a race condition. To be pragmatic, all that really matters is that a race condition means the result you get at runtime varies in ways that you might not have expected in a single threaded program.

The classic race condition is when two or more threads attempt to access a single resource and what happens depends on the order they access it. Notice that in this sense a race condition can only occur if at least one of the threads is modifying the resource whereas a shared resource can be read without restriction or potential problems. Reading is safe, writing is dangerous.

This is also the reason that immutable data structures are preferred.

Of course, to communicate, threads have to write to shared data and this makes things harder. Finding a good but simple example of a race condition is difficult, especially so since the improvements in the way the GIL is managed. Unless a thread gives up the GIL it can run for up to 5 ms without interruption and this makes it difficult to capture an example where two threads are accessing the same resource close in time. For example, prior to the update you could simply use an increment `a += 1` to demonstrate a race condition – two threads incrementing the same global variable soon displayed problems. The cause of the problem is that `myCounter += 1` isn't an "atomic" instruction as it is composed of a number of actions.

That is the update is:

1. Retrieve the value in `myCounter`
2. Add one to it
3. Store the value back in `myCounter`

These three steps occur one after the other and it is quite possible that another thread will take over after any of the steps. If the new thread is running the same code then it too will perform the three steps, but it will retrieve the same value of `myCounter` as the first thread. Suppose `myCounter` is 42 and the first thread retrieves its value and is then replaced by another thread which also retrieves the value in `myCounter`, i.e. 42. The second thread will add one and save the result, i.e. 43 and then the first thread is restarted and it too adds one and stores the result, i.e. 43. Of course, the correct answer should be 44 as both threads should have incremented `myCounter`.

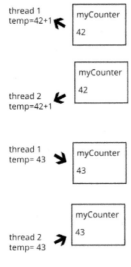

It should be easy to write a program that demonstrates this classic race condition, but the way that the GIL works makes this difficult as the 5 ms runtime makes the probability that another thread will interrupt the running thread during the increment very low, but not zero. To improve the chances of seeing the problem we need to spread the increment over a longer time to make it more likely that a race condition will occur. For example:

```
from cmath import sqrt
import threading
import time

myCounter=0

def count():
    global myCounter
    for i in range(100000):
        temp=myCounter+1
        x=sqrt(2)
        myCounter=temp

thread1= threading.Thread(target=count)
thread2= threading.Thread(target=count)
t1=time.perf_counter()

thread1.start()
thread2.start()
thread1.join()
thread2.join()

t2=time.perf_counter()
print((t2-t1)*1000)
print(myCounter)
```

The count function simply adds one to the global counter, but it does so via a local variable. The time between retrieving the initial value and updating it before storing it back is large enough for another thread to take over execution in the middle. To make this even more likely, a sqrt is calculated as this calls a pure C function to do the calculation and so frees the GIL, inviting another thread to take over. You could use time.sleep(0) in place of sqrt, but this demonstrates that the GIL can be released even when you don't explicitly try to do so.

Even so, when you run this program occasionally you will see the correct answer of 200000 but you should see a smaller value much more often. The value is smaller because of the number of times two overlapping increments occurred and count was only incremented by one instead of two.

The important point is that you cannot predict what this very simple program will produce when it is run. In a system that is organized to not allow a thread to interrupt a running CPU-bound thread then you will get the "correct" answer of 200000. On a machine that allows threads to interrupt each other with less restraint you will get a lower value. The actual behavior of the program depends on its timing and the way that the GIL interacts with the operating system's scheduling method.

The point is that this code is not deterministic in the sense that you cannot predict what it does just by reading its code.

You might object that the function being used to demonstrate this is contrived and would never be created in practice, but it is a simplified model of what most functions do when they access a shared resource – read the resource, do some computation and finally save the new result to the resource. In practice the reason for the race condition is usually much more difficult to see.

Hardware Problem or Heisenbug?

The example of a race condition just given is optimized to increase the probability that the condition will occur. In the real world programs generally have a lower probability of creating a race condition and the result might well be what you are expecting when you run it many times. Eventually, however, the conditions will be right and the program will give the wrong result. This means that the program will likely pass testing and only show an error very occasionally, usually when most damage can be incurred. Such bugs are usually referred to as "non-deterministic" because you can run the program under the same conditions and get different results.

Often the first response is to test, or even replace, the hardware and this increases the time it takes even to realize that there is a software bug waiting to be found. Such bugs are very difficult to locate because they are very difficult to reproduce. They are often labeled as Heisenbugs because any attempt to find them tends to make them disappear. Running a program with a race condition in a debugger, for example, can make the probability of it occurring go to zero. Similarly, adding debugging statements can modify the timings so as to make the problem vanish – until they are removed and the program put back into general use.

The only secure and reasonable solution to the problem is to use locking.

Locks

A lock is a co-operative mechanism for restricting access to a resource. The important point here is "co-operative". It needs to be clear right from the start that a locking mechanism only works if you implement it correctly in all of the code that makes use of the shared resource. There is nothing stopping code that does not make use of the lock from accessing the resource. This is a general feature of locking in most operating systems and isn't specific to Python.

The simplest type of lock has just two states – locked and unlocked. Any code that wants access to a resource that will not be interrupted by another thread has to acquire the lock by changing it to the locked state. If a thread tries to acquire the lock that is already locked then the thread has to wait for it to be unlocked.

The `Lock` class behaves exactly as described. It is a wrapper for a lock that is implemented by the operating system. In other words, the Python `Lock` is an operating system construct. It corresponds to the most basic type of lock, usually called a mutex, for Mutually Exclusive lock. It has an `acquire` method:

`Lock.acquire(blocking=True, timeout=- 1)`

and a `release` method:

`Lock.release()`

The `blocking` parameter determines what happens if the lock cannot be acquired. If it is `True`, the default, then the thread simply waits until the lock is available. The `acquire` returns `True` when the lock is acquired and you can set a `timeout` for the wait. Its default is -1 which means "wait forever". If the `acquire` returns because of the timeout then it returns `False`. Alternatively you can set blocking to `False` and then `acquire` returns immediately with `True` if the lock has been acquired or `False` if it has not. In this case you cannot specify a timeout.

If a thread has the lock then it has to release it when it has finished modifying the resource, using the `release` method. Any thread, not just the thread that has the lock, can release it and this can be a problem. If you try to release a lock that isn't locked then you generate a `RuntimeError`. When a lock is released the thread that released it carries on running until it gives up the GIL and another thread gets a chance to run. If there are multiple threads waiting to acquire the lock then the operating system picks just one of them to run and the others have to again wait until it releases the lock that it has just acquired.

Notice that which thread gets to run when a lock becomes available depends on the operating system and you cannot rely on any particular order of execution. That is, if threads A, B and C attempt to acquire the lock in that order they don't necessarily run in that order when the lock is released.

If we add a lock to the function in the previous example then it always returns the correct result no matter how many threads are used to execute it:

```
myCounter=0
countlock=threading.Lock()
def count():
    global myCounter
    for i in range(100000):
        countlock.acquire()
        temp=myCounter+1
        x=sqrt(2)
        myCounter=temp
        countlock.release()
```

In this example we acquire the lock before accessing the global variable myCounter and release it after it has been completely updated. As long as all threads use the same locking then only one thread can access the resource and the program is fully deterministic. It never misses an update due to overlapped access.

This works, but it slows things down. The unlocked, but incorrect version, runs two threads in about 70 ms whereas the locked version takes 150 ms. The overhead isn't due to any loss of parallelism as with the GIL in place there isn't any. The overhead is entirely due to the cost of locking and unlocking. In principle, you should always arrange for a thread to keep a lock for the shortest possible time to allow other threads to work. However, this doesn't take the GIL into account. If you change the program so that it keeps the lock for the duration of the loop. i.e. until it has very nearly finished. then it is still deterministic, but it only takes about 70 ms with two threads:

```
myCounter=0
def count():
    global myCounter
    countlock.acquire()
    for i in range(100000):
        temp=myCounter+1
        x=sqrt(2)
        myCounter=temp
    countlock.release()
```

In other words, as the GIL only allows one thread to run at a time and as all of the threads are CPU-bound, there is no time advantage in releasing the thread early. The story would be different if some of the threads were I/O-bound because then releasing the lock might give them time to move on to another I/O operation and so reduce the overall runtime.

Locks and Processes

The multiprocessing module supports the same locks that the Threading module does and they work in exactly the same way. The only difference is that a lock isn't automatically shared between processes – recall that processes are independent entities with their own set of variables. This is the big difference between threads and processes. To overcome this problem we have to share the lock with any process that needs to use it by creating the lock in, say, the main program and then passing it as a parameter when the process is created, for example:

```
import multiprocessing
import time

def myProcess(lock):
    lock.acquire()
    time.sleep(4)
    lock.release()

if __name__ == '__main__':
    myLock=multiprocessing.Lock()
    p1=multiprocessing.Process(target=myProcess,args=(myLock,))
    p2=multiprocessing.Process(target=myProcess,args=(myLock,))
    t1=time.perf_counter()
    p1.start()
    p2.start()
    p1.join()
    p2.join()
    t2=time.perf_counter()
    print((t2-t1)*1000)
```

This runs a function which simply waits for four seconds. The lock is created in the main program and passed to each of two processes. As only one of the two processes can acquire the lock the total time taken is more than eight seconds. If you remove the locking the total time drops to just over four seconds as both processes run concurrently.

With this one change all of the examples in this chapter work with processes as well as threads. Notice the Lock has to be created in the main program to avoid it being created as a new object in each of the child processes – there should only be one shared Lock object. In principle it should not be possible to pass a Lock as a parameter because call parameters are passed by being pickled and transferred to the child process via a pipe. Lock objects are treated as a special case by the multiprocessing module and passed as a handle to a system wide lock. You cannot use the same technique when using processes created by the Pool object – see Chapter 8.

To summarize:

- ◆ To use one of the lock objects supported by the multiprocessing you have to create an instance in the main program – so that only one instance is created – and you then have to pass the object, as a parameter in the Process call, to any object that needs to use it.

Deadlock

The problem with locks is not only that they tend to slow things down, they are also prone to deadlock. As already described in Chapter 2, deadlock is where one thread acquires lock A and wants to acquire lock B but there is already a thread which has lock B and wants to acquire lock A. Of course, both threads cannot make progress and so they sit waiting for each other to give up the lock that the other wants.

It is quite easy to demonstrate deadlock using just two threads, but we also need two resources and their corresponding locks. It is also necessary for the threads to attempt to acquire the locks in the opposite order and for this we need two different count functions:

```
import threading
import time

countlock1=threading.Lock()
countlock2=threading.Lock()
myCounter1=0
myCounter2=0

def count1():
    global myCounter1
    global myCounter2
    for i in range(100000):
        countlock1.acquire()
        myCounter1+=1
        countlock2.acquire()
        myCounter2+=1
        countlock2.release()
        countlock1.release()

def count2():
    global myCounter1
    global myCounter2
    for i in range(100000):
        countlock2.acquire()
        myCounter2+=1
        countlock1.acquire()
        myCounter1+=1
        countlock1.release()
        countlock2.release()
```

```
thread1= threading.Thread(target=count1)
thread2= threading.Thread(target=count2)
t1=time.perf_counter()

thread1.start()
thread2.start()
thread1.join()
thread2.join()

t2=time.perf_counter()
print((t2-t1)*1000)
print(myCounter1)
```

You can see that if these two functions are run one-per-thread sooner or later
thread1 will have acquired countlock1 and be interrupted by thread2
which immediately acquires countlock2 and then waits for countlock1 to be
released. Of course when thread1 starts running again it tries to acquire
countlock2 which is already taken by thread2.

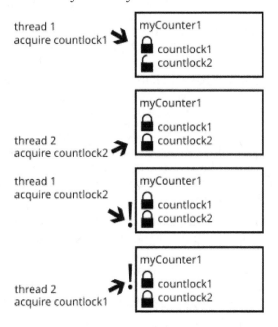

What can we do about deadlock?

This is a very deep question and it is something that has occupied computer scientists for a long time. There are automatic deadlock detection systems, but they aren't often used. The reason is that deadlock can involve many threads and many resources in a locking loop – result, deadlock:

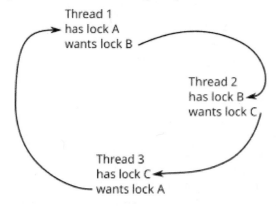

You can avoid deadlock by restricting yourself to a single lock – this is why the GIL is a single global lock. With a single lock in use there can be no deadlock. The problem with this solution is that a single lock isn't fine-grained enough to allow different shared resources to be locked by different threads and this can reduce performance. With a single lock, all of the resources can only be accessed by a single thread at a time.

The general principle for efficient use of locks is that each one should only restrict access to the smallest set of resources that cannot be in simultaneous use, i.e. when such a set of resources is locked it can only be used by a single thread, and should not contain resources that could be used by another thread at the same time.

If you have multiple locks you can avoid deadlock by always acquiring locks in the same order. Our example only suffers from deadlock because of the different order in which the locks are acquired in each thread. The deadlocked loop given earlier cannot happen if the threads always acquire locks in alphabetic order – how could thread 3 have lock C and want lock A if they were acquired in alphabetic order?

A simpler solution is to always use a timeout or non-blocking form of acquire. The idea is that if you wait for longer than a given time then you can assume that deadlock has occurred and to break the deadlock the thread should give up all of its currently held locks and start over.

For example, to remove the deadlock in our earlier example we just need to add timeouts to the second lock `acquire` calls:

```
countlock1=threading.Lock()
countlock2=threading.Lock()
myCounter1=0
myCounter2=0

def count1():
    global myCounter1
    global myCounter2
    for i in range(100000):
        countlock1.acquire()
        myCounter1+=1
        if countlock2.acquire(timeout=0.01):
            myCounter2+=1
            countlock2.release()
        countlock1.release()

def count2():
    global myCounter1
    global myCounter2
    for i in range(100000):
        countlock2.acquire()
        myCounter2+=1
        if countlock1.acquire(timeout=0.01):
            myCounter1+=1
            countlock1.release()
        countlock2.release()
```

Notice that you don't have to include a timeout for the first lock as the thread needs to hold at least two locks for deadlock. If you try this program you will find that it doesn't suffer a permanent deadlock and you eventually get an answer, but it is very slow. The reason is that each time deadlock occurs the second thread waits for just 0.01 seconds and this brings the program to a halt. If you reduce the timeout then you run the risk of concluding there is a deadlock when there isn't. Finding the right timeout in any given situation is difficult and in general selecting a very long timeout to deal with a hopefully infrequent deadlock is the best option.

Context Managed Locks

Python supports a very general context manager facility that can be used to simplify the use of, among other things, locks. Its basic form is:

```
with expression as variable:
        do something
```

What happens is that the system evaluates the *expression*, which has to result in an object that has two special methods __enter__ and __exit__. Such an object is called a "context manager".

The key idea is that as the body of the `with` statement is entered the
__enter__ method is called and if it returns an object it is assigned to the
variable. When the body finishes, either normally or because of an
exception, the __exit__ method is called. You can see that the execution of
the `with` block is associated with the context manager object and the calling
of its __enter__ method. This is supposed to set things up and optionally
return an object to be used in the `with` clause. When the clause ends the
__exit__ method is called to clean things up.

All of the Python lock classes support the context manager. The __enter__
method calls the `acquire` method and the __exit__ method calls the
`release` method.

So the locking in our example:

```
countlock.acquire()
temp=myCounter+1
x=sqrt(2)
myCounter=temp
countlock.release()
```

can be written:

```
with countlock:
    temp=myCounter+1
    x=sqrt(2)
    myCounter=temp
```

The context form is equivalent to:

```
countlock.acquire()
try:
    temp=myCounter+1
    x=sqrt(2)
    myCounter=temp
finally:
    countlock.release()
```

Notice that the lock is released even if an exception is raised in the code.

If you want to detect and deal with deadlock you may think that specifying a
timeout is a good idea, but this is more complex than you might expect. The
__enter__ method does not accept any parameters to be passed on to the
`acquire` method. The solution is to create a function that returns an object
with modified __enter__ and __exit__ methods, for example:

```
def timeLock(lock, blocking=True, timeout=-1):
    class thing:
        def __enter__(self):
            if not lock.acquire(blocking=blocking,timeout=timeout):
                raise Exception("Possible Deadlock")
        def __exit__(self,exception_type,
                                exception_value, traceback):
            lock.release()
    return thing()
```

This simply returns an object that has __enter__ and __exit__ which call the lock's acquire and release with the specified timeout. Notice that the parameters, lock, blocking and timeout are accessible by the methods because of closure, a concept that is introduced in **Programmer's Python: Everything Is An Object**, ISBN: 978-1871962741. The problem with this approach is that if the acquire times out it is difficult to know what to do. In this case we raise an exception to let the calling program solve the problem. Notice that raising an exception in the __enter__ method stops the body of the with from executing and the __exit__ method is not called to deal with the exception. This is not a great advantage as to handle the deadlock we now have to write things like:

```
def count():
    global myCounter
    for i in range(10000):
        try:
            with timeLock(countlock,timeout=0.001):
                temp=myCounter+1
                x=sqrt(2)
                myCounter=temp
        except Exception:
            print("Deadlock")
```

The additional try/except makes using the context handler less attractive.

All of the Python locks support __enter__ and __exit__ for their acquire and release actions and hence they can be used with context managers.

Recursive Lock

The Lock or mutex is the most basic form of lock, but there are many others with additional properties. Most of the time you don't need elaborations of the basic idea but two, the RLock and the Semaphore, are worth knowing about.

The Rlock, recursive or reenterable lock, is based on the Lock class and has the same methods and attributes. Its acquire method supports blocking and timeout and it works within a context manager. Its distinctive feature is that a thread can acquire the lock as many times as it needs to without being blocked, but another thread cannot. That is, when a thread acquires the lock it can call acquire again and it returns immediately, but if a different thread calls acquire it blocks until it is unlocked by the original thread. To unlock it, the original thread has to call release as many times as it called acquire. Rlock keeps a count of how many times it has been acquired and it needs that many calls to release to unlock it. That is, if an Rlock has been acquired n times it takes n releases to unlock it. The number of times acquire has been called by the same thread is known as the recursion depth, but there is no way to access this in a program.

The `Rlock` is easy to understand. What is usually more puzzling is working out what it is used for? The answer is that you can think of a `Lock` as being owned by the section of code it protects, i.e. between the `acquire` and `release`– whereas you can think of an `Rlock` as being owned by the thread that acquires it. Once acquired any code that the thread is running can acquire it again and access the locked resource. This all works as long as the code being run releases the lock as many times as it acquires it, which is ensured if you use context managers. For example if an object has a set of methods which all work with a shared resource, then an `Rlock` can give all of the methods access to the resource as long as they are running on the same thread and they can be called in any combination. The simplest example is:

```
myCounter=0
countlock=threading.RLock()

def incCount():
    global myCounter
    with countlock:
        myCounter+=1

def testCount():
    global myCounter
    with countlock:
        return myCounter==100

def count():
    global myCounter
    with countlock:
        while True:
            incCount()
            if testCount():
                break
        myCounter=0
```

The `incCount` and `testCount` functions simply make use of `myCounter` and lock access using `countLock` in the usual way. The `count` function, However, calls both of these functions and also accesses `myCounter` directly and so it needs to lock it. If we use a standard `Lock` at this point the program would fail because when `incCount` or `testCount` is called it would fail to acquire the lock. Using an `Rlock`, however, works because the lock is already acquired and can be re-acquired. Notice the way that the use of the context manager ensures that the `Rlock` is released the same number of times as it was acquired.

You can think of this use of `Rlock` as the thread acquiring the lock and then any of the functions that use the resource are allowed to access it by acquiring the lock again. If the thread is interrupted by another then the new thread cannot acquire the lock and access the resource.

Another obvious, but not common, use of an `Rlock` is within a recursive function. For example:

```
f=1
flock=threading.RLock()
def fact(n):
    global f
    with flock:
        if n==1:
            return
        f=f*n
        fact(n-1)
```

This is a slightly odd way to write a recursive factorial function as it uses a global variable `f` for its result. To allow the function to be evaluated on more than one thread we need to lock access to `f`. If we used a standard lock then the recursion would fail because the second call to `fact` would discover that the lock was already acquired. To make this work we have to use an `Rlock` which allows the `acquire` as long as the same thread has the lock. Notice that the context manager ensures that the right number of releases occur as the recursion unwinds. If you run this on N threads without resetting `f` the result is $n!^N$.

In most cases you can start out using `Lock` and if you need to call methods that lock the same resource then change to `Rlock`. There used to be a large time penalty in using `Rlock` but this is no longer the case, so avoiding its use is less important.

Semaphore

A `Semaphore` is a lock that keeps a count that relates to the number of current lock holders. The count is set to an initial value and it is decremented after each `acquire` and incremented after each `release`. An `acquire` succeeds only if the count is greater than zero. For example, if you set a `Semaphore` to 3 then the first three calls to `acquire` will immediately return with the result `True` and the fourth will wait because the count is zero. Notice that, unlike `Rlock`, different threads can call `acquire` without blocking. The fourth and subsequent calls will only return when one of the earlier threads releases the semaphore and hence increments the count. In other words, threads only acquire the lock if the count is greater than zero.

You can create a `Semaphore` using:

```
mySemaphore = Semaphore(value = initialcount)
```

and value defaults to 1. Notice that a `Semaphore` with initial value 1 works exactly like a `Lock`, i.e. only one thread can acquire the lock at a time.

The Semaphore acquire method is the same as for Lock, but release can also specify a value to add to the count:

```
release(n = increment)
```

The ability to set the size of the increment, which defaults to 1, takes us a little beyond the basic Semaphore and was added in Python 3.9.

There is also a BoundedSemaphore which raises an exception if the current count exceeds the initial value. In most cases this would indicate that there had been more calls to release than to acquire and hence an error has occurred.

The idea of a Semaphore is easy enough to understand, but it is more difficult to see what it is used for. A Semaphore with an initial value of 1 works as a Lock, but there is little point in using one in place of a Lock. A Semaphore with an initial value of n can be used to restrict the number of threads that access a resource at any one time to n. This clearly isn't about avoiding a race condition because if n threads can access a shared resource a race condition is very likely to happen. If, however, a resource is designed to be safely shared up to a maximum user limit then you can manage it using a Semaphore. For example, if a server can handle n clients then a Semaphore with initial value n can be used to restrict usage to n simultaneous threads. A common question at this point is why not just make the server keep a count of the number of users in a standard variable? Why go to the extra complications of a Semaphore? The answer is that a standard variable would be subject to a race condition as different threads tried to access it. A Semaphore is a thread-safe counter.

While a Semaphore can be used as a lock, its primary use is as a synchronization device, see the next chapter.

Atomic Operations

Although locks are the most direct way of controlling access to a shared resource, there is also the important idea of an "atomic" operation. The basic idea is that an atomic operation is a single action that cannot be interrupted or divided down into other smaller actions. An atomic operation is, in this sense, the fundamental unit that makes up a program, but its importance in this context is that, as it cannot be interrupted, the action that it performs cannot create a race condition in its own right. A race condition can only occur if the thread is interrupted by another in the "gaps" between atomic operations.

Another and more practical way to think of this is that an atomic operation is one where adding a lock has no effect. For example, the update sequence might be composed of three atomic operations:

```
get value
modify value
store value
```

As each of these is uninterruptible there is no point is adding lock to each:

```
acquire lock
 get value
release lock
acquire lock
 modify value
release lock
acquire lock
 store value
release lock
```

However, if you want to avoid race conditions it is worth protecting the entire sequence with a lock:

```
acquire lock
 get value
 modify value
 store value
release lock
```

That is, each operation is atomic, but the sequence is not. There is a very real sense in which adding a lock converts the sequence of atomic operations into a "compound" atomic operation.

If you know that an action that you are about to apply to a shared resource is atomic then you don't need to use a lock. The problem is identifying what constitutes an atomic operation and in Python this isn't defined as part of the language – it is a detail of implementation. This makes relying on an operation being atomic not a good idea – if in doubt use a lock. Of course, using locks when they aren't necessary just slows things down. Notice that for a lock to be effective its acquire and release actions have to be atomic, otherwise two threads might acquire the lock. Making locking operations atomic is where much of the overhead comes from.

Atomic CPython

In CPython, the standard Python interpreter, there are two things that make actions atomic, byte codes and GIL. When a Python program is running it is converted to byte codes and the interpreter runs in a loop, taking one byte code at a time and executing it. Each byte code execution is made atomic by the interpreter and the action of the GIL. Another thread can only gain control of the interpreter between byte codes. So byte codes are made atomic by the action of the GIL, but what isn't clearly defined is which Python instructions actually convert to single byte codes. This isn't documented and it isn't guaranteed to be the same in different versions of Python.

You can find out how many byte codes a line of Python corresponds to in CPython using the `dis` module which provides facilities to disassemble code and display the byte code it corresponds to, for example:

```
import dis
def test():
    a = 0
    a = a+1
    return a
dis.dis(test)
```

displays:

```
3           0 LOAD_CONST           1 (0)
            2 STORE_FAST           0 (a)

4           4 LOAD_FAST            0 (a)
            6 LOAD_CONST           2 (1)
            8 BINARY_ADD
           10 STORE_FAST           0 (a)

5          12 LOAD_FAST            0 (a)
           14 RETURN_VALUE
```

You can see that `a = a+1` corresponds to four byte codes and hence this is not an atomic operation. However, `a += 1` looks as if it should be atomic, but it corresponds to:

```
4           4 LOAD_FAST            0 (a)
            6 LOAD_CONST           2 (1)
            8 INPLACE_ADD
           10 STORE_FAST           0 (a)
```

The CPython documentation states that x = y is atomic, but it corresponds to:

```
5           4 LOAD_FAST            0 (y)
            6 STORE_FAST           1 (x)
```

which is clearly not a single byte code. The reason is that the Python interpreter can release the GIL when it decides to and in this case it doesn't release the GIL between the two byte codes, effectively making them atomic.

In short, there is no sure way to discover if a Python instruction is atomic by examining its byte code!

The documentation lists the following as atomic:

```
L.append(x)
L1.extend(L2)
x = L[i]
x = L.pop()
L1[i:j] = L2
L.sort()
x = y
x.field = y
D[x] = y
D1.update(D2)
D.keys()
```

where the Ls are lists, the Ds dicts, x and y are general objects and I and j are integers. What all this means is that while many Python instructions are atomic the majority aren't and the only way to find out is to read the way CPython implements the byte code. In practice, you cannot rely on any operation being atomic and you should always use an explicit lock when working with a shared resource.

Lock-Free Code

This is an advanced topic and it is included so that you know what the term refers to and roughly how it works. It is a general approach that in principle allows many different techniques to be used to create code which doesn't use locks and yet works. I'm sure that many proponents of the technique would take issue with the description given here but it is broadly correct and conveys the general idea accurately.

There are two general approaches to lock-free code. The first is obvious, use atomic operations. This is easy to understand. If you can complete an update as an atomic operation then you don't need a lock. Of course, in most cases you can't complete an update with a single atomic operation and you will need a lock to convert some section of code into a compound atomic operation. Using atomic operations isn't really lock-free, it is more like using a free lock that the atomic operation provides.

The second approach is much more interesting and very different to using locks. The idea is that you should perform the update to a shared resource in such a way that you can detect that a race condition has indeed occurred. If you do detect a race condition then you repeat the update, so correcting the problem.

For example, the counting example given earlier could be written:

```
def count():
    global myCounter
    for i in range(10000):
        while(True):
            temp = myCounter
            x = sqrt(2)
            if myCounter == temp:
                myCounter = temp+1
                break
```

In this case we check to make sure that `myCounter` hasn't changed since it was first read i.e. stored in `temp`, and if it hasn't we update it. If it has changed then presumably another thread has updated it since it was first read and we have to start over by reading the new value and trying to update it again. Eventually the update will be done correctly and no updates are lost by race conditions because they are detected and corrected. Of course, this approach only works if:

```
 if myCounter == temp:
            myCounter = temp+1
```

is atomic because if it isn't another thread can take over and update `myCounter` between the test and the update. You could, of course, make it atomic by putting a lock around it, but this would no longer be lock-free! Modern processors provide a special compare and swap (CAS) operation which is atomic and can implement exactly the operation of compare and update without the need for a lock. Python doesn't have such an instruction at the moment and so, unless you are making use of a lock-free data structure supplied by a C module, you can't go lock-free.

Notice that there is a disadvantage to lock-free design. In principle the thread could be left retrying forever, or at least a long time. If race conditions occur at all often then the thread will have to redo its update until it finds a time slot when it is the only thread using the resource. This approach to lock-free trades the time it takes to lock and unlock a resource every time it is used for the time needed to redo the update if it fails. Lock-free programs often only promise to work if you wait long enough and if the duration of the update isn't important.

Computing Pi Using Locks

As an example of using locks to allow threads to communicate we can revisit the pi example yet again:

```
import threading
import time
def myPi(m,n):
    pi=0
    for k in range(m,n+1):
        s= 1 if k%2 else -1
        pi += s / (2 * k - 1)
    global PI
    with myLock:
        PI+=pi*4


PI=0
N=10000000
myLock=threading.Lock()
thread1=threading.Thread(target=myPi,args=(N//2+1,N))
t1=time.perf_counter()
thread1.start()
myPi(1,N//2)
thread1.join()
t2=time.perf_counter()
print((t2-t1)*1000)
print(PI)
```

Now we have a global variable `PI` which is protected from race conditions by a global `Lock`, `myLock`. Each thread updates `PI` with its result using a `with` to acquire and release the `Lock`. Notice that we only update the global variable at the end of the function. In principle, both threads could update the global variable each time through their `for` loop, but this would increase the overhead of acquiring and releasing the lock.

Of course, due to the GIL this CPU-bound program still doesn't run any faster than the single-threaded program.

Summary

- A race condition occurs when two or more threads try to update the same resource and interfere with each other in such a way that the final result depends on the exact timing of the operations.

- Race conditions manifest as bugs that seem to occur randomly because of their dependence on the exact timing of operations. Such bugs are often blamed on hardware problems and are hard to find due to the difficulty in reproducing them.

- Locks are a co-operative scheme that restricts access to shared resources to eliminate the possibly of race conditions.

- The simplest lock is Lock which can only be acquired by one thread until is is released. With small changes in how the Lock is shared this works the same way for threads and processes.

- If more than one lock is in use there is the possibility of creating deadlock where a set of threads cannot progress because they are all waiting on locks already owned by other threads in the set.

- One way of avoiding deadlock is to use timeouts in acquiring a lock.

- Rlock is a slightly more advanced lock which keeps track of which thread has it locked and how many times that thread has called acquire. To unlock the Rlock that thread has to call release the same number of times.

- Rlock can be used to give a single thread access to a locked resource from multiple sections of the code it runs.

- The Semaphore is a lock that counts the number of times it has been acquired by any thread. It is initially set to a value which is decremented at each successful acquire and acquire blocks when the count reaches zero. Each release increments the count.

- Semaphores can be used to restrict access to a shared resource to a specific number of threads. They are more useful, however, for synchronization.

- Atomic operations cannot be interrupted by another thread. They don't need to be locked to be free of race conditions.

- It is very difficult to find out what is an atomic instruction in Python.

- Lock-free code is possible if suitable atomic operations can be used instead of locks. Another approach, not available in Python, is to use an atomic compare and swap to check that a shared resource hasn't changed.

Chapter 6

Synchronization

Synchronization is all about how to get threads or processes to do things at the right time. Sometimes we need to wake up a suspended thread or set of threads to do a job only when there is something to do or we need to detect when a thread has completed some part of its task. These and more are synchronization problems.

It should be obvious that any lock can be used to synchronize execution as it is possible to wait on a lock until it is unlocked by another thread or process. In this role locks are not being used to restrict access to a shared resource, but purely to signal that some state has been achieved. In other words, a lock can be used as a simple signaling method.

Join

We have already met the most basic and simple of synchronization primitives – the join. Every thread and process has a join method that can be used to make it wait until another thread or process finishes its execution. Notice that join puts the process or thread to sleep until that other thread or process terminates. The other process or thread has to be recreated from scratch if you need to repeat the action.

What is often overlooked is that join can create a deadlock. For example:

```
import threading
import time

def myThread1():
    time.sleep(1)
    thread2.join()

def myThread2():
    time.sleep(1)
    thread1.join()

thread1= threading.Thread(target=myThread1)
thread2= threading.Thread(target=myThread2)
thread1.start()
thread2.start()
```

If you run this you will discover that it never ends as each thread waits for the other to finish. The sleep is needed to allow time for both threads to be actively running.

Notice that you can use a Lock in place of a join:

```
import threading
import time

joinLock=threading.Lock()

def myThread1():
    time.sleep(1)
    joinLock.release()

thread1= threading.Thread(target=myThread1)
joinLock.acquire()
thread1.start()
joinLock.acquire()
```

The joinLock is used by the main thread to signal the start of thread1 and myThread1 releases the lock when it has finished. Notice that you have to acquire the lock before starting the thread rather than within the thread to avoid a potential race condition.

This is the first example of using a lock as a synchronization primitive.

First To Finish

In Chapter 3 it was explained how to wait for the first process to finish in a group of processes, but this made use of an advanced feature and it didn't work for threads. You can easily implement the same facility using nothing but a Semaphore and it works for both processes and threads.

The idea is that you create a Semaphore and let the main thread acquire it before starting the threads that you want to wait for. Each thread releases the Semaphore and the first one to do so allows the main thread to acquire the Semaphore again and move on to process the data.

This example is based on the earlier one in Chapter 4 that downloads a web page:

```
import urllib.request
import threading

def download(html,lock):
    with urllib.request.urlopen('http://www.example.com/') as f:
        html.append(f.read().decode('utf-8'))
    lock.release()

html1=[]
html2=[]
mySem=threading.Semaphore()

thread1=threading.Thread(target=download,args=(html1,mySem))
thread2=threading.Thread(target=download,args=(html2,mySem))


mySem.acquire()
thread1.start()
thread2.start()
mySem.acquire()

if(html1!=[]):
    print("thread1")
if(html2!=[]):
    print("thread2")
```

Although this is a very simple example there are some things to notice. The first is that a Semaphore is needed only because you can release it multiple times without causing an exception. A BoundedSemaphore would not work in this example as it would cause an exception when it was released too many times. You could set the initial value of the Semaphore to two to stop this from happening, but using a default Semaphore is simpler and you don't need to specify the number of threads being waited for. Another thing to notice is the way that the global variables html1 and html2 are used to pass the results back. This doesn't work with processes.

Finally you cannot be sure that the thread that has released the Semaphore has finished at the time that the main program moves on from the acquire. It is possible that the thread is still terminating after the acquire has allowed the main thread to restart. This is particularly the case with processes where termination is slower and might be concurrent with the main thread on another core. In other words, the release has to be taken to signal that the data is ready, not that the thread or process has ended.

You can use the Semaphore's ability to count to extend the method to signal that m threads of n have completed. The general method is to set the Semaphore to m and then acquire the thread m times before starting the threads. Finally all you have to do is use m acquires to hold the waiting thread until m of the threads have released the Semaphore.

For example, for m = 2 and n = 3 we have:

```
mySem = threading.Semaphore(2)

thread1=threading.Thread(target=download,args=(html1,mySem))
thread2=threading.Thread(target=download,args=(html2,mySem))
thread3=threading.Thread(target=download,args=(html3,mySem))

mySem.acquire()
mySem.acquire()
thread1.start()
thread2.start()
thread3.start()
mySem.acquire()
mySem.acquire()
```

The main thread waits until two of the threads have released the Semaphore.

There are other, arguably better, methods to signal that m threads of a set have reached a particular state, but this shows that the Semaphore is more versatile that usually assumed.

Events

It is important not to think that an Event synchronization object is anything to do with the more general and sophisticated idea of an event as encountered in single threaded asynchronous code. An Event is a simple signal that can be used in place of a Semaphore or Lock. It maintains a single state indicator, an internal flag, that can be atomically set or cleared using the set() and clear() methods. The set() sets the flag to True and the Clear() sets it to False. You can discover the state of the flag using is_set().

A thread or process can wait for the Event to be True using the wait() method. If the Event is already set then the wait() returns at once. When the Event changes state from False to True all of the threads/processes waiting change from suspended to active. You can set a timeout and wait(timeout = t) returns True if it exists because the Event is True and False if it exits due to the timeout.

This means that set and clear can be called by any thread/process any number of times without generating an exception – they simply manipulate the state of the internal flag and you can change the state to True or False without having to also wait on the state.

For example, to wait for the first thread to finish you could use an Event instead of a Semaphore:

```
import urllib.request
import threading

def download(html,event):
    with urllib.request.urlopen('http://www.example.com/') as f:
        html.append(f.read().decode('utf-8'))
    event.set()

html1=[]
html2=[]
myEvent=threading.Event()

thread1=threading.Thread(target=download,args=(html1,myEvent))
thread2=threading.Thread(target=download,args=(html2,myEvent))


myEvent.clear()
thread1.start()
thread2.start()
myEvent.wait()

if(html1!=[]):
    print("thread1")
if(html2!=[]):
    print("thread2")
```

The logic of this is the same as for the Semaphore. The main thread clears the Event and then waits for the first thread to clear it.

The Event is best thought of as a shared Boolean that can be atomically set or cleared and waited on by any thread or process. Because clearing, setting and waiting on an Event are independent actions, there is no sense in which it can be used in a context manager, i.e. there is no sense in trying to write with Event: .

Barrier

The Barrier object is a more complex synchronization object than Event and is more like a Semaphore than a Lock. When you create a Barrier you have to specify the number of "parties", i.e. threads or processes, that have to wait on the Barrier before it is released. It acts like a gate that only allows people to pass when a specified number of people are waiting to go through. For example:

```
myBarrier = threading.Barrier(3)
```

creates a Barrier that lets threads pass when the number waiting reaches 3. To wait on a Barrier a thread/process uses the wait() function, which can also have a timeout specified. As soon as the number of threads/processes that are waiting equals the specified parties then they are all released. When the waiting set is released each wait function returns an integer in the range 0 to parties-1, which can be used to trigger specific behavior in each thread or process.

If a Barrier reaches the threshold and releases the threads or processes waiting on it then it is reset without an error and can be reused.

A Barrier is more difficult to use than other synchronization objects because it is difficult to know what to do if it goes wrong. For example, a Barrier can be reset when each of the waiting threads receives a BrokenBarrierError exception. If you are keen to "break the barrier" you can also call the abort() method, which puts the Barrier into the broken state when any future wait calls fail with an exception. You can also test the broken attribute to see if the Barrier is still functioning. If you want to repair a broken Barrier then call the reset method.

The parties attribute returns the number required to pass the Barrier and n_waiting gives the number currently waiting.

When using a Barrier you have to think about what condition will cause the number of threads or processes waiting to be released. For example, it is easy to arrange for a Barrier to wait for all of a set of threads to complete – you simply set the Barrier to the number of threads plus one. For example:

```
import urllib.request
import threading

def download(html,barrier):
    with urllib.request.urlopen('http://www.example.com/') as f:
        html.append(f.read().decode('utf-8'))
    barrier.wait()

html1=[]
html2=[]
myBarrier=threading.Barrier(3)

thread1=threading.Thread(target=download,args=(html1,myBarrier))
thread2=threading.Thread(target=download,args=(html2,myBarrier))

thread1.start()
thread2.start()
myBarrier.wait()

if(html1!=[]):
    print("thread1")
if(html2!=[]):
    print("thread2")
```

The main thread waits on myBarrier after starting two download threads. When the first download thread finishes the Barrier has two threads waiting, which isn't enough. When the second download thread ends it has three threads waiting, which is the threshold needed to release all of the waiting threads. Notice that the two download threads are not free to end until all of the threads have been released.

You might think that you can arrange to wait for the first n threads to finish by adjusting the number of parties down to two. In that case the main thread waits, making it one waiting for the Barrier and when either of the threads waits the threshold of two is reached and both threads are released. So the first thread that finishes releases the Barrier which resets itself. This seems to work, but when the second thread completes it waits on the Barrier until the threshold of two threads waiting is reached – which of course doesn't happen. The problem is that the Barrier signals that two threads have completed, but it then keeps the third thread suspended forever.

To stop the second thread waiting you could try to reset the Barrier, but this would have to be done after it had started waiting and it would generate an exception in the thread. You could try aborting the Barrier, but this would again generate an exception in the second thread.

If you change the download function to:

```
def download(html,barrier):
    with urllib.request.urlopen('http://www.example.com/') as f:
        html.append(f.read().decode('utf-8'))
    try:
        barrier.wait()
    except:
        pass
```

and the main thread to:

```
html1=[]
html2=[]
myBarrier=threading.Barrier(2)

thread1=threading.Thread(target=download,args=(html1,myBarrier))
thread2=threading.Thread(target=download,args=(html2,myBarrier))

thread1.start()
thread2.start()
myBarrier.wait()
myBarrier.abort()
```

then this works, but it isn't elegant.

`Barrier` has one last feature that is very occasionally useful. You can specify a callable within the constructor using the `action` parameter. If you do this one of the threads freed by the `Barrier` will run the callable before continuing. For example:

```
def report():
    print("Barrier Passed")

myBarrier=threading.Barrier(2,action=report)
```

will print `Barrier Passed` whenever the `Barrier` releases its waiting threads.

Condition Object

The `Condition` object is the most sophisticated of the synchronization methods and some find it hard to understand because of the way it combines a lock with a signaling method. The lock is used to protect the `Condition` object and any shared resources from race conditions. You create a `Condition` object using the constructor:

```
myCond = Condition()
```

this also creates an `Rlock` object to be used internally. If you want to use an existing lock object you can pass it into the constructor using the `lock=` parameter and it has to be a `Lock` or `Rlock` object. In most cases it is simpler to allow the `Condition` object to create a new lock to use.

The `Condition` object has an `acquire` and a `release` method that pass on the call to the internal lock object's methods. You can pass the parameters that are appropriate for the type of lock object in the `acquire` method. There is also a `wait` method which causes the thread to wait until another thread calls the `Condition` object's `notify` method. This is very like the way the `Event` object works to make threads wait until they are signaled to continue.

To avoid race conditions, you first have to acquire the lock before you can call the `wait` method. The clever part is that the lock is automatically released if the thread/process is suspended to wait for a call from some other thread/process to `notify`.

This sounds complicated but the standard sequence to `wait` on a `Condition` object `Co` is:

```
Co.acquire()
        work with locked resource
Co.wait()
```

and the `wait` releases the lock while the thread/process waits, so allowing other threads/processes to acquire the lock. You can use `with` to make this simpler:

```
with Co:
        Co.wait()
```

What wakes the thread up is that another thread calls the `Condition` object's `notify()` method – again the thread has to `acquire` the lock before it can call `notify`. In this case the lock isn't automatically released and any waiting threads/processes are not woken up until the lock is explicitly released. You can also specify the number of threads/processes to wake up in the `notify`. Unfortunately all that is promised is that at least n are started, which could be more than you specify. That is, the standard sequence of using a `Condition` object `Co` to notify other threads that its time to wake up is:

```
Co.acquire()
      work with locked resource
Co.notify()
      work with locked resource
Co.release()
```

and this results in at least one waiting thread or process being started after the lock is released. This is much simpler to write as:

```
with Co:
      work with locked resource
      Co.notify()
      work with locked resource
```

which automatically uses `acquire` when the `with` is entered and `release` when the `with` is exited. You can also wake up all of the waiting threads using:

```
with Co:
      Co.notify_all()
```

Notice that you can use `notify` or `notify_all` as many times as you like.

To summarize:

- You have to `acquire` the lock before calling `wait` or `notify`
- `wait` automatically releases the lock
- `notify` does not automatically release the lock and thread/processes are not restarted until the lock is released.

It is simplest to think of the `Condition` object as being a general lock which allows you to access shared resources as well as the `Condition` object's methods. Its name stems from the idea that you can use it to compute a condition while in the locked state and then respond by waiting or waking up other threads.

This might seem complicated but the idea is that it allows the thread/process to safely access a shared resource, work out its current state and then either use `wait` or `notify` depending on the current state.

A `Condition` object is a lock and a signaling mechanism. As a first example we can use a `Condition` object to wait for the first thread to download a web page:

```
import urllib.request
import threading

def download(html,condition):
    with urllib.request.urlopen('http://www.example.com/') as f:
        html.append(f.read().decode('utf-8'))
    with condition:
        condition.notify()

html1=[]
html2=[]

myCondition=threading.Condition()

thread1=threading.Thread(target=download,args=(html1,myCondition))
thread2=threading.Thread(target=download,args=(html2,myCondition))

thread1.start()
thread2.start()
with myCondition:
    myCondition.wait()

if(html1!=[]):
    print("thread1")
if(html2!=[]):
    print("thread2")
```

This is very simple. The main thread waits on the `Condition` object and the first thread to finish calls `notify` to allow the main thread to wake up. The second thread also calls `notify`, but with no effect as there are no threads waiting.

So far there isn't much new in the `Condition` object. You can use it to control access to shared resources as if it was a simple lock object and you can wait on it until another thread uses a notify method. What this means is that it is very easy to write things like:

```
with Co:
        while condition:
                Co.wait()
```

116

This has the effect of making the thread wait until the condition is `False`. At first sight this looks very inefficient as you have a `while` loop repeatedly testing the value of the *condition*, but this is ignoring the effect of the `wait`.

When the `with` starts we first might have to wait until the lock on `Co` can be acquired. Once the lock has been acquired the thread evaluates the condition and this is safe as the lock should restrict access to any shared resources. If the *condition* is `True` then the thread waits and stays waiting, using no resources, until another thread calls `notify` or `notify_all`. At this point the thread wakes up, checks the *condition* and if it is `True` then the thread waits again. You can see that this is efficient in that the loop and the condition evaluation only happens when one of the threads notifies the waiting threads that it is worth waking up and testing the *condition*. Notice that for all this to work the lock has to be released by the wait, which it is and re-acquired when the condition is re-evaluated.

The wait_for

This repeated testing of the condition and waiting is so standard that there is a method that implements it:

`Co.wait_for(predicate,timeout=None)`

This acquires the lock, evaluates the *predicate* (a function that returns `True` or `False`) and if it returns `True` performs a wait, which releases the lock. When a notification wakes the thread up the lock is acquired again, the predicate is evaluated and the whole process is repeated or the call returns if the predicate is `False`. It is exactly equivalent to:

```
with Co:
     while predicate:
          Co.wait()
```

This is a powerful, simple and efficient signaling method. For example, it can be used to solve the "wait for n threads to complete" problem very easily.

All you need is a global counting variable and to make sure that the threads use a `Condition` object to control access to it and remember to use `notify` to allow any waiting threads to check its value:

```python
import urllib.request
import threading


def download(html,condition):
    with urllib.request.urlopen('http://www.example.com/') as f:
        html.append(f.read().decode('utf-8'))
    global myCount
    with condition:
        myCount+=1
        condition.notify()

myCount=0

html1=[]
html2=[]
html3=[]

myCondition=threading.Condition(threading.Lock())

thread1=threading.Thread(target=download,args=(html1,myCondition))
thread2=threading.Thread(target=download,args=(html2,myCondition))
thread3=threading.Thread(target=download,args=(html3,myCondition))
thread1.start()
thread2.start()
thread3.start()
with myCondition:
    myCondition.wait_for(lambda:myCount>=2)

if(html1!=[]):
    print("thread1")
if(html2!=[]):
    print("thread2")
if(html3!=[]):
    print("thread3")
```

The main thread uses a `lambda` to create the predicate and simply tests for `myCount>=2`. It starts three threads and then waits for a thread to signal a `notify` when it checks the value of `myCount` and continues to wait if it isn't greater than or equal to two. When it is, it stops waiting and carries on. Notice that the condition has to be `>=2` because it is possible that two threads might update `myCount` before the main thread gets to check the value again. This is the sort of thing you have to keep in mind when designing synchronization methods.

You can easily generalize this technique to more complex conditions. As long as the shared resources are only updated while the `Condition` object's lock is held, then everything should work out fine.

An alternative way of doing the job is to make the notifying threads test for the condition:

```
def download(html,condition):
    with urllib.request.urlopen('http://www.example.com/') as f:
        html.append(f.read().decode('utf-8'))
    global myCount
    with condition:
        myCount+=1
        if myCount==2:
            condition.notify()
```

Now a thread only notifies the waiting threads if the condition is satisfied and as the increment and the test are performed under the same lock there is no possibility of the count jumping from one to three so we can test for equality. The main thread now simply waits for the first thread to call `notify`:

```
thread1.start()
thread2.start()
thread3.start()
with myCondition:
    myCondition.wait()
```

The Universal Condition Object

The `Condition` object is very flexible and it can be used for almost any synchronization task you can think of. It can be used as a `Lock`, `Rlock`, `Event` `Semaphore` and `Barrier` and it is worth seeing how.

For a `Lock` or `Rlock` you simply use the `Condition` object's associated lock.

For an `Event` you use a global Boolean variable and implement `set`, `clear` and `wait` as:

```
state=True
def set():
    global state
    with Co:
        state==True
def clear():
    global state
    with Co:
        state==False
def wait():
    global state
    with Co:
        Co.wait_for(lambda:state)
```

For a Semaphore you simply need a global `count` initialized to the desired value and a `release` and `acquire` function:

```
count=3
def release(n=1):
    global count
    with Co:
        if count==0:
            count+=n
            Co.notify(n)
        else:
            count+=n
def acquire():
    global count
    with Co;
        if count==0:
            Co.wait()
            count-=1
        else:
            count+=1
    return True
```

Finally, a `Barrier` object simply needs a global `count` of the number waiting and the number of parties:

```
numWaiting=0
parties=3
def wait():
    with Co:
        numWaiting+=1
        if numWaiting==parties:
            numWaiting=0
            Co.notify_all()
        else:
            Co.wait()
```

You can organize these into objects that do the same job as the supplied synchronization objects and add extra features such as timeout and so on, but it is easier to use the supplied implementations.

The point is that a `Condition` object can do all of the standard synchronizations and more. There is an argument for making it your first choice for any task because once you understand how it works then what it is doing is usually very obvious.

Summary

- Synchronization is about signaling state between threads and processes.

- You can use existing facilities such as locks and `join` to perform synchronization.

- You can use a semaphore to signal that a first thread/process of a group has finished.

- Events are much more useful to signal the state of one thread/process to a group of others.

- The `Barrier` object is specialized and doesn't find wide application.

- The `Condition` object is difficult to understand at first, but it is very logical and very flexible.

- A `Condition` object controls access to a shared resource via a lock and also allows other threads/processes to communicate using a wait/notify system.

- The `wait_for` method is designed to simplify the common requirement to make a thread/process wait for a condition to be true in an efficient way.

- The `Condition` object can perform the duties of all of the other locks and synchronization objects and more.

Chapter 7

Sharing Data

Processes have access to the same range of synchronization primitives as threads. You can use `Lock`, `Rlock`, `Event`, `Semaphore`, `Barrier` and `Condition` with processes in almost exactly the same way as with threads. What is very different, however, is that processes do not share global variables and thus there is very little to lock! Of course, for processes to work together towards some common objective they need to share some data and there are a number of different ways of doing this. There are two shared data structures, the `Queue` and the `Pipe`, which are easy to use and usually powerful enough for most problems. The `Queue` has the advantage of being usable by processes and threads. The `Pipe` is closer to the operating system.

Beyond these two data structures there are some more sophisticated and flexible options. You can use a shared area of memory to transfer data directly between any number of processes. This is made easier by the use of the `ctypes` module which allows the specification of Python types to C types.

Finally we have raw shared memory, which is very close to the way the hardware allows processes to share data. The only problem with this alternative is that everything is done in terms of bytes rather than data structures.

The Queue

The `multiprocessing.Queue` is an implementation of a First In First Out (FIFO) stack that can be shared between processes. It is implemented using a pipe, see later, and some locks. It is a shared data structure at a higher level than the Pipe. In particular, the items that you can add and remove from the queue are Python objects, not just basic data types. If you add an object to a `Queue` it is first pickled to reduce its size and automatically un-pickled when it is retrieved. This is explained in *Programmer's Python: Everything Is Data*, ISBN: 978-1871962598.

A FIFO stack is similar to the standard queue that we are all used to. Items join the queue at that back and leave the queue at the front. This means that the first item to join the queue is the first item out of the queue, hence the name. To create a `Queue` you use the constructor:

```
q=multiprocessing.Queue(maxsize=0)
```

The two basic operations are:

- `q.put(object, block=True, timeout=-1)`
- `object=q.get(block=True, timeout=-1)`

The `put` operation adds the object to the tail of the queue and the `get` removes and returns an object from the head of the queue. You can specify a blocking or non-blocking operation and a timeout. A non-blocking operation returns at once with an object or it raises the `Empty` exception. Notice that both operations can block as locks are used to protect the queue from a data race caused by overlapping access from multiple threads. That is, at any given time only one thread can be getting or putting data from or to the queue. Another reason that the `put` operation can wait is if the `Queue` is full. The `put` will wait until either another process gets some data or a timeout expires when a `Full` exception is raised.

The `Queue` works in a fairly sophisticated way. As long as you don't specify a `maxsize` in the constructor you can store as many items in it as there is memory available. When the first item is added to the `Queue` a thread is started which transfers the data to the pipe, see later, that the `Queue` is built on. This means that the `put` doesn't have to wait and there is always a free place in the `Queue` for new data. If you do specify a `maxsize` parameter then the `Queue` can only hold that number of items – `maxsize` gives the number of items, not the memory allocated. In this case it is possible for a `put` to have to wait until a space in the `Queue` becomes available. Notice that because of the buffering provided by the thread it is possible for the state of the `Queue` to lag behind the `put` operation. For example, you can `put` an item to the `Queue` and then test to see if it is empty using `empty()` only to find that it is. A moment later the thread will send the item to the `Queue` and `empty()` will return `False`.

A simple example demonstrates the basics of using a Queue. An addCount function is run as one process and this stores 1000 integers in the queue and then two processes running getCount read the data back out:

```
import multiprocessing

def addCount(q):
    for i in range(1000):
        q.put(i)

def getCount(q,l):
    while True:
        i=q.get()
        with l:
            print(i)

if __name__ == '__main__':
    q=multiprocessing.Queue()
    pLock=multiprocessing.Lock()

    p1=multiprocessing.Process(target=addCount,args=(q,))
    p2=multiprocessing.Process(target=getCount,args=(q,pLock))
    p3=multiprocessing.Process(target=getCount,args=(q,pLock))
    p1.start()
    p2.start()
    p3.start()

    p3.join()
```

To keep things tidy, a lock is also used to control access to the screen so that results are printed without a race condition.

When using a Queue you can generate the Full and Empty exceptions which don't always mean that the queue is full or empty – they can just mean that a timeout has occurred. To find out which it is you can use:

```
empty()
full()
```

and to find how many items are in the queue:

```
qsize()
```

Each of these methods is described as unreliable in the documentation, but all this means is that it is very possible for the status of the Queue to change between getting a value from one of the methods and doing something with it. For example, a common approach is to check if the Queue is full before trying to put a new value. If you test and find the Queue not full it is possible you could still have to wait when adding a new value because another thread might have filled the Queue before you had a chance to do the job.

You can also control the Queue and the thread that is working with it in the process. The close() method shuts the Queue down so that no more data can be added. The Queue can still be read by other processes. After a close it is recommended that you allow any data put to the Queue to get there using join_thread(). The only problem with this is that if the Queue is full the thread will wait until it has space and if this doesn't happen you have deadlock. Any process that is not the creator of the Queue does a join_thread by default and hence deadlock can occur if the data cannot be entered into the Queue. To avoid this you can use cancel_join_thread(), which results in the process exiting without waiting for the data to be sent to the Queue.

As well as Queue there are also two variations on the basic idea.

SimpleQueue is a reduced version which lacks the ability to restrict its overall size and it doesn't have join or qsize. It only supports:

- get()
- put()
- close()
- empty()

JoinableQueue is a subclass of Queue that makes it easier to wait for a queue to be empty. It has two extra methods:

- join() waits until all items in the queue have been processed, i.e. the queue is empty

- task_done() signals that an item has been removed from the queue and has been processed

The idea is that every time an item is put to the queue the count of unprocessed items goes up by one. The count goes down by one when task_done is called. When the count reaches zero any join unblocks and the waiting thread starts running.

For example you can modify the previous example to use a JoinableQueue by modifying getCount to use task_done():

```
def getCount(q,l):
    while True:
        i=q.get()
        q.task_done()
        with l:
            print(i)
```

Now the main program can wait for the queue to be empty:

```
if __name__ == '__main__':
    q=multiprocessing.JoinableQueue()
    pLock=multiprocessing.Lock()

    p1=multiprocessing.Process(target=addCount,args=(q,))
    p2=multiprocessing.Process(target=getCount,args=(q,pLock))
    p3=multiprocessing.Process(target=getCount,args=(q,pLock))
    p1.start()
    p2.start()
    p3.start()

    q.join()
    print("done")
```

Now the main program waits for the queue to empty and prints done.

Running this example using Python 3.10 under Linux and Windows produces different results. Under Windows the parent process never prints done and waits forever. Under Linux it works correctly – the main process prints done and then waits forever.

Pipes

In most cases you are better off using the higher-level Queue to exchange complex data between processes, but the Queue makes use of the lower-level Pipe, which is provided by the operating system. A Queue is buffered and, unless you restrict the number of items it can hold, a put should not block. In contrast, a Pipe isn't buffered and it is very possible for a writer to have to wait until a reader makes space in the Pipe. For all its disadvantages, a Pipe is about three times faster than a Queue.

A Pipe really is like a data pipe that connects two processes. The Pipe has two ends and each end has a Connection object which the process can use to send and receive data. To create a Pipe you can use its constructor:

```
con1, con2 = multiprocessing.Pipe()
```

By default the Pipe is bi-directional and the connection objects con1 and con2 can be used to send and receive data. If you want a uni-directional pipe you can use:

```
con1, con2 = multiprocessing.Pipe(False)
```

and then con1 can only be used to receive data and con2 to transmit data.

A Connection object has methods to send and receive Python objects:

```
Connection.send(obj)
obj = Connection.recv()
```

The Python objects are reduced to a sequence of bytes that can be sent over an operating system pipe by being pickled. If the object is too big, above around 32MB, you will get a `ValueError` exception.

If you want to send raw bytes as data you can use:

```
Connection.send_bytes(buffer)
buffer=Connection.recv_bytes()
```

or:

```
Connection.recv_bytes_into(buffer)
```

You can specify an offset and size for the send operation and a `maxlength` for the receive operation. The same size limit of around 32MB applies to byte data transfer. The data in buffer is a bytes or `bytearray` object, explained in *Programmer's Python: Everything Is Data*, ISBN: 978-1871962598.

If there is nothing to read from the `Pipe`, the `recv` methods will block until there is or the `Pipe` is closed using `Pipe.close()`. To discover if there is any data waiting to be read you can use `Connection.poll(timeout)`.

A `Connection` object can also be used in as a context manager as if you were working with a file. That is:

```
with con1:
        con1.send("Hello Pipe World")
```

is equivalent to:

```
con1.send("Hello Pipe World")
con1.close()
```

The best way to see a `Pipe` in action is to create a version of the previous example that used a `Queue` to transfer data between two processes:

```
import multiprocessing
from time import sleep

def addCount(con):
    for i in range(500):
        con.send(i)

def getCount(con,l):
    while True:
        sleep(0.005)
        i=con.recv()
        with l:
            print(i,multiprocessing.current_process().name)
```

```
if __name__ == '__main__':

    con1,con2=multiprocessing.Pipe()
    pLock=multiprocessing.Lock()

    p1=multiprocessing.Process(target=addCount,args=(con1,))
    p2=multiprocessing.Process(target=getCount,args=(con2,pLock))
    p3=multiprocessing.Process(target=getCount,args=(con2,pLock))
    p1.start()
    p2.start()
    p3.start()

    p2.join()
```

The Pipe is bi-directional, i.e. duplex, and we pass the connection object for one end to the addCount function and for the other end to the two getCount processes. Notice that there can be any number of readers and writers at each end of the Pipe. The data in the Pipe isn't duplicated to each process that reads it – any process reading an item from the Pipe removes it.

A confusing part of using a Pipe is that it has two ends. In this case we are using the con1 to con2 direction and items that are sent using con1 are read using con2. To send data the other way a process would write to con2 and then other processes could read from con1. In this sense a Pipe behaves as if it was two queues formed by con1 and con2 and by con2 and con1.

The biggest problem with using Pipes is working out when there is data to read and how much. Using Python you can make this a simpler problem by sending and receiving objects, rather than unstructured bytes. A particular problem with this approach, however, is that if the process reading or writing an object is terminated the Pipe might be left in an unreadable state because it contains only part of an object.

Queues for Threads

There isn't much point in using either a Queue or a Pipe to communicate between threads in the same process as the operating system goes to great lengths to implement a pipe which isn't needed. Also given that threads share the same environment all that is needed is a data structure with suitable locks or equivalently atomic operations. If you don't want to do it yourself you can use the queue module. This has a set of ready made queues with updates automatically locked. There are three basic queue objects:

- ◆ queue.Queue(maxsize=0)
  a FIFO queue that works exactly like multiprocessing.Queue

- ◆ queue.LifoQueue(maxsize=0)
  a queue or stack that works exactly like multiprocessing.Queue except the last item added is the first to be retrieved, hence LIFO.

◆ Queue.PriorityQueue(maxsize=0)
A priority queue that stores items and returns them in the order of priority. That is, element x is returned before element y if x<y. If you use a tuple like (priority, data) then elements with the smallest value of priority are returned first and if there is more than one they are returned in data order.

In addition there is also a queue.SimpleQueue class which lacks some of the methods of the other queues.

It is also worth mentioning that collections.deque is thread-safe and you can use its append and pop methods without additional locking. To know more refer to *Programmer's Python: Everything Is Data*.

Shared Memory

Using a queue or any data structure is often more than you need for communication between processes. For example, the program that calculates pi given in previous chapters only needs to share a single variable to allow the different threads to pool their calculation. At the moment such a simple arrangement isn't possible with processes, even though they are ideal for the implementation of a CPU-bound program. To pass simple data between processes the solution is to use shared memory. That is, the system will allocate a block of memory that more than one process can access and this can be used something like a postbox to pass data. This is simple, but the downside is that the shared memory isn't presented as a Python object but as a C data type. Fortunately Python has the ctypes module which provides Python wrappers for all of the standard C data types as explained in *Programmer's Python: Everything Is Data.*

There are two easy-to-use shared data ctypes objects – Value and Array. The Value object wraps a single C variable of a specific type and the Array object wraps an array of C types. It is easier to see how things work by looking at Value first. To create a Value you have to use the constructor in the parent process:

```
value = multiprocessing.Value(type, args, lock = True)
```

This creates a single ctypes object that wraps a shared memory variable of the specified type. The *type* parameter determines which of the ctypes classes is used to wrap the shared memory and one or more *args* is passed to its constructor. You can also specify the type using a single letter code:

```
'c': ctypes.c_char,      'u': ctypes.c_wchar,
'b': ctypes.c_byte,      'B': ctypes.c_ubyte,
'h': ctypes.c_short,     'H': ctypes.c_ushort,
'i': ctypes.c_int,       'I': ctypes.c_uint,
'l': ctypes.c_long,      'L': ctypes.c_ulong,
'q': ctypes.c_longlong,  'Q': ctypes.c_ulonglong,
'f': ctypes.c_float,     'd': ctypes.c_double
```

By default an associated Rlock is created, but you can pass an existing Lock or Rlock to be used instead. The lock can be accessed using get_lock and Value can be used in a context manager.

You can access the shared data using the value attribute. The wrapper automatically locks get/set access to the variable and it is in this sense that the wrapper is "thread-safe". However, you need to be careful in using the value where the lock is released between operations. The only operations that are automatically protected are myVal.value = *expression* and myVar = myVal.value and *expression* can't include myVal. This means that in most cases you have to explicitly lock access to Value. For example, if you want to create a shared integer Value you first have to discover what ctypes class corresponds to the exact type you want, bearing in mind that c_int is a 32-bit integer. Then you create the Value object:

myValue= multiprocessing.Value(ctypes.c_int, 0)

and use it.

To illustrate the problem of keeping a Value object safe, consider the following example which simply sets two processes to count up to 2000:

```
import time
import multiprocessing
import ctypes

def myUpdate(val):
    for i in range(1000):
            time.sleep(0.005)
            val.value += 1

if __name__ == '__main__':
    myValue= multiprocessing.Value(ctypes.c_int, 0)
    p1=multiprocessing.Process(target=myUpdate,args=(myValue,))
    p2=multiprocessing.Process(target=myUpdate,args=(myValue,))
    p2.start()
    p1.start()
    p1.join()
    p2.join()
    print(myValue.value)
```

If you run this program you should find that the total is less than 2000. If it isn't, increase the number of times the for loop executes or the number of threads. The point is that, even though the get implied in val.value+1 is protected by the lock, the lock is released and reacquired before the result is stored back in val.value. The solution is to apply the lock explicitly on the instruction you need to protect. Change the myUpdate function to read:

```
def myUpdate(val):
    for i in range(1000):
            time.sleep(0.005)
            with val:
                val.value += 1
```

As already mentioned, using `val` in the `with` instruction acquires the lock which is released when the `with` ends. This now works and you should always see 2000.

In nearly all cases the automatic locking provided by `Value` is insufficient and you need to add your own explicit lock. As the lock provided by the `Value` object is still applied, even when it isn't needed, the fact that it is slow makes this all the more irritating. What is worse is that the lock is acquired twice and while this is permitted with an `Rlock` it isn't with a Lock. For example, if you change the creation of `myValue` to:

```
myValue = multiprocessing.Value(ctypes.c_int, 0,
                        lock = multiprocessing.Lock())
```

and run the modified program then you will discover that it hangs due to a deadlock. The `with` clause acquires the lock and then the access to `val.value` tries to acquire it a second time and hence the process waits forever.

It is a much better idea to create a `Value` object without a lock, set `lock = False` in the constructor and use an explicit lock. Alternatively you can use a raw `Value` object, see later.

The `Array` object works in much the same way as `Value`, but for an array of the specified type. To create an `Array` you use:

```
multiprocessing.Array(type, size_or_initializer, lock = True)
```

You can specify the size of the array or provide a sequence to initialize the array. If you create an array of `c_char` then you can treat the value attribute as a string. For other data types you can treat the object as a sequence. For example:

```
myArray = multiprocessing.Array(ctypes.c_int, 10)
```

creates an array with ten integer elements initialized to zero. You can sum the array using:

```
for i in range(10):
        sum += myArray[i]
```

or:

```
for v in myArray:
        sum += v
```

Notice that in the both cases you might need additional locking to stop the value in the array changing during the operation.

Shared ctypes

The `Value` and `Array` classes are capable of representing almost any `ctypes` object. They are based on a set of more basic routines in `multiprocessing.sharedctypes` and in most cases you don't need to know about them, even though they are documented as end-user classes in the documentation. In particular, you don't need to use `RawValue` or `RawArray` as they are returned if you use `Value` and `Array` with `lock` set to `False` and you don't need to use synchronized as this is what is returned with `lock` set to `None` or `True`. For example, you can use `Value` to represent a `ctypes` Structure:

```
class Point(ctypes.Structure):
    _fields_ = [('x', ctypes.c_double), ('y', ctypes.c_double)]
```

Point has two fields x and y, which are both floating-point numbers. Once you have the `Structure` class you can use `Value` to create a shared instance:

```
mystruct = multiprocessing.Value(Point,1.0,2.0)
```

This creates a `Structure` with the x and y fields initialized to `1.0` and `2.0` respectively. The general principle is that the parameters that follow the type parameter are passed to the `ctypes` constructor without change. We can now access the `Structure` in the usual way from any process, safe in the knowledge that a lock is used for get and set operations for any of the fields. So expressions like:

```
mystruct.x = 3.0
```

can be regarded as atomic but:

```
mystruct.x += 1.0
```

isn't as it involves two atomic get/set operations. To make the increment safe we have to explicitly lock it:

```
with mystruct:
    mystruct.x+=1.0
```

In most cases it is more efficient to create a synchronized shared object protected by a separate lock:

```
mystruct = multiprocessing.Value(Point,1.0,2.0.lock = False)
myLock = multiprocessing.Rlock()
with myLock:
    mystruct.x += 1.0
```

You can create most `ctypes` as shared objects in this way, but a notable exception is `Pointer`. The reason is that it will share a pointer to a specific memory location, but if the shared object is used in different processes it will reference an area of memory used for a different purpose. Processes have independent memory arrangements and do not share addresses.

133

Raw Shared Memory

As well as the shared ctypes approach to sharing memory, you can also do the job at a much lower level in terms of bytes. This is slightly faster and slightly simpler if you are already working with bytes rather Python data. For example, if you are reading data from a connected device it might well provide the data as a byte sequence.

Using shared memory is easy. Most of the problems that you will encounter are due to the need to convert the data to a byte sequence. To create or connect to an area of shared memory you use:

```
multiprocessing.shared_memory.SharedMemory(name = None,
                                create = False, size = 0)
```

If `create` is `True` the memory block is created and if you don't assign a `name` one is generated. The `name` attribute can be used to retrieve the name. The `size` parameter gives the minimum number of bytes that are allocated to the area. As memory often works in multiples of a fixed page size you may well get more than you asked for. You can use the `size` attribute to discover the number of bytes actually allocated.

Usually one of the processes using the shared area will create the block and the others will connect to it using `create=False` and specifying the `name` of the block. In this case the `size` parameter is ignored.

The shared memory object has a small number of attributes to let you work with the block:

- ♦ `buf` – a memory view of the block that can be treated as a `bytes` object
- ♦ `name` – the name of the block
- ♦ `size` – the size of the block
- ♦ `close()` - disconnects from the memory block, but does not remove the block from memory
- ♦ `unlink()` - requests that the block be removed from memory

Each process should call close when they have finished using the block and one of the processes should call `unlink` to signal that they have all finished and the block can be destroyed.

As a simple example, we can implement the `myUpdate` counting example given earlier. As the shared resource is a byte sequence we can only count up to 255 using a single element of the buffer, but this is sufficient to demonstrate the principle:

```
import time
import multiprocessing
import multiprocessing.shared_memory

def myUpdate(name,lock):
    mySharedMem=multiprocessing.shared_memory.SharedMemory(
                                    create=False,name=name)
    for i in range(127):
        time.sleep(0.005)
        with lock:
            mySharedMem.buf[0]=mySharedMem.buf[0]+1
    mySharedMem.close()


if __name__ == '__main__':
    mylock=multiprocessing.Lock()
    mySharedMem=multiprocessing.shared_memory.SharedMemory(
                                    create=True,size=10)
    mySharedMem.buf[0]=1
    p1=multiprocessing.Process(target=myUpdate,
                            args=(mySharedMem.name,mylock))
    p2=multiprocessing.Process(target=myUpdate,
                            args=(mySharedMem.name,mylock))
    p2.start()
    p1.start()
    p1.join()
    p2.join()
    print(mySharedMem.buf[0])
    mySharedMem.close()
    mySharedMem.unlink()
```

With the lock in use the final count is 255. If you remove the lock the result is lower due to race conditions. Notice that each of the child processes closes the memory block, but only the main process unlinks from it so as to allow the operating system to reclaim the memory.

A simplification is that you can pass the `mySharedMem` object directly to the child process and avoid having to explicitly connect to it:

```
p1 = multiprocessing.Process(target = myUpdate,
                            args = (mySharedMem,mylock))
```

and then you can use `mySharedMem` in `myUpdate` without having to use:

```
multiprocessing.shared_memory.SharedMemory(create=False,name=name)
```

As already stated, the real problem with working with shared memory is that everything has to be reduced to a byte sequence.

For example, if you want to extend the counter example to count to more than 255 you need to interpret the bytes as an integer. This is possible using:

```
int.to_bytes(length, byteorder, signed = False)
```

and:

```
int.from_bytes(bytes, byteorder, signed = False)
```

These methods convert a bignum into a sequence of bytes and back again and are discussed in ***Programmer's Python: Everything Is Data.*** Using them we can convert the previous example to count to more than 255:

```
import time
import multiprocessing
import multiprocessing.shared_memory
import sys

def myUpdate(mySharedMem,lock):
    for i in range(1000):
        time.sleep(0.005)
        with lock:
            count=int.from_bytes(mySharedMem.buf[0:8],
                                    byteorder=sys.byteorder)
            count=count+1
            mySharedMem.buf[0:8]=int.to_bytes(count,8,
                                    byteorder=sys.byteorder)
    mySharedMem.close()


if __name__ == '__main__':
    mylock=multiprocessing.Lock()
    mySharedMem=multiprocessing.shared_memory.SharedMemory(
                                    create=True,size=10)
    mySharedMem.buf[0:8]=int.to_bytes(1,8,
                                    byteorder=sys.byteorder)
    p1=multiprocessing.Process(target=myUpdate,
                                    args=(mySharedMem,mylock))
    p2=multiprocessing.Process(target=myUpdate,
                                    args=(mySharedMem,mylock))

    p2.start()
    p1.start()
    p1.join()
    p2.join()
    count=count=int.from_bytes(mySharedMem.buf[0:8],
                                    byteorder=sys.byteorder)
    print(count)
    mySharedMem.close()
    mySharedMem.unlink()
```

This counts reliably to 2001, unless you remove the lock in which case race conditions ensure that it is smaller. It isn't particularly fast because of all of the packing and unpacking of eight bytes to and from the buffer.

There are ways of converting almost any Python data structure into a byte sequence and back again – this is a topic of ***Programmer's Python: Everything Is Data***. You can even use pickling to convert general objects into a data stream and ctypes to use a C representation, but if you are doing this why not just use the shared ctypes approach. Raw shared memory only has an advantage when the data is already a byte sequence or is very easy and cheap to convert into one.

As well as the raw shared memory class, there is also the ShareableList which is elaborated to allow you to treat the buffer as if it was a Python list, but with some restrictions. A ShareableList isn't dynamic and it cannot change its size via slicing or appending. It is also limited to storing basic data types: int float, bool, string and bytes and each smaller than 10Mbytes.

This is just an implementation of the shared ctypes structure, but one that doesn't need you to explicitly specify the format.

To create a ShareableList use:

```
multiprocessing.shared_memory.ShareableList(
                              sequence = None, *, name = None)
```

This creates a new shared memory block with the format of the specified sequence or, if sequence is None, attaches to the existing block with the specified name.

There are a number of useful attributes:

- ◆ count(value) - returns the number of occurrences of value
- ◆ index(value) - returns the index of value in the list and a ValueError exception is raised if it isn't found
- ◆ Format – The struct packing format that has be deduced from the initial list
- ◆ Shm – The SharedMemory instance being used to store the list

As a simple example, the previous counter can be implemented without the worry of having to convert a bignum to a byte sequence:

```
import time
import multiprocessing
import multiprocessing.shared_memory

def myUpdate(mySharedList,lock):
    for i in range(1000):
        time.sleep(0.005)
        with lock:
            mySharedList[0]=mySharedList[0]+1
    mySharedList.shm.close()


if __name__ == '__main__':
    mylock=multiprocessing.Lock()
    mySharedList=multiprocessing.shared_memory.ShareableList(
                                            sequence=[1])
    p1=multiprocessing.Process(target=myUpdate,
                                    args=(mySharedList,mylock))
    p2=multiprocessing.Process(target=myUpdate,
                                    args=(mySharedList,mylock))
    p2.start()
    p1.start()
    p1.join()
    p2.join()
    print(mySharedList[0])
    mySharedList.shm.close()
    mySharedList.shm.unlink()
```

In practice, you would generally want to use multiple elements of the list and they might well be of mixed type, but this serves to demonstrate the principle. Notice that we have to use the shm attribute to access some of the shared memory attributes.

Shared Memory Manager

Finally there is a shared memory manager which is only worth exploring if you plan to use lots of different shared memory blocks:

```
multiprocessing.managers.SharedMemoryManager(address, authkey)
```

where address and authkey are optional. This creates a SharedMemoryManager instance. If you call its start method a new child process is created which oversees the creation and destruction of all memory blocks – given that this involves an additional process you can appreciate why you would use it only if really needed. To terminate all of the shared memory blocks owned by the manager you would use its shutdown() method which calls the unlink method on all of the blocks.

The two methods SharedMemory(size) and ShareableList(sequence) create a SharedMemory and ShareableList object under the manager's control.

One advantage of using `SharedMemoryManager` is that it can be used in a context manager to automatically start the server and dispose of all the shared memory blocks. For example, we can change the main program of the previous example to use a manager very easily:

```
if __name__ == '__main__':
    mylock=multiprocessing.Lock()
    with multiprocessing.managers.SharedMemoryManager() as smm:
        mySharedList=smm.ShareableList([1])
        p1=multiprocessing.Process(target=myUpdate,
                                    args=(mySharedList,mylock))
        p2=multiprocessing.Process(target=myUpdate,
                                    args=(mySharedList,mylock))
        p2.start()
        p1.start()
        p1.join()
        p2.join()
        print(mySharedList[0])
```

Even though `SharedMemoryManager` is derived from `BaseManager` it doesn't have any facilities for being used as a remote server as it doesn't create proxies, see Chapter 9 for further explanation.

Computing Pi

As a final example, we can make use of `Value` to allow the different processes involved to update a single shared variable in the computation explained in Chapter 3:

```
import ctypes
import multiprocessing
import time

def myPi(m,n,PI):
    pi=0
    for k in range(m,n+1):
        s= 1 if k%2 else -1
        pi += s / (2 * k - 1)
    with PI:
        PI.value +=pi*4

if __name__ == '__main__':
    N=10000000
    PI=multiprocessing.Value(ctypes.c_double,0.0)
    p1=multiprocessing.Process(target=myPi,args=(N//2+1,N,PI))
    t1=time.perf_counter()
    p1.start()
    myPi(1,N//2,PI)
    p1.join()
    t2=time.perf_counter()
    print((t2-t1)*1000)
    print(PI.value)
```

You can see that we create PI, a synchronized double ctype and allow the two processes to update the computed value, which is printed at the end of the program.

The program runs in about half the time of the single-process version. Changing the program to use an explicit lock rather than the lock included in the Value object to avoid locking the get/set access twice makes no different to the runtime. The reason is simply that the double-locking operation only occurs at the end of the loop, i.e. the shared ctypes object is only updated twice. If you change this to an arguably more obvious version of the update using the ctypes object each time through the loop:

```
def myPi(m,n,PI):
    pi=0
    for k in range(m,n+1):
        s= 1 if k%2 else -1
        with PI:
            PI.value += 4*s / (2 * k - 1)
```

This takes 75 times as long as the original and changing to an explicit lock takes 50 times as long.

The moral is that locking is expensive, no matter how you do it.

Summary

- Processes don't share data as a matter of course because they don't share memory. Each process runs in its own allocated memory.

- The multiprocessing `Queue` is the highest level way of sharing data. It is a FIFO stack and is very easy to use because it is buffered. Any number of processes can add or remove data from the queue.

- A standard `Queue` data structure can be used to share data between threads.

- The `Pipe` is a lower level implementation of sharing between processes and is a Python version of a facility provided by the operating system.

- A `Pipe` is bi-directional and you can read and write at each end of the pipe using connection objects. Data written to one end of the pipe can be read from the other end.

- Any number of processes can have access to either end of the `Pipe`.

- An equally fundamental way of sharing data is shared memory and this is supported in hardware and by the operating system.

- You can share a block of memory and use it to exchange data between any number of processes.

- Python lets you use the `ctypes` module to transfer data using shared memory. You have to convert Python data structures to C data structures to transfer via shared memory.

- There is also a more basic way to access shared memory in its raw form. The only problem is that the data takes the form of a byte sequence and so you have to perform the conversion between Python data and byte data manually.

- A slightly easier to use, but still restricted, form of raw shared memory is `ShareableList` which lets you treat the buffers an array of limited types – `int`, `float`, string and `byte`.

Chapter 8

The Process Pool

There are overheads in creating processes and threads and one strategy to reduce the cost of creating them is to use a pool of pre-created items. In most other languages it is the idea of a "thread pool" which is important, but in Python the GIL acts as a deterrent to using many threads. As only one thread can be running Python code at any given time, there isn't a huge advantage is splitting a program into multiple threads. While Python does support a thread pool class, `Threading` in `multiprocessing.pool`, it isn't much used and the newer and more used thread pool features in `concurrent.futures` is described in Chapter 11.

As processes provide a way to improve performance, it is the process pool which is more important. You can create a pool of processes ready to perform jobs which you can submit later, using:

```
multiprocessing.pool.Pool(number, initializer, initargs,
                          maxtasksperchild, context)
```

All of the parameters are optional and often all you need to do is to specify the number of processes to create. Notice that, unlike a typical thread pool, this is not a system process pool that you can assume is already constructed. The processes are created for you when you use the `Pool` constructor and they are destroyed when there is nothing more for them to do or when they have completed `maxtasksperchild` jobs.

It isn't a good idea to keep a process around for too long and give it lots of jobs to do because processes tend to accumulate resources which are only freed when the process ends. A good balance of re-use and re-creation of processes is desirable. If you don't specify the number of processes to create then the number of CPUs as reported by `os.cpu_count` is used. This makes sense for CPU-bound processes, but is less suitable if the processes perform I/O that they have to wait for.

You can also specify an `initializer` function which will be called using `initargs` when the process is started. Notice that this only happens once, even if the process is reused by multiple jobs.

As `Pool` sets up global resources, you cannot simply allow Python to automatically clean up when the object is garbage collected – you need to explicitly use its `close` or `terminate` method to free resources. The difference between the two is that the `close` method allows the processes to finish what they are doing before closing them and the `terminate` method stops the processes immediately. After calling `terminate` or `close` you can call `join` to wait for all of the processes to finish. Notice that it doesn't make sense to call `join` if you haven't used `close` or `terminate` as the processes don't necessarily end when their jobs are complete.

The safest way to use `Pool` is in a `with` as a context manager:

```
with multiprocessing.pool.Pool(2) as myPool:
    use myPool
```

Notice that this uses the `terminate` method when the `with` ends and this means you need to test that everything has completed before leaving the `with`.

Now that you have a pool of processes you need to submit jobs to it and there are a range of `Pool` methods that let you do this. The `Pool` object can only be used by the process that created it – don't try to call `Pool` methods from other processes. In this sense the process that creates the `Pool` object is in charge of what happens.

The most basic job-submitting function is `apply_async`:

```
apply_async(func, args, kwds, callback, error_callback)
```

this submits the callable, specified as *func* with the optional arguments and keywords, to a process in the pool. The optional callbacks can be used to deal with the result of the process, but there are better ways to do this. Notice that the function returns immediately and a pool process starts to run the job. This means you can use `apply_async` to run multiple jobs using pool processes.

There is also an apply method:

```
apply(func,args,kwds)
```

which waits until the pool process has finished before returning and so can only be used to run a single job at at time. For example, we can start two simple jobs and wait for them to finish:

```
import multiprocessing.pool
import multiprocessing
import random
import time

def myProcess():
 time.sleep(random.randrange(1,4))
 print(multiprocessing.current_process().name)

if __name__ == '__main__':
    p = multiprocessing.pool.Pool(2)
    p.apply_async(myProcess)
    p.apply_async(myProcess)
    p.close()
    p.join()
```

After a delay, this displays:

```
ForkPoolWorker-1
ForkPoolWorker-2
```

Note that the print functions used to display the names of the processes are subject to race conditions and should be protected by a lock.

You could specify callback functions to receive the results of the process:

```python
import multiprocessing.pool
import multiprocessing
import random
import time

def myProcess():
    time.sleep(random.randrange(1,4))
    return multiprocessing.current_process().name

def myCallback(result):
    print(result)

if __name__ == '__main__':
        p = multiprocessing.pool.Pool(2)
        p.apply_async(myProcess,callback = myCallback)
        p.apply_async(myProcess,callback = myCallback)
        p.close()
        p.join()
```

The callback is run in the main process and while it is running nothing else can happen, so in general the callback should finish as quickly as possible to avoid freezing the main process. In this example this doesn't matter as the main process is suspended anyway. You can set an error callback in the same way. The problem with using callbacks is getting them to synchronize with the operation of the main process – this is a recurrent theme and the solution is to use something like a deferred object also known as a future.

Waiting for Pool Processes

The apply_async is an easy way to get processes started, the real problem is waiting for them. You can use join after a close to wait for all of the processes to end, but this isn't usually what you want. All of the Pool job methods return an AsyncResult object, which can be used to inquire about the current status of a job and to get results. The AsyncResult object is also interesting because it is the first example of something that programmers in other languages would call a promise and which Python terms a Future, more of which later.

The AsyncResult object is available for the main process to use, but it is also manipulated by the child process and thus provides a means of communication between the two.

The AsyncResult object has four methods:

- ◆ get(timeout) - waits for the optional timeout or when the result is ready and returns the result or raises a TimeOutError
- ◆ wait(timeout) - as for get but doesn't return a result
- ◆ ready() - returns True if complete and False otherwise
- ◆ successful() - returns True if complete without exception and raises an exception otherwise.

Of these the most useful is get as it returns the result of the function that you are running using Pool.

For example:

```
import multiprocessing.pool
import multiprocessing
import random
import time

def myProcess():
    time.sleep(random.randrange(1,4))
    return multiprocessing.current_process().name

if __name__ == '__main__':
    with multiprocessing.pool.Pool(2) as p:
        asr1 = p.apply_async(myProcess)
        asr2 = p.apply_async(myProcess)
        result1=asr1.get()
        result2=asr2.get()
        print(result1,result2)
```

The function now returns the name of the process running it as its result and this is what the get returns. We simply wait for the two processes to complete and return a result. In this case we can use a with because it now completes after the two processes have completed and hence a call to terminate is what we want. This example displays:

```
ForkPoolWorker-1 ForkPoolWorker-2
```

There is no easy way to wait for one of a set of processes to end or similar – the Pool isn't intended for this sort of use. You can try to use knowledge of the internal workings of Pool to access the processes, but this tends to interfere with its overall operation.

The simplest solution is to use the `ready` method in a polling loop with a `sleep` to suspend the main process and allow the child processes access to the CPUs:

```python
import multiprocessing.pool
import multiprocessing
import random
import time

def myProcess():
    time.sleep(random.randrange(1,6))
    return multiprocessing.current_process().name

if __name__ == '__main__':
    with multiprocessing.pool.Pool(2) as p:
        asr1 = p.apply_async(myProcess)
        asr2 = p.apply_async(myProcess)

        waiting=True
        while waiting:
            time.sleep(0.01)
            if(asr1.ready()):
                print(asr1.get())
                break
            if(asr2.ready()):
                print(asr2.get())
                break
```

An alternative is to use `imap_unordered` which presents the results of processes in the order that they occur.

Computing Pi using AsyncResult

Using a process pool makes our example computation of Pi simpler in that we don't have to create individual processes, but also because we don't need to use locks to control access and shared data structures to return the values. All of the communication and timing between the processes is taken care of by the `AsyncResult` objects:

```python
import multiprocessing
import multiprocessing.pool
import time

def myPi(m,n):
    pi = 0
    for k in range(m,n+1):
        s = 1 if k%2 else -1
        pi += s / (2 * k - 1)
    return pi*4
```

```
if __name__ == '__main__':
    N=10000000
    with multiprocessing.pool.Pool(2) as p:
        t1=time.perf_counter()
        asr1=p.apply_async(myPi,args=(1,N//2))
        asr2=p.apply_async(myPi,args=(N//2+1,N))
        PI=asr1.get()
        PI+=asr2.get()
        t2=time.perf_counter()
    print((t2-t1)*1000)
    print(PI)
```

This program runs a little faster than the version that explicitly creates its own process and provides its own locks, but the difference is small. The main advantage of using a Pool is that the process are set up by the time you want to use them.

Map_async

Many multiprocessor problems can be solved by breaking the range of operations up into pieces and giving a section to different processes. This is, after all, what we are doing with the Computing Pi example. The `Pool` object provides a number of methods that attempt to make this easier.

The `map_async` function works like the standard `map` operation in that it applies a function to each element in an iterable, but it uses processes from the pool to evaluate each function. Finding a realistic example of using `map_async` is difficult because there is no point in using a separate process for each function application if the function is small and quick to compute.

To map a function onto an iterable you would use:

```
Pool.map_async(func, iterable, chunksize, callback, error_callback)
```

and *func* will be applied to each element of the *iterable*, each in its own process from the pool. That is, it is equivalent to:

```
[func(x) for x in iterable]
```

but with each function evaluation done in a process from the pool. The comparison is also accurate in that `map_async` returns an `AsyncResult` object which eventually returns a list of results via its `get` method.

You can also specify an optional *chunksize* which will allocate that many items from the *iterable* to the process. By default all of the processes in the pool are used to run function evaluations. So if you have ten processes and ten items each process will be used once. If you set a *chunksize* of 2 then only five of the processes will be used as each process will run two function evaluations. If you don't want to use `asyncResult` then you can optionally specify two callbacks, for the results and for errors.

A very simple example of using `async_map` is to form a list of squares:

```python
import multiprocessing
import multiprocessing.pool

def myFunc(x):
    return x**2

if __name__ == '__main__':
    with multiprocessing.pool.Pool(10) as p:
        asr=p.map_async(myFunc,[1,2,3,4,5,6,7,8,9,10])
        res=asr.get()

    print(res)
```

Each item in the list is used as an argument to the function call and the result is:

```
[1, 4, 9, 16, 25, 36, 49, 64, 81, 100]
```

Notice that the results are in the same order as the input iterator. Also notice that the call to `get` waits until all of the ten processes have completed. If you specify a *chunksize* of 2 only five of the processes in the pool are used but the results are the same. Obviously using `async_map` only makes sense if the functions take sufficient time to make it worth using separate processes.

As another simple example consider the pi example using `async_map`:

```python
import multiprocessing
import multiprocessing.pool
import time

def myPi(r):
    m,n=r
    pi=0
    for k in range(m,n+1):
        s= 1 if k%2 else -1
        pi += s / (2 * k - 1)
    return pi*4

if __name__ == '__main__':
    N=10000000
    with multiprocessing.pool.Pool(2) as p:
        t1=time.perf_counter()
        asr=p.map_async(myPi,[(1,N//2),(N//2+1,N)])
        res=asr.get()
        t2=time.perf_counter()

    print((t2-t1)*1000)
    PI=res[0]+res[1]
    print(PI)
```

In this case the iterable is a list of tuples that give the range that the myPi function should compute. The function has to be modified to unpack the tuple to give m and n. This is a general strategy as the `map_async` method only ever passes a single argument from the iterable to the function. The result is a list of the return values of the functions and this generally has to be processed to produce a final result. There are no speed advantages in using `map_async`, it is just a higher-level abstraction.

There is also a `Pool.map` function which does the same thing as `async_map`, but it waits for the results to be ready before returning. It is exactly equivalent to:

```
map_async(func, iterable, chunksize).get()
```

Starmap_async

The problem of having to unpack the arguments passed to a function by `map_async` is so common that there is a method that does the job for you. The cutely named `starmap_async` will unpack each item in the iterable to the function's parameters. It is called `starmap_async` because it implicitly uses the * operator to unpack items. That is:

```
starmap_async(func,[(1,2),(3,4)]
```

calls `func(1,2)` and `func(3,4)`. Obviously the function has to have the number of parameters corresponding to the items to be unpacked from the iterable element. For example the Computing Pi calculation can be written even more simply as:

```
import multiprocessing
import multiprocessing.pool
import time

def myPi(m,n):
    pi=0
    for k in range(m,n+1):
        s= 1 if k%2 else -1
        pi += s / (2 * k - 1)
    return pi*4

if __name__ == '__main__':
    N=10000000
    with multiprocessing.pool.Pool(2) as p:
        t1=time.perf_counter()
        asr=p.starmap_async(myPi,[(1,N//2),(N//2+1,N)])
        res=asr.get()
        t2=time.perf_counter()

    print((t2-t1)*1000)
    PI=res[0]+res[1]
    print(PI)
```

Notice that now there is no need to modify the myPi function.

There is also a starmap function which blocks until the results are completed.

Immediate Results – imap

Both map_async and starmap_async wait until all of the processes have completed and all of the results are available. Sometimes you want to process a result as soon as it is available. This is what imap and its associated method imap_unordered allow you to do. Instead of returning an AsyncResult object, they return an iterator:

```
Pool.imap(func,iterable,chuncksize)
```

You can use the next method of the iterator or you can use it in a for loop. For example, the squaring program introduced in the section on map_async, can be rewritten as:

```
import multiprocessing
import multiprocessing.pool

def myFunc(x):
    return x**2

if __name__ == '__main__':
    with multiprocessing.pool.Pool(10) as p:
        results=p.imap(myFunc,[1,2,3,4,5,6,7,8,9,10])
        for result in results:
            print(result)
```

This prints the results as soon as they are available, but if you run the program you will find that it prints them in the same order as the input. That is, the iterable returned waits for the processes to end in the same order in which they were started. If a result is available later in the sequence it won't be printed until all of the results before it are available and have been printed.

If you want a real "deal with the result as soon as available" approach then you need the Pool.imap_unordered(func, iterable, chunksize) method. This returns an iterable that waits for the next process to complete and hence returns its results in any order.

For example:

```
import multiprocessing
import multiprocessing.pool

def myFunc(x):
    return x**2

if __name__ == '__main__':
    with multiprocessing.pool.Pool(10) as p:
        results=p.imap_unordered(myFunc,[1,2,3,4,5,6,7,8,9,10])
        for result in results:
            print(result)
```

This program prints the results in any order. As the computation is so slight the order is usually the one in which they were submitted, but typically you will see something like:

4
16
9
25
36
49
64
100
81
1

MapReduce

The map_async method and its variations are a very typical approach to using concurrency to speed up computations. Usually when processing data there is some function which has to be applied to each item of data and then a final processing of the intermediate results to give a single value. This pattern is usually called "MapReduce. It can be implemented in sophisticated ways so that processes run on different machines and are then gathered together to give a single answer. Systems such as Hadoop implement a high level approach to MapReduce but it is easy enough to implement similar schemes in Python.

We already have the map part of the scheme and we could implement the reduce part using for loops but the functools module has a reduce method:

```
functools.reduce(func, iterable, initializer=None)
```

This calls func for each item in the *iterable* and is roughly equivalent to:

```
value = initializer
for item in iterable:
        value = func(value,item)
return value
```

If you don't include an initializer then *value* is set to the first element in iterable. For example, if you just want to sum all of the elements in the iterable then you could define *func* to be:

```
def mySum(value,element):
        return value + item
```

Each time mySum is called *value* is increased by the size of the *item*. For example to find the sum of the squares that the previous examples calculated you could use:

```
import functools
import multiprocessing
import multiprocessing.pool

def myFunc(x):
    return x**2

def mySum(value,item):
    return value+item

if __name__ == '__main__':
    with multiprocessing.pool.Pool(10) as p:
        asr=p.map_async(myFunc,[1,2,3,4,5,6,7,8,9,10])
        res=asr.get()
    sumsquares=functools.reduce(mySum,res)
    print(sumsquares)
```

Notice that the reduce phase involves collecting the individual results in a single process and then using reduce to form a single result. Of course, the mySum function could be better implemented as a lambda function.

Sharing and Locking

The Pool module doesn't provide anything new when it comes to sharing resources and locking. One thing that has changed is that the processes in the pool are created ahead of time and then used to run a function by one of the Pool methods. What this means is that the parameters are passed to the function that you are trying to run in a different way. Python objects are passed via a pipe and they have to be pickled and unpickled to reduce the amount of data moved.

This is a problem when it comes to the multiprocessing synchronization objects such as Lock and Value as these cannot be pickled as they contain an external state – a system-wide lock. The solution is to use the initialization parameters when the pool is created to specify a function to run when the process is first created. The idea is to use this to create global variables that reference the shared resources, for example:

```python
import multiprocessing
import multiprocessing.pool
import time
import ctypes


def counter():
    global count
    for i in range(10000):
        with count:
            temp=count.value+1
            count.value=temp

def setup(var):
    global count
    count=var


if __name__ == '__main__':
    myCounter=multiprocessing.Value(ctypes.c_int,0)
    with multiprocessing.Pool(2,initializer=setup,
                                initargs=(myCounter,)) as p:

        t1=time.perf_counter()
        asr1=p.apply_async(counter)
        asr2=p.apply_async(counter)
        asr1.wait()
        asr2.wait()
        t2=time.perf_counter()
        print(myCounter.value)
    print((t2-t1)*1000)
```

You can see that the setup function simply uses the object passed to it to set up a global variable in the process. The function that is run on the process simply makes use of the global variable without doing anything special. If you take the with statement out of the function you will discover that count doesn't usually reach 20000 because of race conditions. Including the with, the lock that comes with the Value object ensures that no race conditions occur.

There is another way to share resources to Pool process involving process managers, which is the topic of the next chapter.

Summary

- A process pool, a set of processes created and ready to run, can be used to avoid the high cost of repeatedly creating processes.

- The `Pool` object creates a specified number of processes ready to be used.

- The `apply_async` method will run a function using a process from the pool.

- All of the `Pool` methods return an `AsyncResult` object which acts like what would usually be called a deferred, a promise or, in Python's terminology, a future. This can be used to wait for a result.

- There are a range of map-like functions which allow you to run a set of functions on a set of processes from the process pool.

- `map_async` maps a single function onto a range of values, each run on a process from the pool.

- `starmap_async` works like `map_async`, but automates the passing of multiple parameters.

- `imap` works like `map_async`, but returns an iterator that allows you to step through results as they become available.

- The map functions are one half of a standard approach to parallel programming called MapReduce. The `functools` module provides a `reduce` function.

- You can't pass objects like `Lock` and `Value` to a process from the process pool because the process is already running and parameters are passed as pickled data. Lock, `Value` and any object that has state cannot be pickled.

- To share important resources like locks you have to use the initialization parameter when the `Pool` is first created to supply a function which creates the shared resources in each of the processes.

Chapter 9

Process Managers

Process managers are a higher level way of sharing data between processes. They make sharing data easy and extend the whole concept of a process that Python can make use of to include processes running on different machines. This is a powerful, but not so commonly required, feature that makes it possible to build more sophisticated distributed systems.

The important feature of process managers is that they are completely general. A process manager can be used to share resources between a set of processes, no matter how they have been created. That is, you can use a process manager with basic processes created using the multiprocessing module or pool processes created with the multiprocessing.pool module or the concurrent.futures module that is described in Chapter 11.

To be clear, the main purpose of a process manager is to create a central data structure which can be shared by any number of processes running on the same machine or on remote machines connected via the network.

The SyncManager

The simplest manager to use is the SyncManager because it comes with a range of pre-defined data types that can be shared. You can create your own managers with custom data types, but it is simpler to start with SyncManager. To create a SyncManager you use:

```
multiprocessing.Manager()
```

Unlike custom managers the SyncManager is automatically started and it creates a server in a separate process. The server keeps the master copies of all of the shared data that you want to work with and it creates proxy objects that processes can use to access the master copy.

Initially no shared data objects are defined and you have to create them using one of a range of methods all of which accept the same parameters as the corresponding constructors for the basic objects that they proxy:

- `Barrier(parties)`
- `BoundedSemaphore(value)`
- `Condition()`
- `Event()`
- `Lock()`
- `Namespace()`
- `Queue([maxsize])`
- `RLock()`
- `Semaphore([value])`
- `Array(typecode, sequence)`
- `Value(typecode, value)`
- `dict()`
- `dict(mapping)`
- `dict(sequence)`
- `list()`¶
- `list(sequence)`

Each method creates an object of the specified type and returns a proxy for it.

How Proxies Work

To understand how managers work you need to understand proxies. In this section we look at the general ideas that are important to appreciating how managers share data. Later we will look in detail at the implementation of a proxy.

All of the methods listed above create the object in the server, the "referent", and return a suitable proxy object to the calling process. The proxy object has a set of methods that correspond to methods in the referent, but these pass on the call to the referent for execution. The result of the referent's method is returned as the result of the proxy method.

This means that using a process manager involves an additional process – running the server that hosts the referent objects. It also means that when you call a method on a proxy, the call is transferred to the referent via a pipe and the result is transferred back to the proxy via a pipe. This makes sharing using a process manager easy, but not particularly efficient. Using a process manager can be more than ten times slower than using basic multiprocessing objects and `ctype`-based data.

Notice that every time you call one of the proxy methods a new referent is created by the server and a new proxy is returned which references it. This means you can create as many shared Value objects as you need. To be clear, it is the proxying of methods that implement the data sharing rather than any actual sharing of the data. Managers share objects and their methods, not raw data, and managers are best thought of as implementing "remote procedure calls".

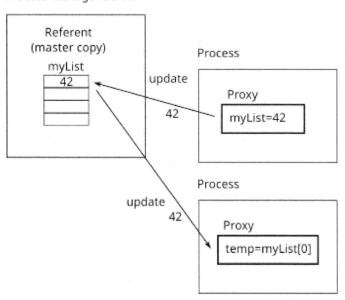

This sounds restrictive, but in Python most data is accessed via methods and if the proxy makes these available then it can look as if you are sharing data. For example, if the proxy has a get and set method for an attribute then a process calling set on the proxy has that call passed on to the server and so changes the attribute. If another process then calls get on the proxy this too is passed on as a call to the server and the result reflects the current value of the attribute.

As long as the proxy supports the data access methods that are "natural" for the data type and passes these on to the referent then it does look as if you are sharing the data.

For example, work out the squares of the elements of a list:

```
import multiprocessing
import multiprocessing.pool
import time

def myFunc(x):
    for i in range(len(x)):
        x[i]=x[i]**2

if __name__ == '__main__':
    man=multiprocessing.Manager()
    myList=man.list([1,2,3,4,5,6,7,8,9,10])
    p=multiprocessing.Process(target=myFunc,args=(myList,))
    t1=time.perf_counter()
    p.start()
    p.join()
    t2=time.perf_counter()

    print((t2-t1)*1000)
    print(myList)
```

This works by creating a Manager and using its list method to create a shared list in the server, the referent, initialized to 1 to 10. The proxy is returned and stored in myList and then passed to myFunc, which changes each element of the shared list using the index operator [ ]:

```
x[i] = x[i]**2.
```

Of course, when you use indexing, Python calls __getitem__ or __setitem__ to do the job and these are the methods that the proxy passes to the referent. In other words, what looks like indexing in the process results in remote method calls to the server.

This is simple, but it has some subtle problems in that only changes to proxy data results in calls to the referent. If you store non-proxy data in, say, a proxy list then you cannot expect an automatic update. For example, you can create a dictionary as an element of a list, but it has to be created by the manager. That is, you should use:

```
myList1=manager.list()
myList1.append(manager.dict())
```

rather than:

```
myList2=manager.list()
myList2.append({})
```

The reason for this is that changes to the dict stored in myList2[0] will not be passed on to the shared copy of the list as there is no way for the proxy to know that there has been a change.

That is:

```
myList2=manager.list()
myList2.append({})
d=myList2[0]
d["a"]=1
```

will not update `myList2` as `d` is not a proxy and any updates to it are not passed on to the referent. You can force an update by assigning `d` back to the list element:

```
myList2[0]=d
```

A better method is just to make the dictionary a proxy:

```
myList1=manager.list()
myList1.append(manager.dict())
d=myList2[0]
d["a"]=1
```

which now does update the referent as the dictionary is a proxy as well as the list.

Locking

Any updates to the proxy object that calls a proxied method will update the referent. This update is atomic in the sense that the state of the referent and proxy cannot be corrupted by changes during the update, but this doesn't make shared data safe from race conditions. For example, if we implement the counter example given earlier using a shared counter provided by a manager then we find that race conditions occur very easily:

```
import multiprocessing

def count(myCounter):
    for i in range(1000):
        myCounter.value=myCounter.value+1

if __name__ == '__main__':
    man=multiprocessing.Manager()
    counter=man.Value(int,0)

    p1=multiprocessing.Process(target=count,args=(counter,))
    p2=multiprocessing.Process(target=count,args=(counter,))
    p1.start()
    p2.start()
    p1.join()
    p2.join()
    print(counter.value)
```

If you try this out you will find that the number printed is generally closer to 1000 than to 2000 due to lost updates. If not increase the size of the count until you see the effect of the race condition.

To make it work you need to add an explicit lock:

```
import multiprocessing

def count(myCounter,lock):
    for i in range(1000):
        with lock:
            myCounter.value=myCounter.value+1

if __name__ == '__main__':
    man=multiprocessing.Manager()
    counter=man.Value(int,0)
    lock=man.Lock()

    p1=multiprocessing.Process(target=count,args=(counter,lock))
    p2=multiprocessing.Process(target=count,args=(counter,lock))
    p1.start()
    p2.start()
    p1.join()
    p2.join()
    print(counter.value)
```

This now displays 2000 every time it is run, but it takes twice as long to run.

To understand what is going on all you need to keep in mind is that when you access a proxy you activate its get/set methods and these contact the server to make sure the local and remote data are synchronized.

The previous example of working out the squares also needs a lock as x[i] = x[i]**2 is not atomic. If you want it to be atomic you have to use explicit locking:

```
def myFunc(x,lock):
        for i in range(len(x)):
                with lock:
                        x[i]=x[i]**2
```

Computing Pi with a Manager

You can use a manager to share a single value between processes and implement a manager version of the Pi computation example:

```
import multiprocessing
import time

def myPi(m,n,PI,lock):
    pi=0
    for k in range(m,n+1):
        s= 1 if k%2 else -1
        pi += s / (2 * k - 1)
    with lock:
        PI.value += pi*4
```

162

```
if __name__ == '__main__':
    N=10000000
    man=multiprocessing.Manager()
    PI=man.Value(float,0.0)
    myLock=man.Lock()
    p1=multiprocessing.Process(target=myPi,
                          args=(N//2+1,N,PI, myLock))
    t1=time.perf_counter()
    p1.start()
    myPi(1,N//2,PI,myLock)
    p1.join()
    t2=time.perf_counter()
    print((t2-t1)*1000)
    print(PI.value)
```

This runs at about the same speed as the `ctypes` and `async_result` version. The only advantage of this approach is that it works with Python data types and it is easy to extend to remote processes, see later. Notice that the update of `PI` isn't atomic and needs a lock to ensure that it is.

Custom Managers

Although the `SyncManager` is very handy, it is only when you implement your own custom manager does the approach become really useful. You need to create a custom manager if you want to share a custom class or if you want to make the manager supply proxies to clients. To create a custom manager you simply have to inherit from `BaseManager`. This has some methods that control the lifecycle of the server:

`multiprocessing.managers.BaseManager(`*`address`*`, `*`authkey`*`)`

The two parameters are optional and specify an address to use for the server and an authorization key for security. They default to workable values if you don't specify them.

`BaseManager` has the following methods:

- ♦ `start(`*`initializer`*`, `*`args`*`)` - creates the server in a new process. If you specify a callable for *initializer* then it is called when the server starts with the specified arguments.

- ♦ `get_server()` - returns the Server object that is associated with the manager. This has a `serve_forever()` method which starts the server running and an address attribute which gives the address of the server.

- ♦ `Connect()` - connects a local manager to a remote server

- ♦ `shutdown()` - stops the server. Can only be called if `start` was used.

The most important method is:

```
register(typeid, callable, proxytype, exposed,
                        method_to_typeid, create_method)
```

This is the method used to add custom data types to the manager. All but the first parameter are optional and *typeid* is a string that identifies the new type that you are adding to the manager. It is the name of the method you use to get a proxy for the type.

The *callable* is a function that actually creates an object of the type and is usually the constructor. It can be None if the manager isn't going to create a shared instance.

The *proxytype* is usually left as a default and the manager creates a suitable proxy from BaseProxy, but you can create and specify your own if you need to.

The *exposed* parameter is a list of method names that the proxy will support. If you don't specify this then all public methods, i.e. those that do not start with an underscore _, are exposed.

The *method_to_typeid* parameter specifies a proxy type to return. In most cases this can be ignored and the return will be copied by value, i.e. it won't be a proxy for a shared object.

What is most important to understand is the way that the first three parameters interact. The *typeid* gives the name of the new attribute added to the manager that you call to create a referent/proxy pair. When you use:

```
myList=Manager.typeid()
```

the *callable* is called on the manager's server to obtain a referent and the *proxytype* is called in the process to return a proxy linked to the referent.

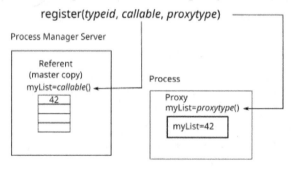

myList=Manager.*typeid*()

The exposed parameter determines which methods are supported by the proxy, i.e. only the methods listed will be included in the proxy.

You can also use a manager in a with clause – start is called on entry and shutdown on exit.

164

A Custom Data Type

This all sounds complicated, but in most cases the defaults are appropriate and hence everything is much simpler. If you register a new data type to a manager then all of its "public" methods are shared via an auto-generated proxy AutoProxy. Notice this only shares methods – sharing attributes or properties is a more complicated problem that involves creating a custom proxy, see the next section. For example, if we create a new class that represents a two-dimensional x,y point then we need to provide access methods that can be shared to the internal _x and _y properties:

```
class Point():
    def __init__(self):
        self._x=0
        self._y=0

    def setxy(self,x,y):
        self._x=x
        self._y=y

    def getxy(self):
        return (self._x, self._y)
```

To share this via a manager all we have to do is derive a new manager class and register the new data type:

```
class myManager(multiprocessing.managers.BaseManager):
    pass
myManager.register("point",Point)
```

Following this myManager has a point attribute that in turn has setxy and getxy methods.

A full example is:

```
import multiprocessing
import multiprocessing.managers

class Point():
    def __init__(self):
        self._x=0
        self._y=0

    def setxy(self,x,y):
        self._x=x
        self._y=y

    def getxy(self):
        return (self._x, self._y)

def myFunc(point):
    point.setxy(42,43)
```

```
class myManager(multiprocessing.managers.BaseManager):
    pass
myManager.register("point",Point)

if __name__ == '__main__':
    man=myManager()
    man.start()
    point=man.point()
    p1=multiprocessing.Process(target=myFunc,args=(point,))
    p1.start()
    p1.join()
    print(point.getxy())
```

If you try this out you will see 42,43 displayed. When any process runs
getxy or setxy, the proxy, that has the copy of the Point object that is shared
by all of the processes, calls the getxy and setxy in the server. Notice that no
locking is applied during the method calls. It is up to you to ensure that
things are thread-safe.

Notice that you can create as many point referents and proxies as you need.
The manager creates new instances each time you call man.point() because
it calls the Point constructor on the server which returns a new referent
which is linked to the returned proxy.

To understand custom managers we need to look at the proxy object in more
detail.

The BaseProxy

So far we have allowed the manager to create a default proxy for us, but
there are times when you need to define your own custom proxy to control
precisely how things work. All of the proxy classes that we have used so far
are derived from the BaseProxy class and this is what we have to use to
implement our custom proxy. The BaseProxy class has the very important
method:

_callmethod(*methodname, args, kwds*)

This calls and returns the result of a method of the proxy's referent, where
args is an iterable of positional parameters and kwds is a dictionary of
keyword parameters. It is this method that implements the remote procedure
call to the server. It is the link between the referent and the proxy.

That is if, in the client process, you use:

```
value = proxy._callmethod(methodname, args, kwds)
```

it runs:

```
methodname(*args, **kwds)
```

on the server. The returned value will be a copy of the result of the call or a proxy to a new shared object. In most cases a value is what you need.

If an exception is raised by the call, then it is re-raised by _callmethod(). If some other exception is raised in the manager's process then this is converted into a RemoteError exception and is raised by _callmethod().

There are three other useful methods:

♦ _getvalue() - returns a copy of the referent. For this to work the custom class has to be pickleable

♦ __repr__() - returns a representation of the proxy object

♦ __str__() - returns the representation of the referent

The basic principle in implementing a managed shared class is that first you implement the class as it will be instantiated and run on the server, i.e. the referent, and then you implement the proxy class that will be instantiated and run on the local process. Finally, you register the two and start using them.

A Property Proxy

The autoproxy generator usually does a good job of creating a proxy suitable for all of the public methods of a class. What it doesn't do at all, at the time of writing, is create proxy methods for any properties a class may have, so this is a good starting point for an example.

First you need the custom class that you want to share and this can be written with no reference to the fact that it is going to be used with a manager:

```
class Counter():
    def __init__(self):
        self.myCounter=0
    def getCount(self):
        return self.myCounter
    def setCount(self,value):
        self.myCounter=value
    count=property(getCount,setCount)
```

The Counter class provides a single count property that can be get and set in the usual way. This is the class that the manager instantiates on the server – it is the referent.

Next we need a suitable proxy that the manager can instantiate on the local process and which redirects any methods to the server object:

```
class CounterProxy(multiprocessing.managers.BaseProxy):
    _exposed_ = ('getCount', 'setCount')
    def get(self):
        return self._callmethod('getCount')
    def set(self, value):
        return self._callmethod('setCount', (value,))
    value = property(get, set)
```

The `CounterProxy` inherits from `BaseProxy` and sets up a property called `value`. Notice that the property name used in the proxy and the custom class don't have to be the same, though they often are. Different names have been used for the two classes in this example to make sure that it is clear which class something refers to. You can see that all the proxy does is to transfer the calls to the `get` and `set` methods to the equivalent methods on the referent.

The `CounterProxy` is instantiated in the local process and when you try to access its value property `set` or `get` is called which in turn call `setCount` or `getCount` on the server instance. Notice that you have to list the server instance's methods that the proxy is allowed to call in the `_exposed_` attribute. You can also set the list of exposed methods when you register the class, but it is usually better to do the job in the proxy itself. In this case the registration is just:

```
myManager.register("counter",callable=Counter,
                             proxytype=CounterProxy)
```

The `callable` is the constructor for the server object i.e. the referent, and the `proxytype` is the constructor for the local object, i.e. the proxy.

The complete program is:

```
import multiprocessing
import multiprocessing.managers

class Counter():
    def __init__(self):
        self.myCounter=0
    def getCount(self):
        return self.myCounter
    def setCount(self,value):
        self.myCounter=value
    count=property(getCount,setCount)

class CounterProxy(multiprocessing.managers.BaseProxy):
    _exposed_ = ('getCount', 'setCount')
    def get(self):
        return self._callmethod('getCount')
    def set(self, value):
        return self._callmethod('setCount', (value,))
    value = property(get, set)
```

```
class myManager(multiprocessing.managers.BaseManager):
    pass

myManager.register("counter",callable=Counter,
                                proxytype=CounterProxy)


def count(myCounter):
    for i in range(1000):
        myCounter.value=myCounter.value+1

if __name__ == '__main__':
    man=myManager()
    man.start()
    counter=man.counter()

    p1=multiprocessing.Process(target=count,args=(counter,))
    p2=multiprocessing.Process(target=count,args=(counter,))
    p1.start()
    p2.start()
    p1.join()
    p2.join()
    print(counter.value)
```

If you run this you will find that it all works, but the counter value is much less than 2000. This is because of race conditions that lose increments. The standard solution is to include a lock, as in previous examples. To do this you have to register a lock object:

```
myManager.register("Lock",threading.Lock,
multiprocessing.managers.AcquirerProxy)
```

As before you can use man.counter() to create as many linked referents and proxies as you need.

The problem with adding standard objects to your manager is that the proxy objects that work with them aren't documented. The only way to find out that you need an AcquirerProxy for a lock is to read the code. Notice also that the lock being used is a thread lock that runs on the server. The non-server processes use the lock via remote procedure calls – they don't really make use of a lock object at all and the lock that they are using isn't implemented as a process-wide lock via the operating system.

A much simpler solution is to inherit from SyncManager rather than BaseManager so that you get all of the standard proxy classes pre-registered:

```
class myManager(multiprocessing.managers.SyncManager):
    pass
myManager.register("counter",callable=Counter,
                                proxytype=CounterProxy)
```

Following this you can use Lock on myManager and use all of the other proxy types listed earlier.

Remote Managers

The connection between the server and the proxy is via an operating system pipe. This is a double-ended queue that can be used to connect two or more processes together, but it can also be used to connect processes running on different machines using the network as the transport. What this means is that a process manager can run on a machine and create a server which can accept connections from managers and proxies running on other machines.

Although the basic mechanisms are the same, there are some differences when you use a manager to create and connect to a remote server. The most important is that now the manager has to supply a proxy to a client without creating a new instance of the referent.

Normally the referent is shared by passing an instance of the proxy to other processes. This works because the processes are running on the same machine and are created using a fork or a spawn and this means that they automatically have definitions of global resources such as the proxy. A remote process, however, doesn't have any association with the server process and it doesn't share anything at all. This means we need the server to supply the proxy to the remote machine. This is achieved using the mechanisms we already have.

The first stages of creating a manager proceed in the usual way. For example, if you simply want the remote server to supply a shared initialized list you need to create a custom class to share:

```
class SharedList():
    def __init__(self):
        self.list=[1,2,3,4,5,6,7,8,9,10]
    def getData(self):
        return self.list
    def setData(self,value,index):
        self.list[index]=value
```

This simply creates a list and provides two access methods getData and setData. Normally we would register this class as the callable, but if we do this the client will automatically create a new instance each time it uses myList=man.sharedList() to get a proxy. The solution is to not register a constructor for the class, but a function that returns a particular instance:

```
_sharedList=SharedList()
def SharedList():
    return _sharedList
```

This creates an instance on the server which is shared between all the processes that use the manager. This also means that there is no way to create additional instances – you are sharing a single referent object created by the process that created the manager.

Now all that remains is to create the proxy and this is nothing new:

```
class SharedListProxy(multiprocessing.managers.BaseProxy):
    _exposed_ = ('getData', 'setData')
    def getData(self):
        return self._callmethod('getData')
    def setData(self,value,index):
        self._callmethod('setData', (value,index))
```

Finally we register the function that returns the object and the proxy:

```
class myManager(multiprocessing.managers.BaseManager):
    pass
myManager.register("SharedList",callable=SharedList,
                                proxytype=SharedListProxy)
```

Once we have a custom manager we can start it running, but now direct it to listen for connections on the local address:

```
if __name__ == '__main__':
    man=myManager(address=("192.168.253.14,50000),
                                authkey=b"password")
```

This creates a manager that will create a server listening for connections on the local IP address port 50000. As these connections can come from untrusted external machines we need to specify an authorization key, which in this example is just set to password. Any remote machine trying to connect has to supply the authorization key.

We can use the manager to share the list with a process running on the same machine in the usual way:

```
if __name__ == '__main__':
    man=myManager(address=("192.168.253.14",50000),
            authkey=b"password")
    man.start()
    myList=man.SharedList()
    print(myList.getData())
```

which displays

```
[1, 2, 3, 4, 5, 6, 7, 8, 9, 10]
```

The proxy that man.SharedList() returns connects with the local server and makes its remote procedure calls directly to it.

Now we are in a position to allow a remote manager to connect to the server, but we have a problem – the server stops running when the program ends. To keep the server running ready to accept connections we could simply keep the main thread from coming to an end by adding man.join(). This works but it leaves the main process suspended and awaiting resources.

171

A better way is to use the `serve_forever` method which causes the main thread to stop running but keeps the server thread alive:

```
if __name__ == '__main__':
    man=myManager(address=("0.0.0.0",50000),authkey=b"password")
    s=man.get_server()
    s.serve_forever()
```

Notice that you cannot have any instructions following `serve_forever()`.

Putting all this together gives us the code for the complete remote server:

```
import multiprocessing
import multiprocessing.managers

class SharedList():
    def __init__(self):
        self.list=[1,2,3,4,5,6,7,8,9,10]
    def getData(self):
        return self.list
    def setData(self,value,index):
        self.list[index]=value

class SharedListProxy(multiprocessing.managers.BaseProxy):
    _exposed_ = ('getData', 'setData')
    def getData(self):
        return self._callmethod('getData')
    def setData(self,value,index):
        self._callmethod('setData', (value,index))

_sharedList=SharedList()
def SharedList():
    return _sharedList

class myManager(multiprocessing.managers.BaseManager):
    pass
myManager.register("SharedList",callable=SharedList,
                                proxytype=SharedListProxy)

if __name__ == '__main__':

man=myManager(address=("192.168.253.14",50000),authkey=b"password")
    s=man.get_server()
    s.serve_forever()
```

Now we can write a client to connect to the remote server. To do this we need to know the IP address of the server. You can use a URL, but this only works if your local network is set up correctly. For your first experiments with remote servers it is better to use their IP addresses.

The first thing we have to do is create a manager that supports the same proxies as the remote manager:

```
class myManager(multiprocessing.managers.BaseManager):
    pass
myManager.register("SharedList",proxytype=SharedListProxy)
```

Notice that we simply register the name of the shared object and the name of the proxy. We also need to include a definition of the proxy in the client as it has to run it locally and has no other way of acquiring it. Now we can get an instance of the manager as usual, but instead of getting it to start a server we use its connect method to connect it to the remote server:

```
man=myManager(address=("192.168.253.14",50000),authkey=b"password")
man.connect()
```

Notice that we have to specify the address of the remote machine and the authorization key before we use connect. There are things that can go wrong at this point – you can get the IP and port wrong, the authkey wrong or the firewall might not let the port through, although most systems will allow the port through if the connection is on the local network. If it doesn't work and you are sure of the IP address, port and authorization key then the only options are that the server isn't running or the firewall is blocking traffic. Whenever a remote connection failed during testing of this code, it was always the configuration of the firewall on the server that was causing the problem.

Once the manager has made the connection to the remote server we can get a proxy and use it:

```
    myList=man.SharedList()
    print(myList.getData())
```

When you call getList the proxy performs a remote procedure call to the method running on the remote server. Again you will see:

```
[1, 2, 3, 4, 5, 6, 7, 8, 9, 10]
```

which looks boring, but the data has come from the remote server and from here you can add standard or custom proxies to make the manager more useful.

The complete client program is:

```
import multiprocessing
import multiprocessing.managers

class SharedListProxy(multiprocessing.managers.BaseProxy):
    _exposed_ = ('getData', 'setData')
    def getData(self):
        return self._callmethod('getData')
    def setData(self,value,index):
        self._callmethod('setData', (value,index))

class myManager(multiprocessing.managers.BaseManager):
    pass
myManager.register("SharedList",proxytype=SharedListProxy)

if __name__ == '__main__':
    man=myManager(address=("192.168.253.14",50000),
                                    authkey=b"password")
    man.connect()
    myList=man.SharedList()
    print(myList.getData())
```

Of course, if you want to run this as a separate Python program on the same machine it will still work as it will if the remote machine is connected via the Internet and many miles away. All that matters is that the two programs, the client and the server, can communicate using IP.

In this case the AutoProxy class works so we can simplify the program by not bothering to define and register a proxy in both the server and the client. The custom proxy is included in this example to demonstrate how it is done.

A Remote Procedure Call

To emphasize the idea that the process manager is a remote procedure call facility that is used to implement shared data, it is worth implementing a pure remote procedure call. If you have been following the way that proxies work this should seem very straightforward.

First we need a server. This provides an implementation of the function that computes pi:

```
import multiprocessing
import multiprocessing.managers

class Math:
    def myPi(self,m,n):
        pi=0
        for k in range(m,n+1):
            s= 1 if k%2 else -1
            pi += s / (2 * k - 1)
        return pi*4
```

```
_math=Math()

def getMath():
    return _math

class MathProxy(multiprocessing.managers.BaseProxy):
    _exposed_ = ("myPi",)
    def myPi(self,m,n):
        return self._callmethod('myPi',m,n)

class myManager(multiprocessing.managers.BaseManager):
    pass
myManager.register("math",callable=getMath, proxytype=MathProxy)

if __name__ == '__main__':
    man=myManager(address=("192.168.253.14",50000),
                                authkey=b"password")
    s=man.get_server()
    s.serve_forever()
```

You can see that we have a class which contains the pi function as a method. As before we create an instance of the Math class and a function, getMath, that returns the instance. A simple custom proxy, MathProxy, provides access to just the myPi function.

Now all we need is a client and this is very similar to the previous client:

```
import multiprocessing
import multiprocessing.managers

class MathProxy(multiprocessing.managers.BaseProxy):
    _exposed_ = ('myPi')
    def myPi(self,m,n):
        return self._callmethod('myPi',(m,n))

class myManager(multiprocessing.managers.BaseManager):
    pass
myManager.register("math",proxytype=MathProxy)

if __name__ == '__main__':

man=myManager(address=("192.168.253.14",50000),authkey=b"password")
    man.connect()
    math=man.math()
    print(math.myPi(1,100))
```

As before we register MathProxy and connect to the server. The call to math.myPi uses the proxy to run the calculation on the remote server and returns the result as a value.

In this case we don't need MathProxy as AutoProxy works perfectly well so we could simplify both the server and the client.

Final Thoughts

The big problem with using process managers is that they are poorly documented and there is a tendency to think that they do more than they really do. If you think about the process manager as a remote procedure call facility then it starts to make more sense. It is particularly important that you don't assume that programs that share data using a manager are automatically free of race conditions – in general you still need to add explicit locking.

Should you use process managers? More direct approaches to sharing data and synchronizing processes are likely to be more efficient and possibly less error-prone than the high-level manager approach. On the other hand, the abstraction of the process manager provides a way to organize data sharing and to build more sophisticated architectures. It also provides a uniform way to work with local and remote servers.

Summary

- Process managers are provided as a way of sharing complex data with any number of processes, irrespective of how the processes are created.

- They work by implementing a remote procedure call mechanism. This allows data to be shared because all Python complex data types use methods for access.

- Remote process calls are implemented by a central server which keeps a master copy of an object, the referent, and via the use of proxies in the client processes.

- The easiest way to use a process manager is via the `SyncManager`. This provides a long list of standard referents and proxies for Python data types such as lists, dictionaries and locks.

- If `SyncManager` doesn't do what you need you can implement a custom manager by deriving a new class from `BaseManager`. This has a method which allows you to add a new shared data type, complete with a function to create the referent and one to create the proxy.

- The system provides `AutoProxy` which creates a proxy which gives access to all of the public methods of the referent.

- To create a custom proxy you derive a class from `BaseProxy` which provides a method that can be used to call any of the referent's methods.

- `AutoProxy` doesn't share properties, but it is relatively easy to implement properties using a custom proxy.

- Process managers can share data, or more accurately provide remote procedure calls, to servers and clients running on different machines that are connected via the network.

Chapter 10

Subprocesses

So far the processes that we have been creating have hosted Python code. That is, the process has a complete copy of the Python interpreter and a Python program ready to run. Sometimes it is useful to be able to run other languages in a separate process and use a Python program to control and make use of it. This is what the subprocess module allows you to do. It is a replacement for low level interaction with foreign code via the os.system and os.spawn modules.

The subprocess module gives you an easier to use approach to running foreign code. However easy the general idea may be, the actual implementation is usually difficult due to the non-standard ways programs can be run under different operating systems. Put simply, the differences between Windows and Linux, or more generally Posix, operating systems are many and time consuming. The simplest situation is only having to target a single operating system. In this case you can adjust parameters to get things to work and not worry about finding something that works across operating systems.

A second problem is the way that programs interact with a human client. The range of ways this can happen is more varied than you might think and it is generally far from regular. Writing code that recognizes when a program has finished sending messages to the user and is now waiting for input is difficult. You are essentially mimicking human behavior, reading the screen and typing appropriate responses. At the extreme this needs AI, but in most cases it only requires simple string manipulation.

It is worth noting that the asyncio module also provides facilities similar to subprocess but modified for asynchronous use. It is worth considering because asyncio doesn't suffer from the same buffering problems as subprocess. However, it is based on the subprocess module and if you simply want to add external programs to an existing, otherwise non-async, program then subprocess is the way to go.

Running a program

The simplest of the `subprocess` functions is `run`. It is built on top of the more flexible `Popen` class and it works well for simple situations. The `run` and `Popen` functions support a very large number of parameters to allow you to customize the way a program is run. These are described in the documentation and most are very specific to particular operating systems and conditions. In this chapter we will deal only with the most important ones.

The `run` command is useful if you just want to run a program and get a result. The `Popen` class is useful if you need to run and interact with a program to get a result. In most cases you can start with a simple version:

```
subprocess.run(command line)
```

where `command line` is a list of items that you would use if running the program from the command line. The program specified is run in a new process and the calling process waits for it to complete. You can specify a `timeout=` parameter if you don't want to wait more than the specified time. For example, if you want to get a directory listing then under Linux you would use:

```
dir /
```

and under Windows:

```
dir \
```

To run these programs, under Linux you would use:

```
import subprocess
subprocess.run(["dir","/"])
```

and under Windows:

```
import subprocess
subprocess.run(["dir", "\\"])
```

Notice the need to escape the backslash.

You can see that each separate item on the command line has to be converted into an item in the list. One of the problems is working out what corresponds to a separate item. The reason that the parameters are specified as items in a list is that the `run` method processes them to try to make them correct for the system. For example, you cannot use:

```
subprocess.run(["dir /"])
```

as this generates the error:

```
No such file or directory: 'dir /'
```

The point is that run doesn't simply submit the items as written, it processes them and the first item is always regarded as the name of the file to be executed.

It can be difficult to work out how to split a command line into suitable items correctly. The easiest option is to use the shlex lexical analysis object. For example:

```
import shlex
print(shlex.split("dir /"))
```

displays

```
['dir', '/']
```

The lexical analysis is designed for Linux/Unix shells and isn't guaranteed to work for Windows but the changes needed are usually small.

Input/Output

When you use the run command the calling process waits for the subprocess to complete and then returns a CompletedProcess object with attributes that provide information about what happened:

- ◆ args – the arguments used to launch the process, i.e. a copy of the first arguments used in run

- ◆ returncode - exit status of the child process where 0 usually indicates success

You can use check_returncode() which raises a CalledProcessError if the return code was non-zero. You can also return the output of the subprocess into the stdout and stderr attributes, but for this to work you have to request that the output is captured by setting the capture_output to True, for example:

```
import subprocess
result = subprocess.run(["dir","/"],capture_output = True)
print("results",result.stdout)
```

This suppresses any output from appearing on any console that might be in use and it allows you to process the returned string.

You can also arrange to send some data to the program. The important thing to realize is that such data is treated as if it was typed on the keyboard to the running program. To send input you simply use the input parameter. As an example designed to demonstrate automating user input, the command:

```
rm test -i
```

checks that the file exists and asks if it is OK to delete it. The user then types a Y or an N and the file is treated accordingly.

To delete the file without the question, you need to specify `input`:

```
import subprocess
result = subprocess.run(['rm', 'test', '-i'],
                        capture_output = True, input=b"y\n")
```

The input string will be "fed" into the running program as it demands input. Notice the use of "\n" to throw a newline. For example to delete two files:

```
import subprocess
result = subprocess.run(['rm', 'test1', 'test2', '-i'],
                        capture_output = True,input = b"y\ny\n")
```

The first "y\n" is used as input to the question to delete the first file and the second is used for the second.

This raises the issue of what the encoding of the input and output text is. By default all text input and output is performed using a byte sequence, something that is discussed in *Programmer's Python: Everything Is Data*, ISBN: 978-1871962598. This is often all you need as most command line programs work in ASCII or the ASCII subset of UTF-8 depending on how you want think of it. If a command line program goes beyond basic UTF-8 or uses a different encoding then you can opt to build your own byte sequences that represent the text or you can specify the encoding and work with Python strings and allow the system to deal with the encoding/decoding.

Essentially the default mode is to open the pipe that connects the two processes in binary mode. This means that no encoding/decoding is performed and the data is transported between the two processes without modification.

You can open the pipe in text mode and accept default encoding/decoding by setting the text parameter to `True`. This means that the data is presented as Python UTF-8 strings and in addition line endings are all converted to \n. You can set the encoding in use with the encoding parameter. A common approach is to first use binary mode to discover exactly what codes are being transferred between the two processes and then change to text mode with the specific encoding.

Popen

The `run` command is a simplifying wrapper around the `Popen` class which gives you much more control over what happens, but at the expense of increased complexity. All of the parameters that we have looked at in using the `run` command can be used in `Popen` and they have the same meaning – as run passes them on to an internal call to `Popen`. The `Popen` class makes the use of pipes to connect the processes more obvious and direct manipulation of these pipes is the way it gains its flexibility. The fact that `Popen` is lower level means that there are many features which depend on the operating system you are using.

The most important thing to know about `Popen` is that it returns immediately and leaves the child process running – unlike `run` which waits for the child process to complete before returning. You can see that this is the case by comparing the output of:

```
import subprocess
subprocess.Popen(["dir","/"])
print("finished")
```

which displays `finished` followed by the directory listing, and:

```
import subprocess
subprocess.run(["dir","/"])
print("finished")
```

which displays the directory listing and then `finished`.

The main process can check what the child process is doing with the `poll` method `Popen.poll()` which returns `None` if the child process is still running and a `returncode` if it has terminated.

You can wait for a child process using `Popen.wait(timeout=None)` which waits for the process to terminate or the timeout to be up and returns a `returncode` if it has or raises a `TimeoutExpired` exception otherwise. If a child process refuses to stop you can terminate it using `Popen.terminate()` or `Popen.kill()`. These work in the same way as for general processes, see Chapter 3.

The fact that `Popen` returns at once means that the main process can get on with other tasks while the child process runs, but more specifically it allows the main process to interact with the child process. To do this the `Popen` has to specify that input and output from the child process is redirected to the main process via pipes. By default the I/O is not modified and connects to the console and keyboard with variable results depending on the system and the exact operating environment.

To specify where the standard I/O streams should be redirected you need use the `stdin`, `stdout` and `stderr` parameters. By default these are set to `None`. If you want to redirect them to a pipe that can be used by the main process then use `PIPE`. If you want to simply discard the data use `DEVNULL`. A more complex option is to specify a valid file object that will be used to store the data for later processing. You can also redirect the `stderr` stream to `stdout` by setting the `stderr` parameter to `STDOUT`.

To understand how this all works you have to understand that a command line program generally writes all its output to the `stdout` stream and reads any data it needs from `stdin`. Any error reports are written to `stderr`. When these streams are redirected to pipes everything works in exactly the same way, but the main process now plays the role of the user. The output data will sit in the pipe until the main process reads it. The child process will also wait for the main process to write data to the pipe if it performs an input operation. What this means is that the main process can interact with the child process by reading data and responding to it by writing data to the stdin pipe.

This sounds easy, but in practice it is generally much more difficult as humans are much more flexible in their interpretation of data than a program can easily mimic. Also notice that any program that doesn't simply use stdin, stdout and stderr isn't going to be controllable via Popen. In particular, any program that has a GUI interface is completely unsuitable.

The simplest, but not the most flexible, way to communicate with the child process is to use the communicate method:

```
Popen.communicate(input=None, timeout=None)
```

This sends the data assigned to input, if any, to stdin and then waits for the process to end before reading the pipe associated with stdout. If the timeout occurs first an exception is raised. In this sense using Popen with communicate doesn't give you anything beyond the run function. For example, the dir program can be written to use Popen:

```
import subprocess
p = subprocess.Popen(["dir","/"],stdout=subprocess.PIPE)
stdout_data,stderr_data=p.communicate()
print(stdout_data)
print("finished")
```

and it works in much the same way.

Interaction

If you want to interact with a subprocess then things become much more complicated. The reason is that most of the programs you are likely to want to run are written in C and this changes the way that they work when you redirect their I/O to a pipe. Some even avoid using stdin and stdout, instead preferring to send data directly to the console. If you are working with such a program there is nothing you can do. Even if you are using a perfectly standard C program there is still a problem. By default, data sent to stdout and stdin is line buffered, that is the buffer is cleared and the data sent to the device a line at a time. In an effort to be more efficient, the standard library code switches to using the available buffers when stdout and stdin are redirected to files or pipes.

This is usually a good idea, but it makes using programs interactively very difficult and sometimes impossible. If a program sends a question to stdout connected to a pipe then the data may not be transmitted to the client because the buffer isn't full. This can leave the client stalled while it waits for input. If the client then executes an input to get the answer to the question from the client we have deadlock. This is the reason that the documentation warns that reading and writing a pipe is dangerous and you should use communicate.

If you do use `communicate` then there is no chance of any interactive behavior. For example, consider this very simple script, firstly for Linux:

```
#!/bin/sh
echo "user name: "
read name
echo $name
```

Secondly for Windows:

```
@echo off
echo "User name:"
set /p id=
echo %id%
```

This simply displays a prompt for a user name, reads it in and then displays it. This is a simple model for part of an interactive sequence from almost any command line program. To automate this we have to read the prompt, perhaps test to see what it is, and then write a suitable name. For example under Windows:

```
import subprocess
p = subprocess.Popen(["myscript.bat"],
        stdout=subprocess.PIPE,stdin=subprocess.PIPE, text=True)
ans=p.stdout.readline()
print("message",ans)
p.stdin.write("mike\n")
ans=p.stdout.readline()
print("message",ans)
```

A Linux version just needs the name of the script changed to `["./myscript.sh"]`

If you try this out you will discover that it hangs at the last `readline`. The first `readline` works because the output buffer is flushed by the script's input command (read or `set`) but the `write` simply sends the data to the buffer waiting to be sent to the script. As a result the script doesn't read it and so doesn't move on to send the data back to the parent and hence the final `readline` waits forever.

There are a number of solutions to this problem but, as the problem is that the Python buffer isn't being cleared, the best is to use the `flush` method:

```
ans = p.stdout.readline()
print("message",ans)
p.stdin.write("mike\n")
p.stdin.flush()
ans = p.stdout.readline()
print("message",ans)
```

This makes the program work, but the same situation can occur due to the subprocess not flushing its buffer and then the parent process cannot solve the problem using a `flush` command as it can flush its own buffers but not those of the subprocess.

185

The point is that communicating over buffered pipes is difficult to get right and very fragile. You can make thing a little easier by switching to line buffering, i.e. the buffer is flushed each time a complete line is present. To do this you simply set bufsize to 0 and universal_newlines to true:

```
import subprocess
p = subprocess.Popen(["myscript.bat"],stdout=subprocess.PIPE,
        stdin=subprocess.PIPE, bufsize=0,
            universal_newlines=True, text=True)

ans=p.stdout.readline()
print("message",ans)
p.stdin.write("mike\n")

ans=p.stdout.readline()
print("message",ans)
```

This now works without the parent needing to flush its buffers, but it only works because the script sends a newline after the prompt. If you change the script to read:

(Linux)

```
#!/bin/sh
echo -n "User name: "
read name
echo $name
```

(Windows)

```
@echo off
set /p id= "User name"
echo %id%
```

Now the prompt "User name" is delivered without a newline before the user's responses. This, of course, makes the program hang because the first readline never completes as the child process's buffer isn't flushed.

Non-Blocking Read Pipe

What we really need to stop all of these deadlocks caused by pipe buffering is a non-blocking read. The problem is that the subprocess module doesn't support non-blocking pipe operations, although asyncio does. However, as we know all about threading it is easy to change a blocking function call into a non-blocking call. The trick is to run the blocking function on another thread and provide a way for the main thread to check that there are some results ready to be processed.

In the case of `pipe.read` the job is very simple because we can arrange for a new thread to always read ahead by one character and have that character ready for the main thread to consume. As there is a good deal of static data needed to maintain the state, it is better to use an object rather than a function:

```
class AsyncReader():
    def __init__(self,stream):
        self._stream = stream
        self._char = ""
        self.t = threading.Thread(target=self._get,daemon = True)
        self.t.start()
```

The object is linked to a particular pipe via the `stream` parameter, which is specified as part of the constructor and saved for later. The initializer creates a thread which attempts to read the pipe even before it has been requested:

```
    def _get(self):
        self._char=self._stream.read(1)
```

This is run on a separate thread and so it simply waits until a single character is ready to read. It doesn't matter how long it waits as it isn't holding up the main thread. When a character is ready it stores it in _char and the thread comes to an end. What this means is that if the thread is still running we haven't read a character and if it has terminated a character is waiting. Notice that we don't have to lock the access to _char as only this new thread is accessing it. Now we can write a read method which doesn't block:

```
    def get(self):
        self.t.join(0.04)
        if self.t.is_alive():
            return ""
        else:
            result=self._char
            self.t=threading.Thread(target=self._get,daemon=True)
            self.t.start()
            return result
```

First we `join` the thread for four hundredths of a second. If the thread has finished the `join` continues without waiting. The reason we wait is to give the script at the other end of the pipe time to send a character. Without the `join` we could read the pipe too fast and conclude that the message being sent was complete. Next we check to see if the thread is still running. If it is then it is still waiting for the pipe to produce a character and we return a null string to indicate that there is no character available. If it has finished we create a new thread to read the next character and return the character stored in _char.

The reason for storing _char in the local variable `result` before starting the thread again is to avoid any race condition without locking. At this point the thread isn't running and so we can safely read the data in _char without locking. Once the thread has started then it could change the value in _char before the method returns and so lose a character. Doing things in this order means that we can avoid locking, employing a lock-free algorithm.

The `get` method reads a single character, but we generally want to read a complete message from the child process. Usually a complete message ends with a newline but not always. Sometimes the child process will simply display a message and then wait for the user to input something on the same line. What does mark the end of a message that needs a response is that the flow of characters stops while the user is given a chance to type a response. This "pause" detection is already included in the `get` method. Now we can use it to write a method that builds up a complete message:

```
def readmessage(self):
    ans=""
    while True:
        char=self.get()
        if char=="":
            break
        ans+=char
    return ans
```

Now we have an object which provides a non-blocking read of a pipe we can put this together to read a message from the child process:

```
p = subprocess.Popen(["myscript.bat"],
                    stdout=subprocess.PIPE,stdin=subprocess.PIPE,
bufsize=1,universal_newlines=True, text=True)

aRead=AsyncReader(p.stdout)
ans=aRead.readmessage()
print("message",ans)
p.stdin.write("mike\n")
ans=aRead.readmessage()
print("message",ans)
```

This now works irrespective on whether or not the message ends with a newline and it works under Windows and Linux (with a change to the name of the script).

The complete program is:

```
import subprocess
import threading

class AsyncReader():
    def __init__(self,stream):
        self._stream=stream
        self._char=""
        self.t=threading.Thread(target=self._get,daemon=True)
        self.t.start()

    def get(self):
        self.t.join(0.04)
        if self.t.is_alive():
            return ""
        else:
            result=self._char
            self.t=threading.Thread(target=self._get,daemon=True)
            self.t.start()
            return result

    def _get(self):
        self._char=self._stream.read(1)

    def readmessage(self):
        ans=""
        while True:
            char=self.get()
            if char=="":
                break
            ans+=char
        return ans


p = subprocess.Popen(["myscript.bat"],
                stdout=subprocess.PIPE,stdin=subprocess.PIPE,
bufsize=1,universal_newlines=True, text=True)

aRead=AsyncReader(p.stdout)

ans=aRead.readmessage()

print("message",ans)
p.stdin.write("mike\n")

ans=aRead.readmessage()
print("message",ans)
```

This is not an ideal implementation, but the idea is sound. In particular, it uses the state of the thread to signal whether or not there is a character ready to read and this means creating and destroying a thread per character. This is inefficient, but in this application this doesn't matter too much – user I/O is slow. A better solution would be to use a thread pool, but an even better solution is to use a queue to store characters as they are read. This introduces another layer of buffering to the I/O, but at least it is one that is under your control.

Using subprocess

The idea of using Python to control another program written in another language is an attractive one, but it is difficult to make work. As already mentioned, many programs don't use `stdin` and `stdout` even though they are command line, character-based applications. Sometimes this is for security reasons – typing in passwords is the most common application. Sometimes this is for flexibility – text editors need to control the screen layout in sophisticated ways. Even if a program does use the standard I/O streams it can still be difficult to get right even with the use of buffering and the assumption that a flexible human will be reading and interpreting what to do next. The only way to find out if a program can be automated is to try it.

You will also find that there are a great many parameters that apply to `Popen` that we haven't covered. The documentation is often vague about what they do and they tend to be system-dependent. This is yet another challenge to getting a subprocess to work. This said, when you can make it work it can be a shortcut that makes something possible.

It is worth knowing that `asyncio` also provides facilities to work with subprocesses and these fit in with the wider asynchronous approach. `asyncio` also seems to be free of the buffering problems we encounter using a pipe.

Summary

- The subprocess module is designed to allow you to run other programs under the control of Python. This is not an easy task given that programs are generally designed to work with a human user.

- The run function is the simple way to run a program and interact with it.

- The run function blocks until the program has finished and then returns any output it might have produced.

- The run function is easy to use but restricts how you can interact with the program. The Popen function returns immediately and lets you interact with the running program as if you were the user.

- A big problem is that I/O between the program and Popen is via a buffered pipe. To avoid deadlock when reading from a buffered pipe the communicate method is provided.

- A better approach to working with a buffered pipe is to provide a non-blocking read which can be done with the help of another thread.

- Even if you have mastered the art of interaction with another program, it can still be difficult to do the job reliably. Humans interact with programs in subtle ways and replicating this using a Python program can be very difficult.

- The only way to discover if you can automate the use of a program is to actually try it.

Chapter 11

Futures

So far we have dealt with the problem of coordinating what happens to the results of asynchronous programs as a low-level concern or as no problem at all. In practice, getting asynchronous results is a major distortion of the usual logic of a program and "futures" are an attempt to restore this logic.

Futures are called "promises" or "deferred" objects in other languages and Python does things differently, as you might expect, in that it automates the way that futures are generated. In other languages, it is up to the programmer to create functions which return a promise object. In Python a standard function is automatically converted to return a `Future` just by the way that it is invoked.

Another important difference is that in most cases promises are implemented in a single-threaded environment. The `concurrent.futures` module is a multi-threading, multi-process implementation of a futures-based framework built on top of the `multiprocessing` module. The ability to use futures in a multi-threaded/process environment is unusual and very useful.

The `asyncio` module also implements futures, but in a more restricted and more conventional single-threaded environment. In a single-threaded environment futures are even more important because they solve the problem of keeping the single thread free to get on with other tasks while preserving much of the logical structure of the program.

In a multi-threaded, multi-process environment futures are still very useful but they are not as essential. They provide a clean way for asynchronous code to return results and handle errors.

In this chapter we look at multi-threaded, multi-process-based futures and their associated executors. The executors are used from within `asyncio` so they are worth knowing about, even if you don't plan to use `concurrent.futures` directly.

Futures

We have already encountered a basic future-style object in the form of the `AsyncResult` object used in connection with the process pool, see Chapter 8. The `concurrent.futures` module has a more complete and general implementation of a `Future` object.

In most cases you don't have to worry about creating a `Future` as they are automatically returned from asynchronous functions run by one of the module's executor objects. The `concurrent.futures` module adds futures to your functions without you having to do anything at all. That means you can write a function that simply raises exceptions when errors occur and returns a result in the usual way and if you use it with `concurrent.futures` it will automatically return a `Future` which handles both the results and the exceptions.

Futures are a better alternative to the ad-hoc approach of returning and waiting for results from asynchronous programs. When we move on to look at futures in a single-threaded environment we will discover that they also lead on to higher-level ideas such as `await`.

The basic idea is that a `Future` is an object that lives in the main thread/process that the child thread/process can use to signal its state and to return a result at some time in the future, hence the name.

A `Future` can be in one of three states:

- Resolved – the function has completed and returned a result, which may be an exception, which is now available in the Future
- Pending – the function is still running and no result is available yet
- Canceled – the function has been canceled and an exception has been returned

The main thread/process can make use of the `Future` via its methods.

- `result(timeout=None)` - waits for a result to be ready
  If the call times out a `TimeoutError` is raised. If the `Future` is canceled a `CancelledError` is raised. If the call completed its result is returned by the `Future`.
- `exception(timeout=None)` - returns the exception raised by the call, `TimeoutError` or `CancelledError`
- `cancel()` - tries to cancel the call. You can only cancel a call if it isn't running, i.e. it is still in the queue waiting for a thread/process from the pool to be available. If you want to cancel a running call then you need to implement a signaling mechanism and deal with any clean up that is required.
- `cancelled()` - True if the call has been successfully canceled
- `done()` - True if the task is complete or successfully canceled
- `running()` - True if the call is executing and cannot be canceled

Although it seems like a retrograde step back to callbacks you can also use add_done__callback(*function*) which attaches the *function* as a callback when the call is done, canceled or has finished running. The callback function receives the Future as its only argument and this can be used to retrieve the result of the call.

Notice that add_done_callback has the advantage that there is no need for the function being run asynchronously to support callbacks, it is all handled by the framework.

Executors

The concurrent.futures module supports both a thread and a process pool and provides easy ways to create and make use of them via the idea of an executor. There are two executors, ProcessPoolExecutor and ThreadPoolExecutor which work in the same way as the ProcessPool described in Chapter 8. To create an Executor you use the appropriate constructor:

```
concurrent.futures.ThreadPoolExecutor(max_workers=None,
                                  thread_name_prefix='')
```

or:

```
concurrent.futures.ProcessPoolExecutor(max_workers=None)
```

In either case if max_workers isn't specified the number of processors available is used.

Although currently not documented you can also specify two additional parameters, initializer = *function* and initargs = *arguments tuple* which call *function* with the specified *arguments* before each thread/process starts. This is a way of getting Python global objects set up before a process runs. It is less useful for threads as they already share global objects. Notice that the initializer is only called once when the thread/process is created as part of the pool. If the pool is reused to run other functions the initializer is not rerun.

Once you have an `Executor` you can run a single function using:

```
Executor.submit(function, args, kwargs)
```

As long as a thread or process is available for use, the function runs immediately, otherwise it queues and waits for a thread or process to become available. A `Future` is returned immediately and you can use this to monitor the function and get a result. Notice that the parameters aren't passed as an explicit list and dictionary as with other similar methods.

That is:

```
Executor.submit(function, 1, 2, myParam = "3")
```

calls:

```
function(1, 2, myParam = "3")
```

If you want to run multiple functions in one operation then you can use:

```
Executor.map(function, iterables, timeout=None, chunksize=1)
```

This is similar to `map_async`, see Chapter 8, but in this case you can specify more than one iterable and these will be used to supply more than one parameter to the function. `chunksize` works in the same way, it determines the number of tasks submitted to each process – it is ignored for threads. An iterator over the results is returned and this gives the next result available and will time out if specified. Also the `multiprocessing.pool` module has a range of much more advanced `map`-like functions.

Finally we have `Executor.shutdown(wait = True)` which closes the executor and frees resources. Calls to `submit` or `map` raise `RuntimeError` after the `Executor` has been shut down. If `wait` is `True` the `shutdown` will block until all `Futures` are resolved. If it is `False` then it returns immediately, but the Python program will not exit until all futures have resolved.

You can use an `Executor` in a `with` clause:

```
with ThreadPoolExecutor() as e:
      e.submit(myfunction)
```

This creates the `Executor` and shuts it down with `wait = True` – i.e. it waits for all of the futures to resolve.

Neither the thread or the process Executor help with the problem of shared resources, race conditions and deadlock. You need to use the techniques we have outlined in previous chapters to share data safely.

I/O-Bound Example

Using `concurrent.futures` is very like using `processpool` but you also have a `threadpool` and a better `Future` at your disposal. To demonstrate how similar they are, consider the problem of using a threadpool to download some HTML files:

```
import concurrent.futures
import time
import urllib.request

def download():
    with urllib.request.urlopen('http://www.example.com/') as f:
        html= f.read().decode('utf-8')
    return html


with concurrent.futures.ThreadPoolExecutor() as executor:
    t1=time.perf_counter()
    f1 = executor.submit(download)
    f2 = executor.submit(download)
    t2=time.perf_counter()
    print((t2-t1)*1000)
    print(f1.result()[:25])
    print(f2.result()[:25])
```

This is very similar to the earlier example, but now we have the advantage of having a `Future` returned from the `download` function. The `download` function returns a string with all of the HTML from the site and the `print` just displays the first 25 characters. What is remarkable is that you can convert this program to work with processes rather than threads by changing the `with` clause to read:

```
with concurrent.futures.ProcessPoolExecutor() as executor:
```

If you are not using a fork you will also need to add:

```
if __name__ == '__main__':
```

before the `with` to stop the main program running in the child process.

Waiting On Futures

Futures also make waiting for results easier. You can use the `wait` function to wait for the first completed, first exception or all completed:

```
concurrent.futures.wait(listOfFutures, timeout = None,
                        return_when = ALL_COMPLETED)
```

This waits for the futures listed to resolve according to the setting of `return_when`:

- `FIRST_COMPLETED`   first future to finish or be canceled
- `FIRST_EXCEPTION`   first future to finish by raising an exception (if no future raises an exception it is equivalent to `ALL_COMPLETED`)
- `ALL_COMPLETED`   wait for all Futures to resolve

The function returns a named tuple (`done`, `not-done`) with each item being a set containing the resolved and the unresolved futures respectively. Notice that the `not-done` set includes all of the futures that correspond to tasks that are still running. For example, to wait for the first thread to download a web page, we would change the main program to:

```
t1=time.perf_counter()
with concurrent.futures.ThreadPoolExecutor() as executor:
    f1 = executor.submit(download)
    f2 = executor.submit(download)

    t2=time.perf_counter()
    print((t2-t1)*1000)

    res=concurrent.futures.wait([f1,f2],
            return_when=concurrent.futures.FIRST_COMPLETED)
    for f in res.done:
        print(f.result()[:25])
```

You can also use `as_complete` to deal with tasks as they complete:

```
iter=concurrent.futures.as_complete(listOfFutures, timeout=None)
```

This returns an iterator which can be used to step through futures as they resolve, for example:

```
with concurrent.futures.ThreadPoolExecutor() as executor:
    f1 = executor.submit(download)
    f2 = executor.submit(download)
    for f in concurrent.futures.as_completed([f1,f2]):
        print(f.result()[:25])
```

Future Done Callbacks

Although callbacks are difficult to handle there comes a time when a main thread/process is so busy that it can't afford the time to wait for a future to resolve. Notice, however, that in a multi-threaded/process environment the cost of waiting is low as you can always use another thread/process to get on with important work. This situation doesn't apply in a single-threaded environment and here we need to be careful to keep the main thread doing useful work. This is what `asyncio` is all about, see Chapters 12 to 14. The `asyncio` module allows you to keep the single thread busy without having to use callbacks.

If you do need to use a callback then you can use:

```
Future.add_done_callback(function)
```

When the `Future` resolves, the `function` is called with the `Future` as its only parameter. This is an improvement over the basic idea of a callback because it is automatically added to your `async` function – you don't have to make any modifications. It also standardizes the form of a callback to a function with a single `Future` parameter.

Another important point is that the callback is executed on the thread that added it to the `Future`. You can add more than one callback and they will be executed in the order that they have been added, for example:

```python
import concurrent.futures
import urllib.request

def download():
    with urllib.request.urlopen('http://www.example.com/') as f:
        html= f.read().decode('utf-8')
    return html

def processDownload(f):
    print(f.result()[:25])

with concurrent.futures.ThreadPoolExecutor() as executor:
    f1 = executor.submit(download)
    f2 = executor.submit(download)
    f1.add_done_callback(processDownload)
    f2.add_done_callback(processDownload)
    print("waiting")
```

The callback `processDownload` is now called as soon as either `Future` resolves. Notice that the main thread waits for both threads to complete because of the `with` block which ends with a call to `shutdown`, which by default waits for all threads or processes to end. The callback is also run on the main thread and it may have to wait for the main thread to be free to run it.

Notice that in a single-threaded environment callbacks are often used to sequence asynchronous operations. For example, suppose you need to download fileA and then fileB, but only if fileA has completed. The only reasonable solution in a single-threaded environment is to use chained callbacks. For example:

```
import concurrent.futures
import urllib.request

def download():
    with urllib.request.urlopen('http://www.example.com/') as f:
        html= f.read().decode('utf-8')
    return html

def processDownloadA(f):
    print(f.result()[:25])
    f2 = executor.submit(download)
    f2.add_done_callback(processDownloadB)

def processDownloadB(f):
    print(f.result()[:25])

with concurrent.futures.ThreadPoolExecutor() as executor:
    f1 = executor.submit(download)
    f1.add_done_callback(processDownloadA)

    print("waiting")
    while True:
        pass
```

In this case we have two callbacks processDownloadA and processDownloadB. The first is set up when the first download starts and the second is set up by processDownloadA when the page has finished downloading. You can see that this "chains" the downloads one after another. Notice that you need to keep the with block running because it will end when f1 resolves and this closes the executor which means that processDownloadA cannot start a new thread. The executor has to be kept running until all of the downloads are complete.

This approach of chaining downloads is standard practice in a single-threaded environment, but it is completely unnecessary in a multi-threaded/process environment. The reason is that in a single-threaded environment it is vital not to make the thread wait and hence be unable to do anything. In a multi-threaded/process environment there is no reason not to wait as a waiting thread/process doesn't take CPU time and you can always use another thread/process to get the important jobs done.

That is, in a multi-threaded/process environment there is little reason not to use:

```
with concurrent.futures.ThreadPoolExecutor() as executor:

    f1 = executor.submit(download)
    print(f1.result()[:25])
    f2 = executor.submit(download)
    print(f2.result()[:25])
```

The use of `f1.result()` causes a wait until the `Future` resolves and only then is the second download started.

Dealing With Exceptions

Using asynchronous code becomes much more difficult when you have to deal with the possibility of errors. In synchronous code we usually deal with errors by using exception handling:

```
try:
      a = b/0
except(list of exception classes) as err:
      deal with exception
```

Exceptions in Python are classes that define a hierarchy of possible exceptions. If the code in the `try` block raises an exception, the `except` clause is tested to see if the exception raised matches any of the classes in the list of exception classes. If it does match, `err` is set to reference it and the code in the `except` clause is executed. There can be multiple `except` clauses and an optional final `else` which is used if nothing else matches.

How can we do something similar when dealing with errors in threads or processes? So far it has been assumed that the implementation of the asynchronous task would deal with errors in a custom way and send back a result that indicated an error. However, `Futures` use a different and very clever method to make exceptions work well, even for asynchronous functions.

The idea is that if an exception occurs within an asynchronous function the exception is handled and by default the `Future` is resolved, but now the `exception` method returns the *exception* object. If you use the `result` method after an exception then the exception is automatically raised in the new thread. If you want to manually handle the exception then you can use the `exception` method which returns `None` if there was no exception and the *exception* object otherwise.

What this means is the you can easily handle exceptions that occur in a child thread in the main thread. For example, if we change the download function to always raise an exception:

```
def download():
    with urllib.request.urlopen('http://www.example.com/') as f:
        html= f.read().decode('utf-8')
    raise ValueError("Test Exception")
    return html
```

Then we can use a try-except clause to deal with it:

```
with concurrent.futures.ThreadPoolExecutor() as executor:
    try:
        f1 = executor.submit(download)
        print(f1.result())
    except:
        print(f1.exception())
```

In this case using result causes the exception raised by the download function to be raised in the main thread. This causes the print to abort and the except clause is run and this prints:

```
Test Exception
```

You can see that this makes it look as if the exception was generated by the function running on the same thread and it makes handling async errors much like synchronous exception handling. If you don't want to use the exception mechanism you can manually handle the exception by testing exception before trying to use result. For example:

```
with concurrent.futures.ThreadPoolExecutor() as executor:
    f1 = executor.submit(download)
    if f1.exception:
        print(f1.exception())
    else:
        print(f1.result())
```

this will either print the result or the text of the exception. The only real reason for doing this is to raise a different, perhaps custom exception, for example:

```
class myException(Exception):
    pass
if f1.exception:
        print(f1.exception())
        raise myException("test custom exception")
    else:
        print(f1.result())
```

This causes the system to break on the exception and display "test custom exception".

If you change your mind and do want to raise the original exception you simply use the instance:

```
with concurrent.futures.ThreadPoolExecutor() as executor:
    f1 = executor.submit(download)
    if f1.exception:
        print(f1.exception())
        raise f1.exception()
    else:
        print(f1.result())
```

Locking and Sharing Data

Of course, you need to avoid race conditions even with futures and executors. They both make using threads and processes easier, but any shared resources still need to be locked if you want to avoid the problems of multiple access. There really should be no reason to repeat this here as concurrent.futures is no different from using raw threads and processes in this respect, but there is a tendency to think that such problems go away as the level of sophistication increases.

Although concurrent.futures provides a similar approach to threads and processes, they differ in the way they work with shared data and locks. As already explained in detail, threads automatically share global data simply because they run in the same address space, i.e. they run in the same process. By contrast, processes are isolated and don't share global resources. As a result you cannot generally take a program that works with threads and change it to work with processes by just changing the executor object. For example, the counter example from earlier automatically shares the global myCounter, but has to use a threading.Lock to avoid race conditions:

```
import concurrent.futures
import threading
import time
from cmath import sqrt

myCounter=0
countlock=threading.Lock()

def count():
    global myCounter
    for i in range(100000):
        with countlock:
            temp=myCounter+1
            x=sqrt(2)
            myCounter=temp
```

```
with concurrent.futures.ThreadPoolExecutor() as execute:
    t1=time.perf_counter()
    f1= execute.submit(count)
    f2= execute.submit(count)
    concurrent.futures.wait([f1,f2],
            return_when=concurrent.futures.ALL_COMPLETED)
    t2=time.perf_counter()
print((t2-t1)*1000)
print(myCounter)
```

If you remove the with countlock then you will usually see a much smaller final count than 200000 due to race conditions.

Locking and Process Parameters

Converting the counter example to use processes is complicated because you have to implement the sharing of the counter and the lock. As was explained in Chapter 8, passing locks and any object which cannot be pickled is a problem for processes. The multiprocessing.pool module treats locks as special and arranges to pass them to child processes in a way that works. The concurrent.futures module doesn't do this and this often causes problems when you first try using it.

You cannot pass lock objects to concurrent.futures processes as parameters. This also means you cannot pass shared ctypes, like Value, as these contain a default lock. If you try something like:

```
myCounter=multiprocessing.Value(ctypes.c_int,0)
with concurrent.futures.ProcessPoolExecutor(2) as execute:
    f1= execute.submit(counter, myCounter)
```

where the counter function is assumed to accept a single parameter which is a Value object, you will discover that it doesn't work. It doesn't generate an error message, it simply dies silently because the future, f1, absorbs the exception. You can see the problem by adding:

```
 print(f1.exception())
```

which displays:

```
Synchronized objects should only be shared between processes
through inheritance
```

and isn't entirely helpful. The problem really is that synchronized objects cannot be pickled and hence cannot be passed to a process.

There are two solutions to this problem and the first isn't well known. You can use the initializer parameter to set up some global objects ready for the process to start. The second is to make use of a process manager to share resources. The process manager approach is very general in that it makes use of its own process to share resources and proxy objects that run in any other processes. This means that it works with almost anything, but it isn't particularly efficient. Lets look at each approach in turn.

Using initializer to Create Shared Globals

If you want an efficient implementation using multiprocessing synchronization objects then you have to set up an initialization function and make sure it is called before each process starts:

```
import concurrent.futures
import multiprocessing
import time
import ctypes

def counter():
    global count
    for i in range(10000):
        with count:
            temp=count.value+1
            count.value=temp

def setup(var):
    global count
    count=var


if __name__ == '__main__':
    myCounter=multiprocessing.Value(ctypes.c_int,0)
    with concurrent.futures.ProcessPoolExecutor(2,
            initializer=setup,initargs=(myCounter,)) as execute:

        t1=time.perf_counter()
        f1= execute.submit(counter)
        f2= execute.submit(counter)
        concurrent.futures.wait([f1,f2],
            return_when=concurrent.futures.ALL_COMPLETED)
        t2=time.perf_counter()
        print(myCounter.value)
    print((t2-t1)*1000)
```

The setup function simply converts its parameter into a global. In general this could be used to create multiple global objects, but in this case we only need multiprocessing.Value as this includes a basic lock. The initializer parameter is used to ensure that each process gets the Value object as a global. The count function uses this as a lock before it updates it. Notice that the initializer is only called once when the process is created. If the process is reused the globals that are created are not reset. Usually this is what you want as they are a communication between processes, but sometimes this can be a problem.

If you take out the with count statement then you will see that the reported count is less than 20000 due to race conditions.

Using a Process Manager to Share Resources

If you want to use a more sophisticated resource sharing method then you need to create a manager and pass the proxy objects it creates to the processes:

```
import concurrent.futures
import multiprocessing
import multiprocessing.managers
import time
import ctypes

def counter(count,lock):
    for i in range(10000):
        with lock:
            temp=count.value+1
            count.value=temp


if __name__ == '__main__':

    with multiprocessing.Manager() as man:
        with concurrent.futures.ProcessPoolExecutor(2) as execute:

            myCounter=man.Value(ctypes.c_int,0)
            myLock=man.Lock()

            t1=time.perf_counter()
            f1= execute.submit(counter,myCounter,myLock)
            f2= execute.submit(counter,myCounter,myLock)
            concurrent.futures.wait([f1,f2],
                return_when=concurrent.futures.ALL_COMPLETED)
            t2=time.perf_counter()
            print(myCounter.value)
    print((t2-t1)*1000)
```

In this case we need to pass both a Value object and a Lock object because the manager's Value object doesn't have a built-in lock. The lock is used in the with statement in the counter function. If you remove it you will find that the result is less than 20000 due to race conditions.

Notice that we don't need to use the initializer as now the shared objects are passed as parameters. To be more accurate, the proxies to the shared objects are passed as parameters and these are standard Python objects which are pickleable. The proxy objects connect to the manager's server running in a separate process. This means we not only have one more process running, we also have the overhead of using a pipe to allow the proxy objects to communicate with the shared object. As a result this is slow. Compared to the use of the basic multiprocessing shared objects this takes more than ten times as long to complete.

Sharing Futures and Deadlock

There is another difference between using threads and processes when it comes to futures. In a threaded environment futures are generally accessible by more than one thread. The reason is that they are usually global to make sure that they live long enough to resolve and deliver their result. What this means is that not only can the use of locks result in deadlock, so can the use of futures by multiple threads. For example, consider what happens if we define two functions, taskA that waits for Future f2 and taskB waits for Future f1:

```
import concurrent.futures
import time

def taskA():
    time.sleep(1)
    ans=f2.result()
    return ans

def taskB():
    time.sleep(1)
    ans=f1.result()
    return ans

with concurrent.futures.ThreadPoolExecutor(2) as execute:
    f1= execute.submit(taskA)
    f2= execute.submit(taskB)
    concurrent.futures.wait([f1,f2],
             return_when=concurrent.futures.ALL_COMPLETED)
    print(f1.result())
```

Of course the result is deadlock. The sleep at the start of taskA is necessary to allow taskB to be started and create f2 before taskA tries to use it.

This may be a contrived example, but in real life deadlocks due to waiting on futures happen in ways that are much more difficult to detect. Notice that this can't happen with process-based futures because these aren't shared between processes. If you can avoid accessing futures on threads that didn't create them then you can avoid deadlock.

Computing Pi with Futures

Computing pi using futures is very similar to the previous example using a process pool. It would seem to be more instructive to implement the example using a thread pool but as this would show no speed advantage due to the GIL, a version using the process executor is more interesting. Converting the code to use a thread pool is a matter of changing one line:

```python
import concurrent.futures
import time

def myPi(m,n):
    pi=0
    for k in range(m,n+1):
        s= 1 if k%2 else -1
        pi += s / (2 * k - 1)
    return pi*4

if __name__ == '__main__':
    N=10000000
    with concurrent.futures.ProcessPoolExecutor(2) as execute:
        t1=time.perf_counter()
        f1=execute.submit(myPi,1,N//2)
        f2=execute.submit(myPi,N//2+1,N)
        PI=f1.result()
        PI+=f2.result()
        t2=time.perf_counter()
    print((t2-t1)*1000)
    print(PI)
```

Notice that now we pass the parameters to the called function without the need to use a list or tuple and the calls to result makes the main process wait until the relevant future resolves. If there is an exception in the function this is passed to the main process. Also notice that no locking is required as the threads do not make use of shared resources and they return their results using a future.

If you change the with to read:

```python
    with concurrent.futures.ThreadPoolExecutor(2) as execute:
```

then, with no other changes, you have a version which works with threads. This takes more than twice as long to run as the process version, which is what you would expect.

Process Pool or Concurrent Futures?

Python seems to have two modules which do similar things. `ProcessPool` provides a futures-like approach using `AsyncResult` and a wide range of map-like operations. However, it doesn't do a good job of supporting a thread pool equivalent.

The `concurrent.futures` module, on the other hand, provides a more complete futures approach and both process and thread pools are well supported. You can also make use of `multiprocessing` managers, which isn't surprising as the sharing by proxy approach does work with almost any type of process, irrespective of how it has been created.

In most cases the best choice is `concurrent.futures` backed up by multiprocessing. Only use `multiprocessing.pool` if you need the more advanced map-style functions.

Summary

- A Future is an object that lives in the main thread/process that the child thread/process can use to signal its state and return a result at some time in the future – hence the name.

- A Future can be in one of three states: Resolved – the function has completed, Pending – the function is still running, Canceled – the function has been canceled.

- You can wait on a Future to either return a result or an exception.

- Executors are objects which can run a function on a thread/process from the thread/process pool.

- Functions can be submitted to the pool using the submit method. Parameters are transferred to the submitted functions by being pickled and transmitted over a connecting pipe. The result of the function is returned as a future.

- The wait function can be used to wait for all futures to complete, the first to complete or the first to give an exception.

- You can also set callbacks which are activated when the future resolves. This is mostly useful in a single-threaded environment.

- One of the big advantages of using futures is that they capture any exceptions that happen in the child thread/process and return them to the parent thread/process. This makes error handling as easy as for synchronous code.

- Even if you are using futures you still have to worry about race conditions and locking is still necessary.

- Threads share global resources like locks, but processes don't. You can't pass a lock to a process as a parameter because the lock isn't pickleable.

- To pass a lock to a process you can use the initializer parameter to run a function which creates global objects when the process is first created.

- An alternative way to pass a lock is to use a process manager, but this is slow.

- Futures shared between threads can cause deadlock.

Chapter 12

Basic Asyncio

So far we have looked at processes as a way of increasing the speed of CPU-bound programs, and threads as a way of increasing the speed of I/O-bound programs. In the following chapters the emphasis changes to using a single thread to speed up I/O-bound processes. This uses an event queue or some other form of cooperative scheduling-based asynchronous programming. The basic idea is that you can use a single thread more efficiently if you simply arrange for it to do something else instead of just waiting for I/O to complete. That is, if you have a set of tasks that are I/O-bound then a single thread can manage all of them if you allow it to run other tasks while waiting for others to complete I/O.

Some are of the opinion that the alternative of allocating n threads, one to each I/O bound task, is actually slower than sharing a single thread between them all. This is certainly true for Python with the GIL restricting threads to one per Python interpreter. If the GIL is removed in the future it would still be likely that one thread for all I/O-bound tasks is going to be faster than one thread per task. There are examples of Python `asyncio` programs handling thousands of network connections with few problems but clearly what the limits are in any particular case depends on the task and the machine.

The key to keeping the thread busy is the event queue. This is a queue of tasks waiting to be run and the scheduler selects a task to run. This then uses the thread until it has to wait for something when it releases the thread back to the event queue and another task is selected to run on the thread. The task that had to wait is added back into the event queue and gets a chance to run when it has finished waiting. This way the single thread always has a task to keep it occupied. Notice that if the thread empties the queue then it just waits for something to do and this is the only time the thread waits.

In the rest of this chapter the focus is on using the `asyncio` module and this single-threaded multi-tasking approach is a different mindset to the earlier approaches using multiple threads or processes. Not only does it introduce new approaches, it also introduces new problems. It is also worth realizing that `asyncio` is focused on network operations rather than being a general purpose single thread asynchronous module. In particular, it isn't an event processing system of the sort you would find as part of a typical GUI such as

Tkinter or Qt. This doesn't stop it from being used as a general purpose approach to async, but the main application in the mind of its creators is to handle network connections.

In this account of basic `asyncio` we only use the high-level API. This is the part that programmers using, rather than extending, `asyncio` should restrict themselves to. The deeper low-level API, which is the subject of Chapter 14, should only be used to create frameworks based on `asyncio`. Notice that many accounts of `asyncio` were written before the high-level API was complete and so tend to use low-level functions. Even worse, many examples and tutorials mix the use of high- and low-level functions simply because they haven't caught up with best practices.

Callbacks, Futures and Await

The drawbacks of using callbacks have been extensively described in earlier chapters, but it is not until we restrict our attention to single-threaded asynchronous code do callbacks become a common approach – but they are not a good approach. The `async` and `await` features introduced with `asyncio` mean you can avoid using callbacks, but it is worth knowing what horrors they save you from.

The idea of a callback is that if you call a function that is going to have to wait to complete a task then you pass it a function, the callback, which it calls when the wait is over. This allows the thread to get on with other things instead of just waiting for the task to complete.

We have already seen that while callbacks are a simple solution they have a number of disadvantages. These have been explained in earlier chapters but it is worth summarizing them here:

1) Callbacks distort the logic of your program. Instead of:

```
TaskA
Wait for TaskA
Process the result of TaskA
TaskB
```

we have:

```
TaskA callbackA
Do something else            callbackA:
                             Process the result of TaskA
                             TaskB
```

You can see that this is a distortion because the original didn't have *Do something else* in it at all and the callback is now what used to be the main program. Another problem with this simple approach is that it is usually far from obvious what the program should do after starting TaskA – i.e. what exactly is *Do something else*? The program's logic is do TaskA, then process the result of TaskA and it is

212

usually difficult to find something else for it to do. This is the reason that single-threaded asynchronous programs generally use an event queue – it automatically provides something for the main thread to do without the programmer having to further distort the logic of the program.

2) It is difficult to sequence callbacks. Assuming you need to do `TaskA` and then when it has completed do `TaskB`. In a synchronous program this would be:

```
TaskA
wait for TaskA
TaskB
```

In a callback this becomes:

```
Task A callbackA
Do something else   callbackA:
                        Process result of A
                    Task B callbackB:    callbackB:
                                            Process result of B
```

Such nested callbacks very quickly become unmanageable.

3) It is difficult to implement "first to complete" and similar forms of waiting. In this case the callbacks have to communicate and this is difficult.

4) Handling exceptions and failures is difficult because they occur within the callback, but the recovery usually has to involve the main program that set up the callbacks.

At first most programmers don't see anything wrong with using callbacks – they seem simple and very easy to use. However, after using callbacks for anything even slightly complicated what you discover is that they become unmanageable. The term "callback hell" is often used and it is perfectly justified.

Futures used with `async/await` aim to reduce the problem of callbacks by avoiding their use entirely. This is what `asyncio` provides and it is the modern way to solve the problem. The basic idea is that asynchronous functions always return a `Future` to the main thread which resolves when the function finishes and returns a result. Typically what happens is:

```
future = TaskA
do something else
process future.result()
```

This is a step in the right direction, but the thread has to wait when it calls `future.result()` until `future` resolves and the result is available. This is fine in a multi-threaded/processing environment, you can simply use another thread to keep things going. In a single-threaded, multi-tasking environment this is unacceptable. The usual solution is to add a method called `then` or something similar to the `Future` to run the specified code when the `Future` resolves. A Python `Future` doesn't have a `then` method, but they do have `add_done_callback` which does the same job. So now you can write:

```
future = TaskA
future.add_done_callback(process result)
do something else
```

Now the main thread doesn't have to check or wait for the `Future` to resolve. But wait – this is a callback! Futures are better than raw callbacks, but they suffer from many of the same problems if you use `add_done_callback`.

The next step is the complete solution and eliminates callbacks altogether. All you need to to is to add the `await` command to the language. The `await` command suspends the code that it is part of and so frees the thread. It then waits for the `Future` to resolve. When it does it "consumes" the `Future`, returns the result and then restarts the code from where it was suspended. With the help of `await` you can now write:

```
result = await TaskA
process result
```

There is now no sign of a `Future`, the task returns a `Future` but the `await` extracts the result and stores it in the variable `result` when the code is restarted. From this point on the program continues as if nothing clever had happened. Notice that now the code that would have been in the callback, i.e. `process result`, is now in the body of the code as it would be if this was pure synchronous code. That is, using `await` means that there is no distortion of the logic of your program because there is no need to use a callback. However, `TaskA` is asynchronous and `await` allows the thread to be freed to run the event queue and run some other task. There are many other advantages of using `await` and these are explained later – but this is the "big idea".

Now we need to look at the details of how this is all implemented in `asyncio`. First we need a new type of function that can be suspended and restarted – the coroutine.

Coroutines

The main idea in sharing a single thread is the event loop, a basic cooperative scheduler. This is simply a queue of tasks that will be run on the thread as and when it can. However, this relies on the idea that a function can be suspended and restarted from where it was forced to wait. In a multi-threaded environment this is nothing special because the thread can just be suspended and restarted by the operating system. In a single-threaded environment the thread has to save its current state, start or resume work on another function and restore the state when it returns to the previous function. A function that can be suspended and restarted in this way is generally called a "coroutine".

Python originally supported coroutines via generators and `yield` and `yield from`. However, support for this was removed in Python 3.10 and trying to understand coroutines via generators is no longer particularly useful. For the rest of this chapter generator coroutines are ignored.

A modern Python coroutine is created using the `async` keyword:

```
async def myCo():
    print("Hello Coroutine World")
    return 42
```

if you call `myCo` it doesn't execute its code, instead it returns a `coroutine` object which can execute the code. This is very similar to a generator returning a `generator` object, but you cannot run a `coroutine` object directly. You have to run it in association with an event loop. To do this you can use low-level functions to create a loop and then submit it. However, it is much easier to use the `asyncio.run` method which creates and manages the event loop without you having knowing anything about it:

```
import asyncio
async def myCo():
    print("Hello Coroutine World")
    return 42

myCoObject=myCo()
result= asyncio.run(myCoObject)
print(result)
```

This runs the coroutine object and displays:

```
Hello Coroutine World
42
```

Instead of passing the coroutine object, the `asyncio.run` call is usually written as a single action:

```
result= asyncio.run(myCo())
```

Also notice that you can pass parameters to the coroutine:

```
import asyncio
async def myCo(myValue):
    print("Hello Coroutine World")
    return myValue

result= asyncio.run(myCo(42))
print(result)
```

It is also important to realize that `asyncio.run` runs `myCo` at once and the thread doesn't return until `myCo` is completed. While running `myCo` an event loop is started and if the thread is freed it starts running any tasks queued before returning to `myCo`. In this sense the call to `asyncio.run` is where the asynchronous part of your program starts and you can think of it as starting the asynchronous main program.

Await

As it stands our coroutine might as well be a standard function as it doesn't suspend and resume its operation. To suspend a coroutine you have to use the `await` keyword to pause the coroutine while an awaitable completes. At the moment you can `await` a coroutine, a `Future` or a `Task`- the `Future` and the `Task` are described in detail later.

- ◆ When you await a coroutine it starts running and the awaiting coroutine is suspended until the awaited coroutine completes and returns a result.

- ◆ A `Future` is awaitable because at some point in the future a function that it is associated with it will complete and resolve the `Future` with either a result or an exception.

- ◆ A `Task` is a subclass of `Future` so it is just a special case. In addition to being a `Future`, it has a coroutine attached which is run and automatically resolves the `Future` according to its result.

In each case an `await` suspends the awaiting program and this means it can only be used within a coroutine, i.e. the only code in Python that can be suspended and resumed. Once you have a coroutine running you can use `await` within it and within any coroutines it awaits. This means that you have to use `asyncio.run` to get a first coroutine running but after this you can use `await` to run coroutines or `Tasks`.

Most asyncio programs are organized so that there is a single `asyncio.run` instruction at the top level of the program and this starts a coroutine – often called `main` – which then runs the rest of the asynchronous program by awaiting other coroutines. That is, a typical `asyncio` program is:

```
async def main():
        call other coroutines using await

asyncio.run(main())
```

The call to `asyncio.run` sets up the event loop as well as starting `main` running. You can call ordinary, i.e. non-coroutine, functions from within coroutines, but these cannot use `await`. Only a coroutine can use `await`, for example:

```
import asyncio

async def test1(msg):
    print(msg)

async def main():
    await test1("Hello Coroutine World")

asyncio.run(main())
```

Notice that even though `main` now awaits the `test1` coroutine there is no new behavior. The program would work in exactly the same way with functions replacing coroutines. The reason is that none of our coroutines actually release the main thread, they simply keep running.

There are two distinct things that can occur when you `await` another coroutine. Some coroutines hold onto the main thread and continue to execute instructions until they finish – they are essentially synchronous coroutines. Some release the main thread while they wait for some operation to complete and only these are truly asynchronous coroutines. At the moment we only know about synchronous coroutines.

Awaiting Sleep

Later we will meet asynchronous coroutines that do release the thread while they wait for I/O operations to complete, but these are complicated by what they actually do. What we need is a simple asynchronous coroutine that releases the main thread and does little more. The simplest asynchronous coroutine is `asyncio.sleep` is:

`asyncio.sleep(delay, result = None)`

which returns after *delay* seconds and returns *result* if specified.

The `asyncio.sleep` coroutine is not the same as the `time.sleep` function used in previous chapters and it is important to understand the difference.

The `time.sleep` function suspends the current thread for the specified amount of time. If you were to use it in a single-threaded environment the result would be that the one thread that you were depending on to do the work would be frozen and so would the event loop. In fact `time.sleep` is a very good way to keep the thread busy and so simulate a coroutine that doesn't give up the thread.

Compare this to `asyncio.sleep` which doesn't suspend the thread at all - it suspends the coroutine. The main thread stops running the coroutine and returns to the event loop to find another coroutine to run. When the time delay is up and the main thread next visits the event loop for more work then the suspended coroutine is restarted. Of course, this means that the coroutine might be suspended for longer than the specified time and this is usually the case. The coroutine is restarted when the main thread is free to run it and the time delay is up.

The `asyncio.sleep` function suspends the current coroutine and not the thread. This means that `asyncio.sleep` really does mimic what happens when other, more complex, async functions are used and hence it is a good but simple example. You can even use the *result* parameter to simulate returning an object.

A standard idiom is to call `sleep` with a value of zero seconds:

```
await asyncio.sleep(0)
```

This gives up the thread to the event loop with the minimum delay if there is nothing to be done in the event loop queue. That is, all that happens is that the main thread is freed and, if there is nothing waiting to be executed in the event loop, it returns at once to running the coroutine. This gives the event loop a chance to run other coroutines and it is a good idea to include any coroutine that runs for a long time. The call `sleep(0)` is equivalent to DoEvents in other languages, i.e. an instruction to process the event loop's queue.

We can easily add an `await` for 10 seconds to our example:

```
import asyncio

async def main(myValue):
    print("Hello Coroutine World")
    await asyncio.sleep(10)
    return myValue

result= asyncio.run(main(42))
print(result)
```

There is now a 10-second delay between displaying `Hello Coroutine World` and the result, i.e. `42`. In this case the main thread is freed when the `await` starts and has `10` seconds in which to run any other coroutines waiting in the event loop. In this case there aren't any and so it just waits for the time to be up. We next need to know how to add coroutines to the event loop so that they can be run when the main thread is free.

Tasks

Tasks are coroutines plus futures. To be more exact, `Task` inherits from `Future` and keeps a reference to a *coroutine* that the `Future` is associated with. Put simply, a `Task` is what you add to the event loop's queue and it is a `Future` plus a *coroutine*. The *coroutine* does the work and the `Future` returns the *result*.

To add a `Task` to the event loop you need to use the:

```
asyncio.create_task(coroutine, args, name = None)
```

This adds the *coroutine* to the current event loop as a `Task`, passing it any *args* you may specify and giving it a *name* if you specify one. The function adds the coroutine to the event loop queue ready to be executed. It doesn't actually get to run until the main thread is free to return to the event loop and run the tasks that it finds there. This only happens when the currently executing coroutine awaits an asynchronous coroutine or terminates.

The `asyncio.create_task` function returns a `Task` which, as already explained, is a future-like object which resolves with the result when the coroutine ends. Anything that is added to the event loop has to behave like a `Future` as it is needed for the `await` to *retrieve* a result. For example, if we create a coroutine that prints a range of numbers then this can be added to the event loop within `main`:

```
import asyncio

async def count(n):
    for i in range(n):
        print(i)
    return n

async def main(myValue):
    t1=asyncio.create_task(count(10))
    print("Hello Coroutine World")
    await asyncio.sleep(5)
    return myValue

result= asyncio.run(main(42))
print(result)
```

The `count` coroutine is added to the event loop before the `print`, but it doesn't get to run until `main` awaits `sleep` for 5 seconds and so frees the thread. If you take out the `await` on `sleep` then the `count` coroutine gets to run when `main` finishes. If you put the `await` before the `print` then `count` gets to print its values before the `Hello Coroutine World` is displayed. When `count` runs depends on when `main` is allowed to run the event loop.

If you look at the program again you will see that `count` returns a result, but the result isn't used in the program. How can we get a result from a `Task`? The simple answer is that we wait for its `Future` to resolve and for `await` to return its *result* after consuming the `Future`, for example:

```
async def main(myValue):
    t1 = asyncio.create_task(count(10))
    print("Hello Coroutine World")
    await asyncio.sleep(5)
    result = await t1
    print(result)
    return myValue
```

In this case `await t1` returns `result` which is displayed.

At this point you should be wondering why we bothered creating a `Task` and adding it to the event loops's queue? Why not just use `await count`? That is:

```
async def main(myValue):
    print("Hello Coroutine World")
    await asyncio.sleep(5)
    result= await count(10)
    print(result)
    return myValue
```

This produces the same answer, but what happens under the hood is very different. The first version adds `count` to the event loop's queue and when `main` sleeps for five seconds the thread is freed and `t1` is allowed to execute. After the five seconds is up the `await` returns at once because `t1` is resolved and there is a `result` which is displayed immediately. The second version doesn't add `count` to the queue and so nothing happens while `main` waits for five seconds. When the wait is up the `await` starts `count` running to get the `result` which is then printed. In other words, when you await a `Task` the `Task` might already have run and have a result. If it hasn't already resolved then it is taken from the queue and run just like a coroutine. That is:

- when you `await` a coroutine it starts running to completion
- when you `await` a `Task` it only starts running if it hasn't already resolved

In both cases the thread might be released and tasks run before the coroutine or the `Task` completes.

You will sometimes see instructions like:

```
value = await asyncio.create_task(count(10))
```

This adds the coroutine to the queue as a `Task` and then immediately awaits it, which of course, starts it running. There is no point in doing this and it is entirely equivalent to:

```
value = await count(10)
```

In general:

```
await asyncio.create(coroutine)
```

is the same as:

```
await coroutine
```

To summarize:

- `asyncio.create_task(coroutine)` runs the *coroutine* at a later time. It adds it to the event loop's queue as a `Task` for execution when the thread is free
- `await coroutine` runs the *coroutine* immediately
- `await Task` runs the associated *coroutine* if the associated `Future` hasn't ready resolved
- `asyncio.create_task(coroutine)` is equivalent to `await coroutine`

Because it is often used in older examples, it is also worth mentioning,:

```
asyncio.ensure_future(awaitable)
```

This takes a coroutine, Future or any awaitable object, converts it and "ensures" that it is a future-like object and adds it to the event queue. In practice, this means that the coroutine is converted into a Task and added to the queue. In other words, it is the equivalent of create_task.

Execution Order

This is all fairly simple, but it can be surprisingly difficult to work out what order coroutines will run in. Consider the following example:

```
import asyncio
async def test1(msg):
    print(msg)

async def main():
    asyncio.create_task(test1("one"))
    asyncio.create_task(test1("two"))

    await test1("three")
    print("Hello Coroutine World")
    await asyncio.sleep(0)

asyncio.run(main())
```

What does this display? The main coroutine adds two copies of test1 onto the event loop queue. Then it awaits a third. Notice that test1 doesn't await anything and so doesn't give up the main thread. As neither test1 or main release the main thread to service the event loop the two coroutines aren't run until main terminates. At this point the event loop runs each of them in turn and what you see displayed is:

```
three
Hello Coroutine World
one
two
```

If we make a small change by adding test2:

```
async def test2(msg):
    await asyncio.sleep(0)
    print(msg)
```

the only difference is that test2 includes an await on sleep which, if you recall, is currently the only coroutine we know of that actually does release the main thread.

Now if we change `main` to use `await test2` then something different happens:

```
async def main():
    asyncio.create_task(test1("one"))
    asyncio.create_task(test1("two"))

    await test2("three")
    print("Hello Coroutine World")
    await asyncio.sleep(0)
asyncio.run(main())
```

In this case the two tasks are added to the event loop queue, but now the first thing that happens is that `test2` awaits `sleep`, which does release `main`. This allows the event loop to run and the two tasks in the queue are executed. So what we see displayed is:

```
one
two
three
Hello Coroutine World
```

You can try out other variations by including `await asyncio.sleep` at other points in the program. The key idea is that as soon as you include an `await` on a coroutine that gives up the main thread then the event loop is processed. For example, see what happens if you change `main` to read:

```
async def main():
    asyncio.create_task(test2("one"))
    asyncio.create_task(test2("two"))

    await test2("three")
    print("Hello Coroutine World")
    await asyncio.sleep(0)
asyncio.run(main())
```

Now the two `Task` coroutines in the queue have `await asyncio.sleep(0)` as their first instruction and this releases the thread. They are added to the queue and then `await test2("three")` releases the main thread as before, but now the first `Task` on the queue starts running, but it too gives up the main thread. This allows the second `Task` on the queue to start running, but it too gives up the main thread – and now there is no `Task` left in the queue. As a result the main thread restarts the first call, `await test2("three")`, and `three` is displayed. When it ends the thread continues to execute `main` and the `Hello Coroutine World` is displayed and finally the two `Task` instructions are restarted.

So what is displayed is:

```
three
Hello Coroutine World
one
two
```

which appears to be the same behavior as the first example, but of course it isn't.

The principle is fairly simple – the main thread only changes what it is running when it is released. Following this rule to find out what is executed can be confusing. This shouldn't matter, however. The whole point of asynchronous programming is that things can happen in any order and your program should be constructed so that things either happen in the order that you impose or the order shouldn't matter. It is helpful to understand how things work, but you should only worry about it when things don't go as you expect.

Tasks and Futures

The `Task` returned by `asyncio.create_task` inherits from `Future` with some additional methods. The standard `Future` methods shared by a `Task` are:

- ◆ `cancelled()` - True if `Task` canceled
- ◆ `done()`- True if `Task` completed, i.e. a result or an exception
- ◆ `result()` - returns the result of the `Task`, but only if it is done. If it is pending then an `InvalidStateError` is raised
- ◆ `exception()` - returns the exception if any – if `Task` not done it raises `InvalidStateError`

There are some other methods, but they are only useful for low-level work or for implementing something that makes direct use of a `Future`.

Notice that the `result` and `exception` methods do not wait and this is the most important difference between `asyncio.Future` and `concurrent.futures` Future. There are also many other minor differences, but the fact that `concurrent.futures.Future` instances cannot be awaited means that they cannot be used within an asynchronous program. It is also the case that `asyncio.Future` is not compatible with the `concurrent.futures.wait()` and `concurrent.futures.as_completed()` functions. Basically this means that you should avoid mixing the two types of future. An additional and important difference is that `asyncio.Future` is not thread-safe – you cannot share an `asyncio` `Task` or `Future` with multiple threads. There is a wrapper function which will convert a `concurrent.futures.Future` to an `asyncio.Future`.

The documentation makes it clear that you should always keep a reference to the Task returned by asyncio.create_task. For reasons of efficiency the event loop only keeps a weak reference to the Task and this means that to stop it from being garbage-collected you need to keep a strong reference to it. However, the Task will only be removed if it isn't running or sleeping i.e. if it hasn't been started. Any Task that is sitting in the queue doing nothing is vulnerable to the problem and in this case you probably do need a reference so that you can await the Task at some later time.

You can create an instance of a Future rather than a Task and it works in exactly the same way, but it has no code associated with it. There is usually some code that works with it to set its state, but it isn't associated in the same way as a coroutine is in a Task. So for example, if you cancel a Task you cancel it and the coroutine it is associated with, but if you cancel a Future you simply set the Future to cancelled state.

Waiting On Coroutines

The basic way to wait on an awaitable, a Future, a Task or a coroutine, is to use await, but this isn't particularly flexible. For example, it provides no way to specify a timeout. Notice that in this case waiting doesn't mean that the thread is suspended. It means that the coroutine is suspended and the thread is free to work with the event loop queue to run another Task.

There are a number of standard coroutines that provide alternative ways of waiting. The most basic is asyncio.wait_for(aw, *timeout*) which waits for aw, an awaitable, to complete or until the *timeout* is up. If *timeout* is None it waits until completion.

- ◆ If the awaitable is a coroutine it is added to the event loop as a Task. If the timeout occurs the Task is canceled and a TimeoutError is raised. If the wait is canceled so is aw. This is like await with a timeout.

A more sophisticated wait function is:

```
asyncio.wait(aws, timeout = None, return_when = ALL_COMPLETED)
```

This is the equivalent of concurrent.futures.wait and runs each awaitable, which has to be a Future or a Task, in the aws iterable by adding them to the event loop. It then waits for the condition specified by return_when which is one of:

- ◆ FIRST_COMPLETED   first to finish or be canceled
- ◆ FIRST_EXCEPTION   first to finish by raising an exception. If none raises an exception then it is equivalent to ALL_COMPLETED
- ◆ ALL_COMPLETED   waits for all to resolve

If the *timeout* occurs there is no exception. Instead the completed and pending awaitables are returned as a tuple of sets *(done, pending)*.

The function:

```
asyncio.as_completed(aws, timeout = None)
```

is the equivalent of `concurrent.futures.as_complete`. It returns an iterator for the awaitables as they complete. Notice that it returns the coroutine and not the result of the coroutine. If a timeout occurs a `TimeoutError` is raised.

You can use `as_completed` in a `for` loop:

```
for coro in as_completed(aws):
    result = await coro:
    print(result)
```

The `gather` function is usually described as being a way of running `Task` coroutines concurrently, but it is better thought of as a way of running and waiting for a set of `Task` coroutines to complete:

```
asyncio.gather(aws, return_exceptions = False)
```

Any coroutine in the `aws` comma-separated list of awaitables is added to the event loop queue as a `Task`. All of the awaitables are then executed as the queue schedules them with the calling coroutine suspended until all of them complete. The function returns a list of results in the same order as the awaitables were originally listed in `aws`. If `return_exceptions` is `False` then any exception is propagated to the calling coroutine, but the other coroutines in the `aws` list are left to complete. If it is `True` then the exceptions are returned as valid results in the list.

If the `gather` is canceled all of the items in `aws` are canceled. If any of the items in `aws` are canceled then it raises a `CancelledError`, which is either passed to the calling coroutine or added to the result list and the `gather` itself is not canceled. Using `gather` is almost the same as adding coroutines to the event loop using `asyncio.create_task` and then waiting for them with `asyncio.wait`.

As an example of using the `wait` coroutine we set up two coroutines on the event loop queue and then await them using `wait` without a timeout:

```
import asyncio
async def test1(msg):
    print(msg)
    return msg

async def main():
    t1 = asyncio.create_task(test1("one"))
    t2 = asyncio.create_task(test1("two"))
    done,pending = await asyncio.wait([t1,t2],
                            return_when = asyncio.ALL_COMPLETED)
    for t in done:
        print(t.result())
    print("Hello Coroutine World")
asyncio.run(main())
```

The results are returned in no particular order.

We can achieve the same sort of result using `gather`:

```
import asyncio
async def test1(msg):
    print(msg)
    return msg

async def main():
    result = await asyncio.gather(test1("one"),test1("two"))
    print(result)
    print("Hello Coroutine World")

asyncio.run(main())
```

The only real difference is that now `result` is a list of return values.

Sequential and Concurrent

It should be obvious by this point, but it is worth making clear, that if you want to run coroutines one after another, i.e. sequentially, then you would use:

```
await coroutine1()
await coroutine2()
await coroutine3()
```

and so on. This adds each coroutine to the event loop queue one at a time and the calling coroutine waits for each one to end in turn. If the called coroutine releases the main thread other coroutines, if any, already on the event loop get a chance to run. You can be sure, however, that `coroutine1` completes before `coroutine2` starts and `coroutine2` completes before `coroutine3` starts.

Compare this to:

```
await gather(coroutine1(), coroutine2(), coroutine3(), …)
```

which adds all of the coroutines to the event loop and then runs each one in turn. If any of the coroutines releases the main thread the other coroutines listed get a chance to run, along with anything that was on the event loop before the `gather`. As a result all of the coroutines in the `gather` make progress to completion at the same time. They are executed concurrently in the sense that you cannot be sure that `coroutine1` completes before `coroutine2` or `coroutine3` starts.

If you want to run coroutines sequentially use sequential awaits. If you want to run them concurrently use `gather`. Being able to run coroutines sequentially or concurrently avoids the problem of callbacks distorting the flow of control and is one of the big advantages of using `async` and `await`.

Canceling Tasks

In a multi-threaded environment canceling a function is synonymous with canceling the thread it is running on and this generally not a good idea. As a result any standard cancel operation provided generally only works in the small window where the function is waiting in a queue to be allocated a thread/process from the pool. Once the function is running canceling it is left to the programmer to include a cancel mechanism based on testing for an event say.

In a single-threaded environment canceling a Task cannot mean canceling the thread because it has other work to do. If you use the task.cancel method then the Task is marked to receive a CancelledError exception the next time it runs on the event loop. If you don't handle the exception the Task simply dies silently. If you have any resources to close then you have to handle the exception to perform the cleanup. You can even opt to ignore the CancelledError exception altogether. For example:

```
import asyncio
async def test1(msg):
    try:
        await asyncio.sleep(0)
    except:
        pass
    print(msg)
    return msg

async def main():
    t1 = asyncio.create_task(test1("one"))
    await asyncio.sleep(0)
    t1.cancel()
    print("Hello Coroutine World")
    await asyncio.sleep(0)

asyncio.run(main())
```

In this case the try suppresses the exception and everything works as if cancel had not been called. If you remove the try/except then you don't see one displayed as test1 is canceled. If you cancel a Future then this sets its state to cancelled and this cannot be ignored.

You can also use the shield coroutine to stop an awaitable from being canceled:

```
result = await shield(awaitable)
```

works like await but if the calling coroutine is canceled the awaitable isn't. If the awaitable is canceled by other means then shield has no effect.

Dealing With Exceptions

The fact that a Task is a Future should immediately tell you how to handle exceptions in asynchronous programs. The Task either returns a result or an exception object and by default the exception object is used to raise the exception in the calling coroutine. For example:

```
import asyncio

async def test(msg):
    print(msg)
    raise Exception("Test exception")


async def main():
    t1=asyncio.create_task(test("one"))
    try:
        await t1
    except:
        print("an exception has occurred")
    print("Hello Coroutine World")
    await asyncio.sleep(0)

asyncio.run(main())
```

In this case test raises an exception as soon as it is called. This is returned to the calling coroutine and raised again by the await operation. If you are running this in an IDE make sure the debugger is set to ignore raised and unhandled exceptions.

If you want to access the exception object and handle it manually you will have to use one of the wait methods as await always consumes the Task and hence raises the exception. For example:

```
import asyncio

async def test(msg):
    print(msg)
    raise Exception("Test exception")


async def main():
    t1 = asyncio.create_task(test("one"))

    done,pending = await asyncio.wait([t1])
    print(repr(done.pop().exception()))

    print("Hello Coroutine World")
    await asyncio.sleep(0)

asyncio.run(main())
```

This displays:

```
one
Exception('Test exception')
Hello Coroutine World
```

You can see that now you have the Exception object and you can choose to do what you like with it or raise it when you are ready.

Finally if you don't await a Task then any exceptions are ignored, just as any results are ignored. The Task fails silently, just as it succeeds silently if it is not awaited.

Shared Variables and Locks

Coroutines share global variables and have their own local variables as is the case for functions that run on different threads. There are some important differences, however, because of the fact that only a single thread is involved. Consider the following example based on the counter given in earlier chapters:

```
import asyncio

async def count():
    global myCounter
    for i in range(1000):
        temp = myCounter+1
        myCounter = temp

async def main():
    t1=asyncio.create_task(count())
    t2=asyncio.create_task(count())
    await asyncio.wait([t1,t2])
    print(myCounter)

myCounter=0
asyncio.run(main())
```

The two tasks t1 and t2 increment the same global variable. If you run the program you will find that 2000 is displayed every time you run it, which might not be what you expected. This holds no matter how large you make the count and it is indicative that there is no race condition involved in this program even though no locks are in use.

The reason why no locks are required should be obvious. Tasks run in a way that is controlled by you. In this case t1 runs and only when it finishes does t2 get to run – the program is sequential and there can be no race condition.

229

However, if t1 and t2 are modified so that they release the main thread then things get slightly more complicated:

```
async def count():
    global myCounter
    for i in range(1000):
        temp = myCounter+1
        await asyncio.sleep(0)
        myCounter = temp
```

Now both t1 and t2 release the main thread in the middle of the update of the global variable. As a result each task updates myCounter at exactly the same time and as a result there is a perfect race condition on every update and the program displays 1000.

The simplest solution to this problem is not to release the main thread in the middle of an operation. As long as the task doesn't release the main thread it is an atomic operation. This is usually one of the benefits of using single-threaded multi-tasking.

If this approach cannot be used then there is no alternative but to add a lock. The asyncio module provides its own locks which are not thread-safe and are implemented using coroutines. The only real difference is that we have to use "async with" rather than "with". This can only be used in a coroutine and it can be suspended during the enter and exit phase:

```
import asyncio
import asyncio.locks

async def count():
    global myCounter
    global myLock
    for i in range(1000):
        async with myLock:
            temp=myCounter+1
            await asyncio.sleep(0)
            myCounter=temp



async def main():
    t1=asyncio.create_task(count())
    t2=asyncio.create_task(count())
    await asyncio.wait([t1,t2])
    print(myCounter)

myCounter=0
myLock=asyncio.locks.Lock()
asyncio.run(main())
```

Now t2 has to wait until t1 releases the lock before it can continue. Notice the use of async with rather than just with. The program now displays 2000.

In this case the problem has been caused deliberately, but when you are using coroutines there are occasions that you cannot modify in which locking is the only option.

The asyncio.locks module contains asynchronous equivalents for most of the standard threading locks:

- Lock
- Event
- Condition
- Semaphore
- BoundedSemaphore

These are all used in the same way as their Threading equivalents, but notice that none of them is thread-safe in the sense that you cannot use them to lock access from different threads. You can also specify an additional loop parameter which specifies the event loop that the lock is associated with.

Context Variables

There is an additional problem that occurs when sharing global variables in a single-threaded multi-tasking system. If you have a Task, the outer Task, that sets the value of a global variable and another Task, the inner Task, called by the outer, which gets the set value? If you use synchronous functions then there is no problem:

```
idGlobal=0

def inner(idparam):
    global idGlobal
    if idparam!=idGlobal:
        print("error")
    print()

def outer():
    global idGlobal
    id=random.randint(0,10000)
    idGlobal=id
    inner(id)
```

The inner function tests the value of idGlobal against the value passed in as the id parameter. Of course, they have to be the same and the whole program seems silly. How can the passed parameter value be different from the global variable!

What isn't so silly is if you now change each of these functions into a coroutine and run each as a `Task`:

```python
import asyncio
import random

idGlobal=0

async def inner(idparam):
    global idGlobal
    await asyncio.sleep(0)
    if idparam!=idGlobal:
        print("error")

async def outer():
    global idGlobal
    id=random.randint(0,10000)
    idGlobal=id
    await inner(id)

async def main():
    await asyncio.gather(outer(),outer())

asyncio.run(main())
```

Now if you run this you will see the error displayed once. This might seem to be impossible, but it is perfectly reasonable because now `inner` isn't guaranteed to be run at the same time as its calling function, `outer`. Suppose the `outer` function sets `idGlobal` to 42 and then calls `inner(42)`. As the first instruction releases the main thread another `Task` gets to run `outer` and let's say this sets `idGlobal` to 43 and then calls `inner(43)`. This immediately releases the main thread and restarts the first call, `inner(42)`, which is expecting to find `idGlobal` set to 42, but it isn't, it's 43 and hence the error. When the second call, `inner(43)`, restarts `idGlobal` is still set to 43 and so no error is displayed.

The problem is that that `inner` tried to use a global variable that has been modified by another version of `outer` that called it leading to a race condition.

This can also happen in a multi-threaded program, but in this case the solution is simple – thread-local variables. If the `idGlobal` variable is made thread-local then the inner function running on the same thread sees the same "version" of `idGlobal` and hence always sees the same value.

Thread-local storage has no effect on coroutines because there is only a single thread involved in running them and the thread-local storage is the same for all coroutines. The solution is to use a context variable. A context is automatically added to a `Task` when it is created and this is automatically made available to the coroutine when it runs.

You create a context variable using:

```
variable = contextvars.ContextVar(name, default=None)
```

The `name` is used internally and the `default` value is used if the context variable hasn't been assigned a value yet. For example, to create a context variable for the global id you might use:

```
idGlobalCtx=contextvars.ContextVar("id")
```

and to assign a value to it:

```
idGlobalCtx.set(value)
```

and to retrieve its current value:

```
myValue = idGlobalCtx.get(default)
```

where *default* is used if the context variable doesn't have a value.

There are many other methods and attributes of a context variable, but for the most common ways of using them `get` and `set` are sufficient.

A context variable is local to a coroutine and using it we can rewrite the previous example as:

```
import asyncio
import random
import contextvars

idGlobalCtx=contextvars.ContextVar("id")

async def inner(idparam):
    await asyncio.sleep(0)
    print(idparam,idGlobalCtx.get(),end=" ")
    if idparam!=idGlobalCtx.get():
        print("error",end="")
    print()

async def outer():
    global idGlobal
    id=random.randint(0,10000)
    idGlobalCtx.set(id)
    await inner(id)

async def main():
    await asyncio.gather(outer(),outer())

asyncio.run(main())
```

With a context variable being used in place of the global variable everything works and the inner coroutine gets the same version as the outer coroutine sets.

It isn't worth getting any deeper into context variables because, apart from some specialized uses, they are best avoided. Just as with thread-local variables, it is usually better to pass the data to the called routine using a parameter and accept any updates via the returned object. Sharing globals is to be avoided if possible and it usually is.

Queues

In the same way that `asyncio` provides implementation of many of the `Thread` synchronization primitives it also provides a single-threaded async version of the `Queue` classes in `asyncio.queues`. You can use any of:

- Queue
- PriorityQueue
- LifoQueue

None of these data structures is thread-safe and you can include an additional parameter loop to specify the event loop that they are associated with. You also have to use `await` to call any of the methods, as you would expect of an asynchronous queue, for example:

```
import asyncio
import asyncio.queues

async def addCount(q):
    for i in range(1000):
        await q.put(i)

async def getCount(q,id):
    while True:
        i = await q.get()
        print(id,i)
        await asyncio.sleep(0)

async def main():
    q=asyncio.queues.Queue()
    t1=asyncio.create_task(addCount(q))
    t2=asyncio.create_task(getCount(q,"t2"))
    t3=asyncio.create_task(getCount(q,"t3"))
    await asyncio.wait([t1,t2,t3])

asyncio.run(main())
```

This sets up a `Queue` and `t1` is a `Task` which adds `1000` elements to it while `t2` and `t3` read items from it. As each one performs a `sleep` after reading an item, the other one gets a turn at reading. If you run this you will see:

```
t2 0
t3 1
t2 2
t3 3
t2 4
t3 5
t2 6
t3 7
t2 8
```

and so on. If you don't include the `sleep` then `t2` reads all of the items and `t3` never gets to run as `t2` waits for more data.

Notice that as there is only one thread involved in running this producer/consumer example, there is no performance advantage unless either the consumers or the producers are performing I/O-bound operations which can free the main thread.

Summary

- The `asyncio` module provides single-threaded multi-tasking.

- The callback is the most common way of implementing single-threaded multi-tasking but it has many disadvantages. A better method is to use a `Future` and an even better method is to use `await`.

- A coroutine is a function that can be suspended and resumed by the use of the `await` instruction.

- A coroutine has to be run in conjunction with an event loop. The `asyncio.run` creates an event loop and runs a coroutine using it.

- A `Task` is a `Future` plus a coroutine and it is what is added to the event loop's queue using `asyncio.create_task`. The `Task` is run when the thread becomes free.

- When you `await` a coroutine it starts running to completion.

- When you `await` a `Task` it only starts running if it isn't already completed.

- The `await` always returns the result of the coroutine/`Task`, including any exceptions that might have occurred.

- If you don't `await` a `Task` its result and any exceptions are ignored.

- You can use `wait_for` as a version of `await` with a timeout.

- The `wait` coroutine can be used to wait for the first to complete, the first to raise an exception or for all complete.

- `Task` coroutines can be executed in sequential order by awaiting each one in turn. They can be run concurrently by adding them to the queue or by using the `gather` coroutine.

- A `Task` can be canceled and this sends the `CancelledError` exception to the `Task`.

- A `Task` returns any exceptions to the awaiting coroutine – these can be raised or processed.

- Locks are less useful for coroutines because unless the thread is released they are atomic. If a race condition can occur there are asynchronous equivalents of all of the standard synchronization objects.

- Shared global variables cannot be protected against race conditions using thread-local variables as only a single thread is in operation. Instead we need to use context variables.

- There are asynchronous equivalents of the `Thread` queue objects.

Chapter 13

Using asyncio

So far in our examination of `asyncio` the only truly asynchronous coroutine we have used has been `asyncio.sleep`. This frees the main thread to run the event loop, but it doesn't really achieve very much other than helping explain what is going on. Put another way, without the use of `asyncio.sleep` we essentially have a synchronous system, even if it does use an event loop. In this chapter we take a look at things that we can do with `asyncio` that are actually useful and demonstrate an efficiency improvement.

The `asyncio` module is primarily designed to work with asynchronous network connections. If you want to go beyond this important, but limited, application you need either to use a library that extends asyncio or to create your own asynchronous extensions.

To be clear, `asyncio` does not help with working with local files asynchronously and it doesn't provide any methods of dealing with asynchronous user interaction, but it is possible to adapt it to do both and there are existing modules for most similar applications.

What is more surprising is that it doesn't provide high-level networking facilities. There is no asynchronous download of an HTML page, for example. Indeed until recently, all network interaction was performed at a low level, but in most cases you can ignore the low-level API and its pipes, sockets and transports and simply use streams.

Streams

Streams are the high-level coroutine implementation of network connections implemented using sockets. They work in much the same way as standard files, but they are asynchronous which enables you to work with many, hundreds or even thousands of, connections using a single thread.

Like a `file`, a `stream` has to be opened:

```
reader, writer = asyncio.open_connection(host = None, port = None)
```

There are a great many additional parameters which you can use to customize the connection, but this simple form does for most connections to internet servers.

Opening a stream returns a tuple consisting of a StreamReader and a StreamWriter. These have methods very similar to any of the familiar file objects and, apart from being asynchronous, they work in the same way. If you want to know more about file objects refer to *Programmer's Python: Everything Is Data,* ISBN: 978-1871962598.

StreamReader

The following methods are commonly used to read streams:

- read(n = -1) - reads up to n bytes as a bytes object
  The default, n = -1, is to read until the end of the file signal (EOF) is received and return all read bytes.
- readline() - reads one line, where "line" is a sequence of bytes ending with \n
  If EOF is received and \n was not found, the method returns partially read data. If EOF is received and the internal buffer is empty, returns an empty bytes object.
- readexactly(n) - reads exactly n bytes and raises an IncompleteReadError if EOF is reached before n can be read
  Use the IncompleteReadError.partial attribute to get any partially read data.

- readuntil(separator = b'\n') - reads data from the stream until separator is found.
  The default is to use \n, i.e. new line, as the separator which makes it the same as readline.

  If the amount of data read exceeds the configured stream limit, a LimitOverrunError exception is raised, and the data is left in the internal buffer and can be read again. If EOF is reached before the complete separator is found, an IncompleteReadError exception is raised and the internal buffer is reset.
  The IncompleteReadError.partial attribute may contain a portion of the separator.
- at_eof() - True if buffer is empty and EOF has been signaled.

Notice that all of the reading methods are coroutines as there may not be enough data ready to satisfy the call. In this case the coroutine is suspended and the main thread is freed. That is calls to functions that read data are asynchronous coroutines. Also notice that while there are references to using EOF to signal the end of a transaction, in general EOF isn't particularly useful when dealing with sockets. Sockets tend to be left open until they are no longer required and data is usually sent in some sort of format that lets you work out when you have read a useful chunk of data that can be processed. Generally, if you wait for an EOF you will wait a long time until the server times out and closes the socket.

StreamWriter

The two key methods used for writing data are:

- write(*data*) - attempts to write the data to the socket, if that fails, the data is queued in an internal write buffer until it can be sent.

- writelines(data)- writes a list (or any iterable) of bytes to the underlying socket immediately. If that fails, the data is queued in an internal write buffer until it can be sent.

Neither of these is a coroutine as they both always return immediately. However, the drain() coroutine, which waits until it is appropriate to resume writing to the stream, should be called after each write operation, for example:

```
writer.write(data)
await writer.drain()
```

The logic of this is that there is no point in performing another write if there is not enough space in the buffer. Instead a better option is to wait until the data has drained out of the buffer, hence the name of the coroutine, and the main thread is released to do something else.

The close() method closes both the stream and the underlying socket and should be used along with the wait_closed() coroutine:

```
stream.close()
await stream.wait_closed()
```

The logic is that there is no point in carrying on until the stream has been closed and so you might as well free the main thread. You can also use is_closing() to test whether the stream is closed or is in the process of closing.

The write_eof() method sends the EOF signal to the reader. Not all streams support the EOF signal so use it in conjunction with the can_write_eof() coroutine, which returns True if the underlying transport supports the write_eof() method and False otherwise.

There are also two lower level methods:

- get_extra_info(name, default = None) - accesses optional transport information

- transport – returns the underlying asyncio transport

Notice that the methods provided by StreamWriter are mostly not coroutines. The reason for this is that write methods generally return at once because the data is either immediately sent via the socket or placed in a buffer to be sent over the socket connection. This means there is usually no reason for them to free the main thread as they don't block. However, as already mentioned, you should use the drain() coroutine to check that there is space in the buffer so that the write operations don't have to wait.

Downloading a Web Page

We have already used the `request` module to download a web page asynchronously using multiple threads. While the `request` module isn't suitable for use with `asyncio`, it is fairly straightforward to modify it to work asynchronously, see later. There is also a module, `aiohttp`, based on `asyncio` that lets you work at a higher level. However, using streams is easy and instructive.

First we need a coroutine that downloads a web page. This starts by parsing the `url` and making a connection to the web server:

```
async def download(url):
    url = urllib.parse.urlsplit(url)
    reader, writer = await asyncio.open_connection(
                                      url.hostname, 80)
```

Of course, most web servers are on port 80, as specified in the `open`, but this does vary. If you want to use `https` then change the `open_connection` to:

```
reader, writer = await asyncio.open_connection(
                            url.hostname, 443,ssl = True)
```

This provides basic SSL security. If you need to specify the certificate to be used or check the server certificate then you need to look into the `ssl` module.

Now we have a bidirectional TCP connection to the server and a `reader` and `writer` ready to send and receive data. What data we actually send and receive depends on the protocol in use. Web servers use HTTP, which is a very simple text-based protocol.

The HTTP protocol is essentially a set of text headers of the form:

headername: *headerdata* \r\n

that tell the server what to do, and a set of headers that the server sends back to tell you what it has done. You can look up the details of HTTP headers in the documentation – there are a lot of them.

The most basic transaction the client can have with the server is to send a `GET` request for the server to send back a particular file. Thus the simplest header is:

```
"GET /index.html HTTP/1.1\r\n\r\n"
```

which is a request for the server to send `index.html`. In most cases we need one more header, `HOST`, which gives the domain name of the server. Why do we need it? Simply because HTTP says you should and many websites are hosted by a single server at the same IP address. Which website the server retrieves the file from is governed by the domain name you specify in the `HOST` header.

This means that the simplest set of headers we can send the server is:

`"GET /index.htm HTTP/1.1\r\nHOST:example.org\r\n\r\n";`

which corresponds to the headers:

```
GET /index.html HTTP/1.1
HOST:example.org
```

An HTTP request always ends with a blank line. If you don't send the blank line then you will get no response from most servers. In addition, the `HOST` header has to have the domain name with no additional syntax - no slashes and no `http:` or similar. We can use Python's f strings and automatic concatenation, topics covered in **Programmer's Python: Everything Is Data**, to create the header data:

```
request = (
    f"GET /index.html HTTP/1.1\r\n"
    f"Host: {url.hostname}\r\n"
    f"\r\n"
)
```

Now we are ready to send our request to the server:

`writer.write(request.encode('ascii'))`

Notice that we specify the encoding as `ascii` because headers are only allowed to contain ASCII characters.

When the server receives the `GET` request it finds the specified file and sends it to the client using the same socket connection. The first part of the message sent to the client is a set of headers which we need to read and process. The first line of any response is always:

`HTTP/1.1 200 OK\r\n`

which gives the HTTP version and the status code which we can assume is going to be `200`, i.e. no error. If you want to write a complete client you need to extract the error code and react to it. In our simple demonstration we can read it and ignore it:

```
headers=""
line = await reader.readline()
```

Next we need to read the headers that the server has sent. These arrive one to a line and the end is marked by a blank like, just like the headers we sent to the server:

```
while True:
    line = await reader.readline()
    line = line.decode('ascii')
    if line=="\r\n":
        break
    headers+=line
```

This loop reads each line in turn, converts it to a Python string using ASCII encoding and builds up a complete string of headers. The loop ends when we read a blank line.

We need to process the headers because the `Content-Length` header tells us how many bytes to read to get the content, i.e. the HTML that makes up the page. We need this because we cannot read data expecting an EOF signal, because there isn't one. The socket stays open in case you have another request to send to the server. If you do wait for an EOF then you will usually wait a long time before the server times out.

We need to read the `Content-Length` header to find the number of bytes to read. We could use some simple string manipulation to extract the header we want, but there is a standard way to parse HTTP headers even if it is obscure because it is part of the email module. It turns out the emails use HTTP as their protocol and hence you can use `email.message_from_string` to parse HTTP headers:

```
def parseHeaders(headers):
    message = email.message_from_string(headers)
    return dict(message.items())
```

This utility function returns all of the headers as a dictionary keyed on the header names with values of the strings they are set to. Now we can use this to get the `Content-Length` header:

```
headers = parseHeaders(headers)
length = int(headers["Content-Length"])
```

As we now know the number of characters to read the rest of the procedure is simple:

```
line = await reader.read(length)
line = line.decode('utf8')
writer.close()
await writer.wait_closed()
return line
```

This time we decode the content using `utf8` because this is what most modern web pages use for their content. To check, we should decode the `Content-Type` header which in this case reads:

`Content-Type: text/html; charset=UTF-8`

So the content is HTML and it is UTF-8 encoded.

To demonstrate all of this we need a coroutine to start things off:

```
async def main():
    start = time.perf_counter()
    results = await asyncio.gather(
                        download('http://www.example.com/'),
                        download('http://www.example.com/'))
    end = time.perf_counter()
    print((end-start)*1000)
    print(results[0][:25])

asyncio.run(main())
```

This creates two tasks to download the same page, starts them both off asynchronously and waits for them to complete. Whenever one of the tasks has to wait for data to be available it releases the main thread and the other gets a chance to run and so on. As a result main mostly has little to do and you can increase the number of downloads without increasing the time it takes by much. For example, adding an additional download on a test machine to the asynchronous program increases the time it takes by about 30 ms, whereas for a synchronous program it adds 220 ms. This means that downloading 100 pages takes about 3 seconds asynchronously, but 21 seconds doing the job synchronously.

The complete program is:

```
import asyncio
import urllib.parse
import time
import email

def parseHeaders(headers):
    message = email.message_from_string(headers)
    return dict(message.items())

async def download(url):
    url = urllib.parse.urlsplit(url)
    reader, writer = await asyncio.open_connection(
                                    url.hostname, 443,ssl=True)
    request = (
        f"GET /index.html HTTP/1.1\r\n"
        f"Host: {url.hostname}\r\n"
        f"\r\n"
    )
    writer.write(request.encode('ascii'))

    headers = ""
    line = await reader.readline()

    while True:
        line = await reader.readline()
        line = line.decode('ascii')
        if line == "\r\n":
            break
        headers += line

    headers = parseHeaders(headers)
    length = int(headers["Content-Length"])

    line = await reader.read(length)
    line = line.decode('utf8')
    writer.close()
    await writer.wait_closed()
    return line
```

```
async def main():
    start = time.perf_counter()
    results = await asyncio.gather(
                        download('http://www.example.com/'),
                        download('http://www.example.com/'))
    end = time.perf_counter()
    print((end-start)*1000)
    print(results[0][:25])

asyncio.run(main())
```

Server

As well as making a stream connection to a server, asyncio also allows you to create a server that will accept incoming connections as streams:

```
asyncio.start_server(client_connected_cb, host = None, port = None)
```

This starts a socket server, with a callback for each client connected. The return value is a Server object. The callback is passed two parameters, a reader and a writer, to communicate with the client. Each client connection is independent and can be continued until the transaction is complete. The callback can be a standard function but this would block the event loop so it is usual to make it a coroutine.

The Server object has the following methods:

- close()
  Stop serving: close listening sockets and set the sockets attribute to None. The sockets that represent existing incoming client connections are left open and can continue to be used until they are closed.

- wait_closed()
  The server is closed asynchronously, use the wait_closed() coroutine to wait until the server is closed.

- start_serving()
  Normally the server is started when created but you can use the start_serving keyword parameter to create it in a non-serving mode. You can call this even is the server has started.

- serve_forever()
  The server will run while the coroutine that created it is alive. If you haven't got anything else for it to do then simply use await a serve_forever() instruction. This runs the server until the coroutine that created it is canceled which closes the server. You can call this method even if the server is already serving but only one coroutine can await a serve_forever().

- ◆ is_serving()
  Return True if the server is accepting new connections.
- ◆ get_loop()
  Return the event loop associated with the server object.
- ◆ sockets
  List of socket.socket objects the server is listening on.

The Server object also supports use as an async context manager. When the with block is exited the server.close method is called.

A Web Server

Implementing a simple web server using the Server object is very easy. It isn't a replacement for a full web server, but it is a practical lightweight alternative when you simply need to provide a web page or some other data to clients.

Getting the server started is easy:

```
async def main():
    server=await asyncio.start_server(handleRequest,"",8080)
    async with server:
        await server.serve_forever()
```

The server will respond to requests on all network connections, i.e. usually one for the IPv4 address and one for the IPv6 address. The port is set to 8080 rather than the usual port 80 to avoid security problems. Most operating systems restrict access to ports below 1024 to programs running with root privileges. After creating the server the coroutine simply waits on serve_forever.

The Server object now monitors incoming TCP packets on the specified address and port. When a client sends a packet, the Server object calls the callback – handleRequest in this case. Each client gets its own copy of handleRequest which run asynchronously on the event loop. This means that you could have many requests handled using just a single thread. Our handleRequest is going to be simple, it will return a fixed HTML page irrespective of what the client asks for. Extending it to more general requests is fairly easy.

The callback has a streamReader and a streamWriter passed to it which enable two-way communication with the client:

```
async def handleRequest(reader, writer):
    headers = ""
    while True:
        line = await reader.readline()
        line = line.decode('ascii')
        if line == "\r\n":
            break
        headers += line
    print(headers)
```

245

Given this is an HTTP connection, the first thing we have to do is read the headers. The first header gives the operation and file that the client is interested in. For example:

GET /test.html HTTP/1.1

is a GET request for the file `test.html`. If you want to respond to this you would have to separate the filename from the header, retrieve the file and then send it to the client. For our example we will send the same HTML and ignore the filename. As required, the end of the headers is marked by a blank line.

The HTML page we send to the client has to have a set of headers including the current date and time and the length of the content:

```
html = ("<html><head><title>Test Page</title></head><body>"
        "page content"
        "</p></body></html>\r\n")

headers=("HTTP/1.1 200 OK\r\n"
        "Content-Type: text/html; charset=UTF-8\r\n"
        "Server:PythonAsyncio\r\n"
        f"Date: {email.utils.formatdate(
                timeval=None, localtime=False, usegmt=True)}\r\n"
        f"Content-Length:{len(html)}\r\n\r\n"
        )
```

We first define the `html` that will be sent. This string is used to define the `Content-Length` header. To generate a date and time stamp we once again use the `email` module which has a function, `formatdate`, that provides the correctly formatted current date and time.

Now we can send the data to the client:

```
data=headers.encode("ascii")+html.encode("utf8")
writer.write(data)
await writer.drain()
await writer.wait_closed()
```

Notice that closing the writer closes only the streams to the current client. The server and all the other copies of `handleRequest` that are running to work with other clients continue to do so.

Putting all this together gives the complete program:

```
import asyncio
import email
import email.utils

async def handleRequest(reader, writer):
    headers = ""
    while True:
        line = await reader.readline()
        line = line.decode('ascii')
        if line == "\r\n":
            break
        headers += line
    print(headers)
    html = ("<html><head><title>Test Page</title></head><body>"
            "page content"
            "</p></body></html>\r\n")
    headers = ("HTTP/1.1 200 OK\r\n"
               "Content-Type: text/html; charset=UTF-8\r\n"
               "Server:PythonAcyncio\r\n"
              f"Date: {email.utils.formatdate(timeval=None,
                        localtime=False, usegmt=True)}\r\n"
              f"Content-Length:{len(html)}\r\n\r\n"
               )
    data = headers.encode("ascii")+html.encode("utf8")
    writer.write(data)
    await writer.drain()
    await writer.wait_closed()

async def main():
    server=await asyncio.start_server(handleRequest,"",8080)
    async with server:
        await server.serve_forever()


asyncio.run(main())
```

If you run the server on a different machine you should be able to see the web page by entering:

192.168.1.32:8080/test.html

where you replace the IP address with the IP address of the machine used. Notice that the test.html is ignored by the server and you could enter any URL.

A typical set of headers sent by Chrome to the server is:

```
GET /test.html HTTP/1.1
Host: 192.168.1.32:8080
Connection: keep-alive
Cache-Control: max-age=0
Upgrade-Insecure-Requests: 1
User-Agent: Mozilla/5.0 (Windows NT 10.0; Win64; x64)
AppleWebKit/537.36 (KHTML, like Gecko) Chrome/103.0.0.0
Safari/537.36
Accept:
text/html,application/xhtml+xml,application/xml;q=0.9,image/avif,im
age/webp,image/apng,*/*;q=0.8,application/signed-
exchange;v=b3;q=0.9
Accept-Encoding: gzip, deflate
Accept-Language: en-GB,en-US;q=0.9,en;q=0.8,es;q=0.7
```

As you can see, we ignore a lot of the information about how the client would like the data sent. Taking notice of client preferences is what takes a web server from being simple in theory to intricate in practice.

SSL Server

If you want to implement an SSL server then things are slightly more complicated because you need to provide a certificate. Getting a certificate can be an involved process. Even popular free certificate issuing sites like Let's Encrypt require proof that you own the domain that the certificate applies to. To do this you have to write code which generates a new key pair and then either create a specific DNS record or store a file on the website. This is easy enough for production purposes, but not so easy when you are in the process of creating a program.

The usual solution is to create a self-signed certificate. If the operation system has OpenSSL installed and Windows and most versions of Linux do, then you can create a key and certificate pair using:

```
openssl req -newkey rsa:2048 -nodes -keyout iopress.key -x509
                  -days 365 -out iopress.crt
```

changing iopress to the name of your server. You will be asked a set of questions for information that is included in the certificate. How you answer these questions only modifies what the user sees if they ask to inspect the certificate so you can simply accept the defaults.

The openssl command creates two files, a .key file and a .crt file, which are used to create an SSL context:

```
    sslContext= ssl.create_default_context(ssl.Purpose.CLIENT_AUTH)
    sslContext.load_cert_chain('iopress.crt', 'iopress.key')
```

If you have created the files in another location you may need to include the path.

Now you can start the server in SSL mode:

```
import ssl
async def main():
    sslContext= ssl.create_default_context(ssl.Purpose.CLIENT_AUTH)
    sslContext.load_cert_chain('iopress.crt', 'iopress.key')
    server = await asyncio.start_server(handleRequest, "",
                                        8080,ssl= sslContext)
    async with server:
        await server.serve_forever()
```

No modifications are necessary for the `handleRequest` coroutine. If you try this out you will find that any web browser will display a warning. The details that Chrome shows are typical:

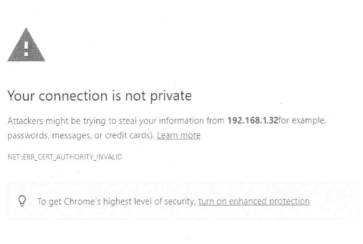

Messages like this are because browsers don't trust a self-signed certificate. However, if you allow the page to download it will use SSL encryption. If you select `Advanced` you will be able to let the page download. You can force a browser to accept the certificate by adding it to its trusted root certification authorities tab. However, for most testing purposes this isn't necessary. If you have a valid certificate and key for a particular web server you can substitute it for the self-signed certificates.

Using Streams

The asyncio module provides a very large range of socket support from raw sockets to streams. The question is, when should you use something other than the highest-level abstraction, the stream? The answer is that you should always use streams unless what you want to do goes beyond what they can do. While there are specific Unix versions of both open_connection and start_server, namely open_unix_connection and start_unix_server, they only work under Linux/Unix and there is little advantage in using them.

The only real reason to abandon streams is if you need a datagram-based protocol. Streams use TCP connections which is the most commonly used socket connection because it is simple and reliable. A datagram connection is used to send and receive individual packets of data without error detection or correction. Datagram is used for fast, low-level, communication and to make use of it you have to use the asyncio low-level API. A datagram UDP example is given in the next chapter.

Converting Blocking To Non-blocking

A programmer who hasn't completely grasped the ideas of asynchronous programming, and asyncio in particular, might well try to download a web page using the familiar urllib.request module with asyncio:

```
import urllib.request
import asyncio
import time

async def download():
    with urllib.request.urlopen('http://www.example.com/') as f:
        html = f.read().decode('utf-8')
        return html

async def main():
    t1=time.perf_counter()
    results=await asyncio.gather(download(),download())
    t2=time.perf_counter()
    print((t2-t1)*1000)
    print(results[0][:25])

asyncio.run(main())
```

If you try this out you will find that the time to download two pages is twice that for one page and so on. The problem is that download() isn't really an asynchronous coroutine. Once this program starts it doesn't give up the main thread until the web page has finished downloading. It performs a sequential download.

There is no simple way to convert the download coroutine into an asynchronous coroutine that will give up the main thread while the web page is downloading as the `urllib.request` functions are synchronous. There is a workaround, but it involves threads.

Running in Threads

You might think that adding additional threads to the main thread is counter to the approach of `asyncio`. Indeed it is, but it is sometimes essential. When an I/O operation releases the thread so that the event loop can continue to run, there is nearly always another thread involved. The additional thread is usually ignored as it is immediately suspended and simply waits for the I/O operation to be complete and to wake it up.

We can use the same technique to convert any synchronous I/O-bound function into a coroutine that frees the main thread while the I/O operation is in progress. The simplest way of doing this is to use:

```
asyncio.to_thread(function, *args, **kwargs)
```

this starts *function* running on a thread taken from the thread pool and passes it any arguments that you care to specify. A coroutine is returned that can be awaited until *function* completes and returns a value. The coroutine returns the same value and the coroutine has access to the default context variables object.

Using this we can use `urllib.request` in an asynchronous way:

```
import urllib.request
import asyncio
import time

def _download():
    with urllib.request.urlopen('http://www.example.com/') as f:
        html = f.read().decode('utf-8')
        return html

async def download():
    return await asyncio.to_thread(_download)

async def main():
    n = 1000
    t1 = time.perf_counter()
    results = await asyncio.gather(*[download() for i in range(n)])
    t2 = time.perf_counter()
    print((t2-t1)*1000)
    print(results[0][:25])

asyncio.run(main())
```

Now the blocking function has been moved by to _download and the asynchronous download function runs it on a new thread. This doesn't block the main thread and surprisingly it is only slightly slower than using a stream to do the same job. The extra time is due to the cost of setting up and using a thread, but the overhead isn't that high and is very preferable to doing the job synchronously. For comparison, downloading 100 pages using streams takes around 3 seconds, using urllib.request on a separate thread takes 3.3 seconds, which should be compared to 21 seconds doing the job synchronously.

It is worth knowing that asyncio uses concurrent.futures to implement the thread pool and the low-level API gives access to the thread pool and the process pool for more control over what is happening.

Why Not Just Use Threads?

At this point you may be thinking that is is crazy. If we are going to use a thread as soon as things aren't asynchronous why not just use threads and forget asyncio? This is indeed a possibility and there are arguments for doing so if you understand threading, the effect of the GIL and race conditions. Single-threaded asynchronous programs are much easier to reason about and usually race conditions don't occur so the need for locking is rare. Running a synchronous function using to_thread automatically gives some of these advantages. In particular, the use of await gives a return value that is a Task and we can use all of the methods of waiting on multiple Tasks Such as the gather coroutine used in the previous section.

The key idea behind gaining these advantages is to keep the synchronous function simple and ensure that for most of its lifetime it is suspended, waiting for an I/O operation to complete. The operating system looks after this efficiently, leaving the thread suspended until the I/O operation is complete. With the thread suspended for most of its life, its scope for creating a race condition is low. However, if it makes use of shared resources it will need locking to protect them. In the main you should avoid sharing resources and ensure that the result is returned via the Task.

The ideal situation is to use a single additional thread to monitor the status of all I/O operations. This is how streams and sockets in general are implemented – see the next chapter for the low-level details. The basic idea is that a single operating system instruction, select, is used to monitor all sockets and its thread is woken up when one of the sockets has some data. This in turn lets the event loop know which coroutine to wake up.

The point to note is that all of asyncio and indeed all single-threaded asynchronous models rely on other threads to do their waiting. Just because you need to use a thread to wait for an operation to complete doesn't mean that "single-threaded async" isn't a valid choice.

CPU-Bound Tasks

It should be obvious that running a CPU-bound task on a new thread doesn't really help with the problem of speeding things up because of the GIL. To speed things up we need to run CPU-bound tasks in a separate process and this can be done using the low-level `asyncio` API – see the next chapter. However, there are advantages to running even a CPU-bound function as a coroutine if you do it correctly.

Consider a version of the program to compute pi running together with a tick coroutine that prints a count at half-second intervals:

```python
import asyncio
import time

async def tick():
    i=0
    while True:
        i+=1
        print("TICK", i)
        await asyncio.sleep(0.5)

def _myPi(m,n):
    pi=0
    for k in range(m,n+1):
        s= 1 if k%2 else -1
        pi += s / (2 * k - 1)
    return 4*pi

async def myPi(m,n):
    return await asyncio.to_thread(_myPi,m,n)

async def main():
    n=100
    t1=time.perf_counter()
    T1=asyncio.create_task(myPi(1,10000000))
    T2=asyncio.create_task(tick())
    done,pending=await asyncio.wait([T1,T2],
                        return_when=asyncio.FIRST_COMPLETED)
    t2=time.perf_counter()
    print((t2-t1)*1000)
    print(done.pop().result())

asyncio.run(main())
```

Once again we have used the coroutine, `myPi`, to call the synchronous function `_myPi`, using a thread. The main program creates two tasks and then waits for the first one to finish – which will always be `myPi` as `tick` is an infinite loop. If you run this what you will see is that `tick` does get a chance to run, even though the `_myPi` function never gives up its thread. The reason is that the GIL scheduler forces a swap of threads running the Python interpreter every 5 ms. So the `tick` function and any other `Task` in the event loop queue does get a chance to run, although perhaps not as often as you might like. The `tick` routine certainly doesn't get to run every half second.

If you want the synchronous function running on another thread to give the event loop a chance to run more often than the GIL allows, all you have to do is include a `time.sleep(0)`. This suspends the thread and lets other threads have a chance to run.

If you change _myPi to read:

```
def _myPi(m,n):
    pi=0
    for k in range(m,n+1):
        s= 1 if k%2 else -1
        pi += s / (2 * k - 1)
        if k&1000:
            time.sleep(0)
    return 4*pi
```

you will see more `ticks`, one every 0.5 s, but, of course, the computation of pi will take that much longer. When you use `time.sleep(0)` it suspends the thread and allows another thread to run – usually the main thread and this runs until there is nothing left in the event loop queue to run or the GIL interrupts it and allows another thread to run.

How often you need to suspend the CPU-bound thread depends on how much you want to keep the event loop active and how long you are prepared to slow the CPU-bound thread down. Often the choices aren't critical and you still get the advantages of using `asyncio`, in particular the result being returned as a `Task` and the reduced need for locking.

Asyncio-Based Modules

Finally it is worth pointing out that there are many modules which provide asynchronous implementations of otherwise synchronous functions. For example, if you want to work with web pages using `asyncio` you might like the `aiohttp` module.

This is not part of the standard library and has to be installed using:

```
pip install aiohttp
```

A program to download the same page as the earlier examples is:

```python
import aiohttp
import asyncio

async def main():
    async with aiohttp.ClientSession() as session:
        async with session.get("http://www.example.com") as response:

            print("Status:", response.status)
            print("Content-type:", response.headers['content-type'])

            html = await response.text()
            print("Body:", html[:25], "...")

asyncio.run(main())
```

You can create clients and servers using `aiohttp`.

There is no facility to perform standard file-based I/O using asyncio. Part of the reason for this is that currently Linux file handling is synchronous, but this is changing. The simplest solution to create async file-handling is to use `asyncio.to_thread` to run open, close, read and write on separate threads. Alternatively you could use the `aiofiles` module which uses exactly the same technique as given earlier to wrap the standard Python file commands. It is not part of the standard library and you have to install it using:

```
pip install aiofiles
```

Once installed you can use it to read and write files as you always have, but now the actions are asynchronous, for example:

```python
import aiofiles
import asyncio

async def main():
    async with aiofiles.tempfile.NamedTemporaryFile('wb+') as f:
        await f.write(b'Line1\n Line2')
        await f.seek(0)
        async for line in f:
            print(line)

asyncio.run(main())
```

There are many similar asynchronous modules based on `asyncio` but they all use the technique of running the synchronous code on a new thread. This is a technique that you can use very easily without additional modules.

Working With Other Event Loops – Tkinter

The `asyncio` module provides us with an all-purpose event loop and in an ideal world every other library that needed an event loop would use it. Unfortunately many such libraries were implemented well before `asyncio` was thought of and have their own event loops. So it is with the Python "standard" GUI, Tkinter, and all of its alternatives.

The question addressed here is how do you cope with hosting two event loops. There are two general solutions and both of them are demonstrated using Tkinter as an example. There is a third solution which is to re-engineer the library to make use of `asyncio`, but this is generally beyond the scope of most projects and is also unlikely to be supported in the future.

It is assumed that you know something about Tkinter, but even if you don't you should be able to see how the following test program works:

```
import tkinter

count=0
root=None
label1=None

def stopProg(e):
    global root
    root.destroy()

def transfertext(e):
    global root,label1
    global count
    count=count+1
    label1.configure(text=count)

def runGUI():
    global root,label1
    root=tkinter.Tk()
    button1=tkinter.Button(root,text="Exit")
    button1.pack()
    button1.bind('<Button-1>',stopProg)
    button2=tkinter.Button(root,text="Click Me")
    button2.pack()
    button2.bind('<Button-1>',transfertext)
    label1=tkinter.Label(root,text="nothing to say")
    label1.pack()
    root.mainloop()

runGUI()
```

The `runGUI` function sets up a simple user interface with two instances of `Button` and one of `Label`. `transfertext` and `stopProg` are a pair of event handlers which are to be called when the buttons are clicked. What happens is that when the buttons are clicked these event handlers are added to an event loop queue and are processed when the thread is freed by any already running event handlers. The function runGUI sets up the GUI and then calls root.mainloop() to run the event loop. If you try this out and click button2 you will see the count incremented and displayed in the label. Clicking button1 exits the event loop and hence the program.

Now that we have an example GUI program we need to integrate it with an asyncio event loop. The first solution is to find an "update loop" function call for the GUI event loop. Most event loops have a function which forces the thread to run the event loop and to make this method of integration work you have to find such a function.

For tkinter there is the update function which runs the event loop, processing all of the event handlers in the queue, but not any that are added during the update. What is more, this works without having to start the event loop. This means we can start the asyncio event loop running and include a Task that calls the tkinter update function every so often to keep the GUI alive.

This is our first example:

```
import asyncio
import tkinter

count=0
root=None
label1=None
T1=None

def stopProg(e):
    global T1
    global root
    T1.cancel()
    root.quit()

def transfertext(e):
    global root,label1
    global count
    count=count+1
    label1.configure(text=count)
```

```
async def updater(interval):
    global root
    while True:
        root.update()
        await asyncio.sleep(interval)

def setupGUI():
    global root,label1
    root=tkinter.Tk()
    button1=tkinter.Button(root,text="Exit")
    button1.pack()
    button1.bind('<Button-1>',stopProg)
    button2=tkinter.Button(root,text="Click Me")
    button2.pack()
    button2.bind('<Button-1>',transfertext)
    label1=tkinter.Label(root,text="nothing to say")
    label1.pack()

async def tick():
    i=0
    while True:
        i+=1
        print("TICK", i)
        await asyncio.sleep(0.5)

async def main():
    global T1,root
    root.tk.willdispatch()
    T1=asyncio.create_task(updater(0.01))
    T2=asyncio.create_task(tick())
    await asyncio.wait((T1,))

setupGUI()
asyncio.run(main())
```

Now the setupGUI function constructs the window but doesn't start the
tkinter event loop running. Instead we use asyncio to run main, which sets
up two Tasks, updater and tick. The updater function repeatedly calls the
tkinter update function to run its event loop. The tick function simply
repeatedly displays a message to show that the asyncio event loop is active.
If you run the program you will find that you can click the buttons and
increment the count while the message is printed. The call to
root.tk.willdispatch() is sometimes necessary as it sets a flag to indicate
to the rest of tkinter that the event loop is running.

To make all this work we need global variables. In general global variables
should be avoided by using a suitable class, but using them here makes the
example simpler to understand. There are no race conditions as they are
used by a single thread. Notice that while tkinter makes use of several
internal threads they never run at the same time.

It is usual to warn against the use of update as it can lead to problems – but often the problems that it might lead to are not made clear. In fact the problem in using update occurs if you call it from an active event handler. In this case the tkinter event loop might already have started the event handler and when it calls update the event loop starts it again – resulting in an infinite recursion. Similarly, you can invent situations where an event handler calls update which runs other event handlers which modify what the original event handler is working on. These are real problems and are caused by the tkinter event handlers not being re-entrant. In this use of update, however, no such problems can arise because update is not being called from within an event handler. Even so, there may be edge cases which cause problems.

The second method is in principle more reliable and less likely to have problems with edge cases. The idea is to run the tkinter event loop in the main thread and the asyncio event loop in a different thread. To do this you need to use the Threading module, but if you have read earlier chapters this should be no problem:

```python
import asyncio
import tkinter
import threading

count=0
root=None
label1=None

def stopProg(e):
    global root
    root.quit()

def transfertext(e):
    global label1
    global count
    count=count+1
    label1.configure(text=count)

def setupGUI():
    global root,label1
    root=tkinter.Tk()
    button1=tkinter.Button(root,text="Exit")
    button1.pack()
    button1.bind('<Button-1>',stopProg)
    button2=tkinter.Button(root,text="Click Me")
    button2.pack()
    button2.bind('<Button-1>',transfertext)
    label1=tkinter.Label(root,text="nothing to say")
    label1.pack()
```

```
async def tick():
    i=0
    while True:
        i+=1
        print("TICK", i)
        await asyncio.sleep(0.5)

def runasyncio():
    asyncio.run(main())

async def main():
    T2= asyncio.create_task(tick())
    await asyncio.wait((T2,))

setupGUI()
t1=threading.Thread(target=runasyncio,daemon=True)
t1.start()
root.mainloop()
```

Running `tkinter` on the main thread involves nothing new. Running the
`asyncio` event loop on another thread simply requires a function to get the
main coroutine started. After this everything works as before, but we now
have two event loops on two threads. The only subtle point is the way
`daemon = True` means that the `asyncio` thread ends when the main thread
does.

There are some problems with this approach, the main one being the GIL.
The two threads will swap every 5 ms by default unless one of them does
something that suspends its thread. You can include a `time.sleep(0)`
command in the `asyncio` event loop to force it to suspend its thread if you
need the `tkinter` event loop to be more responsive. Another smaller
problem is that now you have to use global variables with locks to pass
information between the two event loops.

Notice that you cannot access the `tkinter` objects from the `asyncio` thread,
but you can use `asyncio.run_coroutine_threadsafe` in the tkinter thread
to run a coroutine on the `asyncio` event loop. For example, to display
`clicked` when a `button` is clicked you can add a call to
`run_coroutine_threadsafe`:

```
async def click():
    print("clicked")

def transfertext(e):
    global label1
    global count
    global loop
    count=count+1
    label1.configure(text=count)
    asyncio.run_coroutine_threadsafe(click(),loop)
```

To make this work we need to supply a reference to the currently running loop:

```
loop = None
async def main():
    global loop
    T2 = asyncio.create_task(tick())
    loop = asyncio.get_running_loop()
    await asyncio.wait((T2,))
```

If you want to increase performance and avoid the problems of the GIL you could run the `asyncio` event loop in a child process, but this would increase the complexity and cost of communicating between the two components of the program.

Subprocesses

Although running functions as child processes using `asyncio` isn't part of the high-level API, running general executables as subprocesses is. This is essentially an asynchronous version of the `subprocess` module described in Chapter 10. What this means is that with only minor modifications you can take what you already know about running subprocesses and apply them to running everything asynchronously. If you are using the `subprocess` module then most of the calls are non-blocking and return immediately to a main thread that continues to execute the calling program. If you use the `asyncio.process` module then the methods are coroutines that return the main thread to the event loop. This simplifies the design of the calling program – it can now use `await` to wait for subprocesses – and other `Tasks` get to run while it is waiting.

The creation of an asynchronous subprocess is very like using `Popen`:

```
asyncio.create_subprocess_exec(program, *args,
        stdin=None, stdout=None, stderr=None, limit=None, **kwds)
```

There is also a coroutine that will create a shell instance and run any shell command using it:

```
asyncio.create_subprocess_shell(cmd, stdin=None, stdout=None,
                                stderr=None, **kwds)
```

The big difference is the way that the *program* and *args* are passed. `Popen` passed the program and parameters as a sequence, usually a list, and here we pass the parameters as individual parameters. For example, the `Popen` call:

```
subprocess.Popen(["dir","/"])
```

becomes:

```
await asyncio.create_subprocess_exec("dir","/")
```

The call returns an `asyncio.Process` object which is an asynchronous version of the `subprocess.Process` object. It has all of the same methods apart from `poll` and it lacks timeouts on `communicate` and `await`. You don't need `poll` because you can just `await` the coroutines and you can use `wait_for` in place of a timeout.

Another difference is that `communicate`, `stdin`, `stdout` and `stderr` all use `StreamWriter` and `StreamReader` rather than a raw `Pipe`. You still assign them to a `Pipe`, but to `asyncio.subprocess.PIPE`, which is a `StreamReader` or a `StreamWriter` depending on data transfer direction. This also means that there is no text mode – both `StreamReader` and `StreamWriter` work in terms of byte sequences.

So the async version of the first example in Chapter 10 is:

```
import asyncio

async def main():
    p =  await asyncio.create_subprocess_exec("dir","/",
                               stdout=asyncio.subprocess.PIPE)
    stdout_data,stderr_data = await p.communicate()
    print(stdout_data)
    print("finished")


asyncio.run(main())
```

Notice that while `main` is awaiting the `communicate` coroutine the main thread is free to service the event loop and hence run other coroutines.

This second example is slightly different when implemented as an async coroutine because there is no text mode. If you set `text = True` in the `create_subprocess_exec` call an error message is displayed indicating that the only allowed setting is `False`.

The two scripts being run are (the first for Linux the second for Windows):

```
#!/bin/sh
echo "user name: "
read name
echo $name

@echo off
echo "User name:"
set /p id=
echo %id%
```

The async version of the program is:

```
import asyncio

async def main():
    p = await asyncio.create_subprocess_exec("./myscript.sh",
        stdout=asyncio.subprocess.PIPE,stdin=asyncio.subprocess.PIPE)

    ans=await p.stdout.readline()
    print("message",ans)
    p.stdin.write(b"mike\n")
    ans= await p.stdout.readline()
    print("message",ans)

asyncio.run(main())
```

Change the name of the script to suit what you have called it and it works for both Windows and Linux.

In this case there is no problem with the final readline as the buffers send the data immediately as a byte stream. As a result there is no need to resort to setting the bufsize to zero and the universal_newlines isn't supported as there is only one type of newline character in a byte stream, i.e. \n.

However, we still have the standard problem of dealing with messages sent to the user that don't end in a newline character. As before, the solution is to use a timeout, but with asyncio we don't have to work hard to implement one. If the scripts are changed to:

(Linux)

```
#!/bin/sh
echo -n "User name: "
read name
echo $name
```

(Windows)

```
@echo off
set /p id= "User name"
echo %id%
```

Now the prompt User name appears on the same line as the user types in the answer and there is no newline to end a readline coroutine. The solution, as previously presented in Chapter 10, is to implement a read with timeout.

As already mentioned a timeout is easy to implement using asyncio:

```
import asyncio

async def main():
    p = await asyncio.create_subprocess_exec("./myscript.sh",
     stdout=asyncio.subprocess.PIPE,stdin=asyncio.subprocess.PIPE)
    T=asyncio.create_task(p.stdout.read(100))
    try:
        done,pending=await asyncio.wait([T],timeout= 0.1)
    except asyncio.TimeoutError:
        pass
    print("message",T.result())
    p.stdin.write(b"mike\n")
    ans= await p.stdout.readline()
    print("message",ans)
    await p.wait()

asyncio.run(main())
```

Notice that we create a Task from the read coroutine and limit the input line length to 100 characters – you can set this higher as it is the timeout that determines when the message is complete. Next we set a timeout of a tenth of a second and as long as the running program sends some data and then pauses we can be sure that it will timeout unless it sends 100 characters in that time. Next we handle the timeout exception and move on to use the result stored in the Task, we don't need to examine done and pending because we know that it is the Task that caused the timeout. The final await ensures the subprocess is complete before the coroutine exits.

If the program you are working with always sends its messages to the user one per line then you can use readline. If it places messages and responses on the same line you need to use read with a timeout. Using asyncio subprocesses makes this much easier.

Summary

- The `asyncio` module makes network connections easy and asynchronous.

- Network communication is via streams – `StreamReader` and `StreamWriter` - which work like more sophisticated `Pipes`.

- Implementing a web client is easy, but there is no high-level function which downloads an HTML page. You have to work with the HTTP protocol.

- The `email` module has many useful functions for working with HTTP.

- Creating an SSL client is a matter of changing a single line in the program.

- Creating a web server is only slightly more difficult in that you have to support multiple potential clients.

- Converting the server to SSL requires the generation and installation of a certificate.

- You can use raw sockets which do not support streams. The only reason for doing this is to implement a custom protocol.

- To convert a blocking synchronous function into a non-blocking asynchronous function all you have to do is run it on another thread and release the original thread to service the event loop.

- The `asyncio` module provides a function that allows you to run a function on another thread asynchronously.

- You can use additional threads to run CPU-bound functions asynchronously.

- There are additional modules that provide asynchronous versions of standard operations, usually by running them on an additional thread.

- A particular problem is coexisting with modules that implement their own event loop such as `tkinter`. There are two approaches – to find an update function which can be called from an `asyncio` event loop or to use a separate thread to run each event loop.

- The `asyncio` module provides a very easy way to run subprocesses without having to worry about blocking the thread or dealing with buffers.

Chapter 14

The Low-Level API

In theory there should be no need to explore the low-level API as the high-level API covered in chapters 12 and 13 with the addition, perhaps, of some extra modules can achieve almost any result. There is, however, a lot to be said for understanding what is going on under the covers and there are some things that are only possible using the low-level API.

The Event Loop

The event loop is the key part of the `asyncio` system. `Tasks` are placed on the event loop and executed one after another. Using the high-level API you don't need worry about creating an event loop as one is created for you automatically. There are four low-level functions which create or obtain the event loop

- `asyncio.get_running_loop()` returns the running event loop.
  If there is no event loop a `RuntimeError` is raised.
- `asyncio.get_event_loop()` returns the current event loop.
  If there isn't an event loop one is created.
- `asyncio.set_event_loop()` sets the event loop as the current loop
- `asyncio.new_event_loop()` create a new event loop

To make use of the event loop you have to use one of its methods:

- `loop.run_forever()` runs the event loop forever
- `loop.stop()` stops the event loop
- `loop.close()` close the event loop
- `loop.is_running()` returns `True` if the event loop is running
- `loop.is_closed()` returns `True` if the event loop is closed

There are also basic methods to schedule awaitables and callbacks:

- `loop.run_until_complete(aw)` runs a `Future`/`Task`/awaitable until complete and returns its result or raises its exception.
  You can call this method multiple times on the same event loop.
- `loop.call_soon(function,args)` adds a *function* to the queue that will be called at the next iteration of the event loop.
  It returns a `Handle` object which can be used to cancel the function.

- ♦ `loop.call_soon_threadsafe(`*`function`*`,`*`args`*`)` as for `call_soon`, but used in another thread
- ♦ `loop.call_later(delay,function,args)` invokes function after the given delay and returns a TimerHandle
- ♦ `loop.call_at(when,function,args)` invokes function at the time given by when and returns a TimerHandle
- ♦ `loop.time()` returns the current time according to the event loop's clock
- ♦ `loop.create_task(coro, args, name=None)` converts the coroutine into a Task and adds it to the event queue.
  This is the lower-level equivalent of asyncio.create_task.
- ♦ `loop.create_future()` creates an asyncio.Future.

Using the Loop

To see how all these functions and methods work the best way is to try out a few simple examples.

Running Functions - Callbacks

The first just runs some standard functions making use of the loop:

```
import asyncio

def myFunction(value):
    print(value)

myLoop = asyncio.new_event_loop()
myLoop.call_later(3,myFunction,43)
t = myLoop.time()+2
myLoop.call_at(t,myFunction,44)
myLoop.call_soon(myFunction,42)

myLoop.call_soon(myFunction,45)
myLoop.run_forever()
```

This, of course, displays:

```
42
45
44
43
```

The functions are called in the order in which they were placed in the queue and according to their delay or starting time.

If you want to schedule a function for a given time of day then you need to compare the `loop.time()` function to the usual clock time given by `time.time()`.

Notice that as these are just functions, usually referred to as "callback functions", there is no way that they can release the thread to return to the event loop to run another function. This isn't asynchronous code, it's more like scheduling synchronous code.

The reason for including the ability to run functions on the event loop is to allow for callbacks. A callback is supposed to be a way to make a connection with some existing code and they should be short, so as not to block the event loop, and they don't return a result. They are generally referred to as "fire and forget". For example, a Future and hence a Task, allows you to add a callback using the high level API:

```
Future.add_done_callback(function)
```

The callback *function* is automatically called when the Future or the Task resolves. This is run at a lower level using the call_soon method.

Tasks

The main way of creating asynchronous code is to use the loop's create_task method, which is identical to the high level function, but with the ability to select which event loop is used, for example:

```
import asyncio

async def myFunction1(value):
    await asyncio.sleep(0)
    print(value)

async def myFunction2(value):
    print(value)
    await asyncio.sleep(0)

myLoop = asyncio.new_event_loop()
T1 = myLoop.create_task(myFunction1(42))
T2 = myLoop.create_task(myFunction2(43))

myLoop.run_forever()
```

This displays:

```
43
42
```

because myFunction1 gives the thread back to the loop before printing its value and this allows myFunction2 to run and to print its value before releasing the main thread.

Notice that you cannot await either T1 or T2 because they are not within an async function – you can only use await within an async function.

The run_forever means that this program never ends. Instead the event loop runs forever waiting for a Task that never arrives. The solution to this problem is to use loop.run_until_complete(*aw*) in place of run_forever:

```
myLoop.run_until_complete(T1)
```

or, more reasonably if you want to be sure that both Tasks complete:

```
myLoop.run_until_complete(asyncio.wait([T1,T2]))
```

Use run_until if you want the event loop to stop as soon as an awaitable is resolved. You could also use:

```
myLoop.run_until_complete(T1)
myLoop.run_until_complete(T2)
```

Alternative Event Loops

You can create as many event loops as you like, but there is little point in doing so on the same thread. A single event loop is perfectly capable of managing thousands of Task objects of different types and having more than one event loop has no obvious advantage. However, you may want to structure your application so that the event loop is running on a thread separate from the main thread. While the GIL is in force there is no performance gain in doing this as only one Python thread can be running at any given time. The only reason for doing this is for program structure.

Creating an event loop on another thread using low-level API functions is very easy:

```
myLoop=None
def myThreadLoop():
 global myLoop
 myLoop = asyncio.new_event_loop()
 T1=myLoop.create_task(myFunction1(42))
 T2=myLoop.create_task(myFunction2(43))
 myLoop.run_forever()

t=threading.Thread(target=myThreadLoop)
t.start()
t.join()
```

You can also do the same job using the high-level API, see **Working With Other Event Loops – Tkinter** in the previous chapter.

The setup and use of the event loop is exactly the same as working in the main thread. The only difference is that it is now in a function that is run on another thread. Notice the join means that the program never ends as the event loop runs forever.

The problems start when you try to add a Task from the main thread – or any thread other than the one that the created the event loop. The solution is to use the call_soon_threadsafe function to run a callback that creates the

Task on the original thread. Notice you cannot use `call_soon_threadsafe` to add a coroutine to the event queue. The high-level API way of doing this using `asyncio.run_coroutine_threadsafe` is described in the previous chapter. The low-level way is to create a function that adds a Task and then run this on the other thread:

```
def myMakeTask(cor,value):
    loop=asyncio.get_running_loop()
    loop.create_task(cor(value))
```

This runs a general coroutine which accepts a single value. You could easily generalize this to any number of parameters. Using it you can add a Task to the event loop in the other thread using:

```
myLoop.call_soon_threadsafe(myMakeTask,myFunction1,44)
```

It is neater to package these two actions into a single `myMakeTask` function which does the whole job:

```
def myMakeTask(loop,cor,value):
    loop.call_soon_threadsafe(lambda: loop.create_task(cor(value)))
```

Putting all this together gives:

```
import asyncio
import threading
import time

def myMakeTask(loop,cor,value):
    loop.call_soon_threadsafe(lambda: loop.create_task(cor(value)))

async def myFunction1(value):
    await asyncio.sleep(0)
    print(value)

async def myFunction2(value):
    print(value)
    await asyncio.sleep(0)

myLoop=None
def myThreadLoop():
    global myLoop
    myLoop = asyncio.new_event_loop()
    T1=myLoop.create_task(myFunction1(42))
    T2=myLoop.create_task(myFunction2(43))
    myLoop.run_forever()

t=threading.Thread(target=myThreadLoop)
t.start()
time.sleep(0)
while not myLoop:
    pass
myMakeTask(myLoop,myFunction1,44)
t.join()
```

Notice that we need a `time.sleep` call to allow the new thread to run and we need to test `myLoop` to make sure that the thread has finished setting things up.

A final complication is that if the main thread needs to wait it cannot use an asyncio Future, it has to use a `concurrent.futures` Future. The reason is that asyncio isn't thread-safe but `concurrent.futures` mostly is. The solution is to use a `concurrent.futures` Future as the shared object.

Executing Tasks in Processes

asyncio is built on top of `concurrent.futures` and you can make use of its executors. We have already seen the use of to_thread to run a function asynchronously in a single thread. This provides an advantage for I/O-bound functions, but, because of the GIL, not for CPU-bound functions. Unfortunately at the time of writing there is no simple asyncio function such as to_thread that will run a function on a process. The good news is that there is a low-level API to do the job and it is easy to use and, in the spirit of `concurrent.futures`, it works in the same way for threads and processes:

```
loop.run_in_executor(executor, func, args)
```

runs the function with the specified arguments on the *executor* provided. It returns an awaitable which eventually resolves to the result of the function or an exception. So all we have to do is create a process executor and use the run_in_executor function, for example:

```
import asyncio
import concurrent.futures


def myFunction1(value):
    print(value)
    return value

if __name__ == '__main__':
    pool = concurrent.futures.ProcessPoolExecutor()
    myLoop = asyncio.new_event_loop()

    T1 = myLoop.run_in_executor(pool, myFunction1, 42)
    T2 = myLoop.run_in_executor(pool, myFunction1, 43)

    myLoop.run_until_complete(asyncio.wait([T1, T2]))
    print(T1.result())
    print(T2.result())
    pool.shutdown()
```

This is very simple and you can use it to run the functions in threads by changing the `ProcessPoolExecutor` to a `ThreadPoolExecutor`. Notice that as the main program isn't a coroutine we cannot use `await` directly, but `run_until_complete` is a good substitute. As executors can be used as context managers you could use `with`.

You can code the same thing using a main coroutine and running everything asynchronously, but as you can see you don't have to. What is important is that the two functions are run on separate processes which might be running at the same time on two different cores of the machine. At the same time the main thread is free to process the event loop.

Computing Pi With asyncio

As our function to compute pi is CPU-bound, so far we haven't bothered to implement it using `asyncio`, but now that we have a way to run a function as a process it is worth it:

```
import asyncio
import concurrent.futures
import time


def myPi(m,n):
    pi=0
    for k in range(m,n+1):
        s= 1 if k%2 else -1
        pi += s / (2 * k - 1)
    return pi*4

if __name__ == '__main__':
    pool=concurrent.futures.ProcessPoolExecutor()

    myLoop = asyncio.new_event_loop()

    N=10000000
    with concurrent.futures.ProcessPoolExecutor() as pool:
        t1=time.perf_counter()
        T1=myLoop.run_in_executor(pool,myPi,1,N//2)
        T2=myLoop.run_in_executor(pool,myPi,N//2+1,N)
        myLoop.run_until_complete(asyncio.wait([T1,T2]))
        t2=time.perf_counter()

    PI=T1.result()
    PI +=T2.result()
    print((t2-t1)*1000)
    print(PI)
```

This is very like the earlier version using the process pool, but notice that we now don't have to worry about creating a main program as `asyncio` runs a function in isolation and does not need a complete program plus global variables. As before, the main thread is free to run any `Task` that is in the event loop queue while the processes are running. This version takes about the same time as the pure process pool version in Chapter 8 and half the time that the thread pool version takes.

Network Functions

As one of the main motivations for async is network communications you might expect there to be a lot of low-level API calls dealing with TCP and similar networking. Most of these, however, are simply lower-level versions of functions we have already encountered. What is also true is that they mainly support a great many parameters to control how the connection operates. Dealing with all of these would take us too far into networking protocols and away from the main topic of this book.

The low-level API functions, the first four of which deal with client connections and servers, are:

- `await loop.create_connection()` opens a TCP connection and is an extended form of `open_connection`
- `await loop.create_server()` creates a TCP server and is an extended form of `start_server`
- `await loop.create_unix_connection()` opens a Unix socket connection and is an extended form of `open_unix_connection`
- `await loop.create_unix_server()` creates a Unix socket server and is an extended form of `start_unix_server`

Once you have a connection the you need:

- `await loop.connect_accepted_socket()` wraps a streaming socket into a (*transport, protocol*) tuple
  This is used to allow `asyncio` to work with sockets that are opened by a socket server outside of `asyncio`. That is, it wraps a connection to a client already established by a non-asyncio server.
- `await loop.create_datagram_endpoint()` opens a datagram (UDP) connection
  UDP is the simpler method of communication that you can use when TCP is more than you require. If you require UDP this is the function to use as there is no high-level function for it.
- `await loop.sendfile()` sends a file over a transport
  This is another low-level function that you have to use because there is no high-level equivalent. Of course you can always use a stream to read and send a file.
- `await loop.start_tls()` upgrades an existing connection to TLS
  This adds certificate based encryption to an existing connection. It is mostly used in email transport.

There are also two low-level functions that work with pipes:

- ◆ await loop.connect_read_pipe() wraps the read end of a pipe into a(*transport, protocol*) tuple
- ◆ await loop.connect_write_pipe() wraps the write end of a pipe into a (*transport, protocol*) tuple.

Transports and Protocols

Most of Python's network functions make use of transports and protocols. Transports are about sending and receiving data and protocols are about the finer details such as buffering and opening and closing connections. The two work together to make data transfer possible. Python defines two base classes, BaseTransport and BaseProtocol from which all other transport and protocol classes are derived. A set of standard classes are provided for common connection types:

- ◆ BaseTransport
- ◆ Transport
- ◆ ReadTransport WriteTransport
- ◆ DatagramTransport
- ◆ SubprocessTransport

- ◆ BaseProtocol
- ◆ Protocol
- ◆ BufferedProtocol
- ◆ DatagramProtocol
- ◆ SubprocessProtocol

In most cases you can simply make use of these in the appropriate situation, but if you need something additional you can derive your own classes.

BaseTransport provides the following methods:

- ◆ close()   closes the transport
- ◆ is_closing()   True if the transport is closing
- ◆ get_extra_info()   gets information about the connection

There are also two methods that set and get the associated protocol object:

- ◆ set_protocol(*protocol*)
- ◆ get_protocol()

The derived classes have these methods and add extra methods according to the type of connection. For example, the UDP transport DatagramProtocol also has:

- ◆ sendto(*data*, addr = None) sends *data* to the client specified by addr
- ◆ abort() closes the transport immediately without waiting for operations to complete

The BaseProtocol provides:

- ◆ connection_made(transport) - called when the connection is made It can be customized to store details of the transport.

- ◆ connection_lost(*exception*) - called when the connection is lost If there is no exception the parameter is None.

Other protocol classes add additional methods appropriate for the type of connection. For example the UDP protocol `DatagramProtocol` has two additional methods:

- `datagram_received(data, addr)` - called when a datagram is received where *data* is a `bytes` object and *addr* is the address of the machine that sent the data
- `error_received(err)` - called when a send or receive operation raises the OSError specified by *err*

The details of the various connection types and their transports and protocols are too numerous to go into here, but the only one that isn't covered by a high-level API is the UDP or datagram protocol and this also provides a good example of how to use these low level facilities.

A UDP Server

The UDP protocol is very different from the more usual TCP connection. UDP is very basic. There is no error correction and no guarantee that datagrams will arrive in the order they were sent. All you get is a checksum error detection mechanism that lets you detect any corruption in the data the datagram is carrying. Using IPv4 the data in a datagram is limited to 65,507 bytes, but this limit can be exceeded using IPv6. UDP can also broadcast datagrams simultaneously to as many clients as care to receive them.

After this description you may be wondering why anyone would consider using UDP in preference to TCP. The simple answer is speed. There are few overheads to UDP and it is ideal for sending fast packets of data, as long as packet loss and order don't matter or can be engineered to not matter.

All we have to do to create a UDP server, i.e. a program that can send datagrams, is open a `datagram_endpoint` and the transport's `sendto` to send some data to a specific IP address:

```
import asyncio

async def main():
    loop = asyncio.get_running_loop()
    transport, protocol = await loop.create_datagram_endpoint(
                             lambda: asyncio.DatagramProtocol(),
                             local_addr=("192.168.253.20",8080))

    data=b"Hello UDP World"
    transport.sendto(data,addr=("192.168.253.14",8080))
    transport.close()

asyncio.run(main())
```

In this case we can simply use the `DatagramProtocol` without any changes. The IP address assigned to `local_addr` is the address and port on the local machine that is used to send the datagrams. The IP address used in the `sendto` is the address of the machine the datagram is sent to, i.e. the remote machine. The port used, 8080, isn't typically used for UDP, but it has a higher probability of working through firewalls. If this program doesn't work on a particular machine then it is almost certain that it is a firewall rule that is blocking it or the lack of a rule to allow it.

A UDP Client

The obvious thing to do is to write a client that can receive the datagram sent by the previous example. Many examples of using UDP do so on a single machine, passing the datagram between two programs via the local loopback connection. This usually works, but it doesn't make clear the distinction between client and server. In this case it is assumed that the client is running on a different machine that is reachable by the server running on another machine.

The UDP Client is different from the server because we have to create our own Transport class so as to override the `datagram_received` which is called when there is a datagram to process.

```
import asyncio
class ClientDatagramProtocol(asyncio.DatagramProtocol):
    def datagram_received(self, data, addr):
        message = data.decode("utf8")
        print("Received",message,"from", addr)

async def main():
    loop = asyncio.get_running_loop()
    transport, protocol = await loop.create_datagram_endpoint(
            lambda: ClientDatagramProtocol(),
                    local_addr=('192.168.253.14', 8080))
    await asyncio.sleep(1000)
    transport.close()

asyncio.run(main())
```

As this is just an example, the event loop is left running for 1000 seconds and will respond to incoming datagrams for this time. Unlike TCP and other protocols, there is no start or end of the connection. The server can send datagrams at any time and the client can either be ready to read them or it can just ignore them. The address used for `local_address` is the address of the machine the client is running on. Again the port is 8080 to reduce the chance of firewall problems.

If you run this particular client on the machine with the correct IP address and the server on a machine with the IP it is using then when the server sends a datagram you will see:

```
Received 'Hello UDP World' from ('192.168.253.20', 8080)
```

There is no limit on the number of datagrams that can be received, but as soon as the 1000 seconds is up the client stops working. If you don't see the message when both are running then the only possible reasons are that you are using the wrong IP addresses – check the IP address of both the client and the server machines or, and this is more likely, the firewall on the client is stopping the datagrams arriving.

Broadcast UDP

You can use UDP to send a datagram to all of the machines on the network. Whether this is a good idea or not is debatable. IPv6 has abandoned broadcast UDP in favor of multicasting, which is just as simple from the program point of view, but requires the network to be set up to use it and a router or managed switch that supports it. In short broadcasting is simple, but not supported by IPv6.

Most of the examples of UDP broadcasting make use of raw access to sockets. This isn't necessary. You can set the server given earlier to broadcast with just a few small changes. First you need to change the `create_datagram_endpoint` statement:

```
transport, protocol = await loop.create_datagram_endpoint(
        lambda: asyncio.DatagramProtocol(),
        local_addr=("192.168.253.20",8080),allow_broadcast=True)
```

That is add `allow_broadcast=True`. You don't need to change the IP address that the socket is bound to. The only other change is to the `sendto` call:

```
transport.sendto(data,addr=("192.168.253.255",8080))
```

The IP address has to be in the same subnet, i.e. 192.168.253.x in this case, but the final octet has to be 255. Nothing else has to change and the UDP client works as it did, but now any machine running it will receive the same datagram.

Sockets

Underlying all of the `asyncio` networking is the socket. This is a low-level bidirectional network connection and if you really need to you can work with sockets directly. Most of the time this isn't necessary as `asyncio` provides much better ways of doing the same job. If you want to go the whole way back to using raw sockets then you need to use the `socket` module as well as `asyncio`. Creating a socket using the `socket` module can be complicated. A much simpler solution is to use the `transport` class, `transport.get_extra_info`, to return the underlying socket and then use the socket functions that `asyncio` provides:

♦ `await loop.sock_recv(socket, n)` receives n bytes of data from the socket and returns the data as the result of a `Task`

♦ `await loop.sock_recv_into(socket, buffer)` receives data from socket into `buffer` and returns the number of bytes as the result of a `Task`

♦ `await loop.sock_sendall(socket, buffer)` sends all data in `buffer` to socket and returns number of bytes as result of `Task`

♦ `await loop.sock_connect(socket, address)` connects the `socket` to the `address` ready to send data

♦ `await loop.sock_accept(socket)` starts the socket accepting connections
The returned result is a tuple (*con*, *address*) with *con* being a new socket that can be used to communicate with the client and *address* the address of the client.

♦ `await loop.sock_sendfile(socket, file, offset = 0,`
`                             count = None,fallback = True)`
sends a `file` over the `socket`

For example the UDP server can be written using socket functions as:

```
import asyncio

async def main():
    loop = asyncio.get_running_loop()
    transport, protocol = await loop.create_datagram_endpoint(
        lambda: asyncio.DatagramProtocol(),
        local_addr=("192.168.253.20",8080),allow_broadcast=True)
    sock = transport.get_extra_info('socket')
    print(sock)
    data=b"Hello UDP World"
    await loop.sock_connect(sock,("192.168.253.255",8080))
    await loop.sock_sendall(sock,data)
    transport.close()

asyncio.run(main())
```

If you really need to create a socket directly then you need to use the socket module:

```
import asyncio
import socket

async def main():
    loop = asyncio.get_running_loop()

    sock = socket.socket(socket.AF_INET, socket.SOCK_DGRAM)
    sock.setsockopt(socket.SOL_SOCKET, socket.SO_BROADCAST, 1)

    data=b"Hello UDP World"
    await loop.sock_connect(sock,("192.168.253.255",8080))
    await loop.sock_sendall(sock,data)

asyncio.run(main())
```

Notice that you have to set `socket.SO_BROADCAST` to get permission to send a broadcast packet.

Event Loop Implementation

In most cases you don't need to delve into how the event loop is actually implemented, but knowing how things work can make it easier to reason when things go wrong. The basic idea of an event loop is fairly simple. A queue of tasks is maintained and tasks are executed in order by the main thread. When the main thread is released by a `Task` completing then it starts to run the event loop and finds another `Task` to run. This continues until the event loop queue is empty.

Of course, not all tasks in the event loop queue are ready to be run – some are waiting for I/O to complete. The real question is how does the event loop know when a `Task` changes from "waiting" to "ready"? The whole idea depends on something happening independent of the main thread while the `Task` is waiting. That is, if a `Task` is waiting for some data to be received then that process has to be implemented in such a way that the main thread isn't involved. If it was then the whole event loop would be stalled. You can think of this, very roughly, as "*something going on somewhere else*" while a `Task` is waiting. Notice that this could be another thread dealing with the "*something*". As already explained in Chapter 13, a CPU-bound `Task` can be handled on the event loop as long as it is run on a separate thread. From the point of view of the event loop, the `Task` is suspended and waiting for the other thread to complete the `Task`. When the other thread finishes running the `Task` it informs the event loop that the `Task` is no longer waiting and the event loop returns any results as part of a future-like object to the calling coroutine.

When it comes to real I/O operations, hardware and operating system facilities fill the role of "*something happening elsewhere*". For example, hardware can be left to read data from the Internet and signal to the operating system, using an interrupt, that the data is ready for the software to process. It is this handing off of I/O tasks to the hardware and the operating system that allows the main thread to process the event loop queue and hence get on with useful work. However, we still have the problem of how the event loop is informed that a Task is no longer waiting and is now ready to run?

There are two basic mechanisms for waiting on I/O – selectors in Unix/Linux and Windows and the I/O Completion Port IOCP in Windows – and there is an event loop implementation for each:

 ◆ `class asyncio.SelectorEventLoop` makes use of the `selectors` module
 ◆ `class asyncio.ProactorEventLoop` implements an event loop for IOCP under Windows

`SelectorEventLoop` is the default under Unix/Linux and `ProactorEventLoop` is the default for Windows.

The `SelectorEventLoop` is based on the use of the Linux/Unix `select` system call. This can be given a list of file descriptors and a list of events that you want to wait on. When a call to `select` is made it blocks until at least one of the file descriptors has a specified event, e.g. data is ready, it then returns with a list of file descriptors that have the specified events. Notice that this is a blocking call and therefore to keep things running it has to be called on a thread that isn't the main thread. There are a number of different variations on `select`, including `poll` and `epoll`, and the `selectors` module uses the best available.

Under Linux/Unix you can use `select` to wait on file descriptors that correspond to sockets or pipes. Under Windows you can only wait on file descriptors that correspond to sockets. You can't use `select` to wait on file descriptors that correspond to standard files on any system.

The `ProactorEventLoop` only works on Windows. The IOCP mechanism provides the same facilities as `select` but in an easier-to-use and more efficient form. An I/O process creates a completion port which has a queue that allows threads to register an interest in receiving notification of an event. A single thread can perform the same function as in the `select` case by calling `getQueuedCompletionStatus`, which blocks until a completion packet is available in the queue. In principle, the IOCP can provide asynchronous operations on standard files as well as pipes and sockets, but currently this isn't supported.

What Makes a Good Async Operation?

The key idea is that what the event loop can support as an asynchronous operation all depends on how the operation can be run without blocking the main thread and how the operation can tell the main thread that it is ready to run on it. We have seen that the solution to the first problem is to run the operation on its own thread. Of course, this isn't really an advantage if the majority of the operations have to be run in this way. This is essentially equivalent to multi-threading the program and you might as well give up the single-thread asyncio approach.

If only a small number of the Task objects need a separate thread then it is still worth using asyncio. For example, the network operations involving sockets and pipes only need a single extra thread to make all such operations asynchronous. A single thread can monitor all of the I/O operations in progress and, what is more, most of the time it is suspended. This isn't a great deal of overhead compared to a single-threaded system.

So ideally converting a synchronous operation to asynchronous using a thread should have the following characteristics. It should be possible to handle all of the operations with a small number of threads, much fewer than one per operation. The monitoring thread should also spend most of its time suspended, only to be woken up when the operation needs attention from the main thread.

This makes any CPU-bound operation a bad candidate for conversion using a thread unless it is to fit into an existing, mostly asynchronous, program. Converting more general event handling operations is more promising. If you have a function which checks a set of devices, temperature sensors say, then a single thread could be set up to poll them all every so often and be suspended between measurements. Any time a thread is mostly waiting for something to happen you have an opportunity to convert its treatment from synchronous to asynchronous, but in the final analysis it all depends on being able to make use of the waiting time to do something else.

Summary

- You can avoid the use of the low-level API in nearly all cases apart from some unusual and advanced applications.

- Many tutorials and examples make use of both the high- and low-level APIs because of the way that the `asyncio` module was slowly upgraded.

- The majority of the low-level API is concerned with setting up and working with the event loop.

- You can add callbacks and `Tasks` to the event loop from the current thread or a different one. Most of these methods have high- level equivalents.

- The low-level API has methods to allow you to run a `Task` in both threads and process, whereas the high-level API only supports threads.

- The set of low-level network functions mostly duplicate those of the high-level API, but there are extra functions that let you send and receive UDP protocol.

- Network functions make use of the idea of a transport and a protocol.

- An even lower-level set of network functions lets you work with the sockets that underlie all network connections.

- Event loops need some way of being informed when a `Task` is ready to run. Under Linux/Unix this is via the `selectors` module which uses an additional thread to wait for network operations to complete. Under Windows the I/O Completion Port does the same job in more or less the same way.

- The ideal asynchronous operation is one that spends most of its time waiting for something to happen and offers an easy way to signal when it is ready to run. Ideally a single monitoring thread should be capable of monitoring the state of multiple tasks while itself being suspended.

Appendix I

Python in Visual Studio Code

There are many good IDEs (Integrated Development Environment) available for Python, but VS Code (Visual Studio Code) has the advantage that it works with many different languages.

As VS Code is under constant development, it is probably better to consult its website to find the latest instructions on how to install it and the various components. What is important is to know which components you need to install.

First install the up-to-date stable version of Visual Studio Code appropriate for the platform you are using. It works under Windows, Debian and Mac OS. You can also find versions for other operating systems, but usually without installers.

Next you need to install the Python extension. Without it you cannot run or debug Python programs.

You probably already have Python 3 installed, but if not download and install the latest version. To check that you have Python correctly installed use:

`python3 —version` under Linux
`py -3 —version`   under Windows

You should see the latest version you installed, if not you have to fix this problem before moving on.

When you run VS Code it should find the Python environment and select it. Unfortunately this sometimes isn't the Python you were looking for. To make 100% sure you are using the correct version of Python open the Command Palette (`Ctrl+Shift+P`) and select `Python Select Interpreter`. This will produce a list of all the Python interpreters installed and you can select the one you want to use:

The interpreter you select will be stored in the current folder you are working with.

When you open the File Explorer you will see a list of folders stored in your home folder on the host machine. Create a new folder suitable for storing your Python programs and create a file called `Hello.py` in it. The new file will open in the editor and you can type in:

```
print("Hello World")
```

Next select `Run, Run Without Debugging` and, if asked for the run configuration, select the `Current Python file`. You should see `Hello World` appear in the console at the bottom of the window. You can do the same with `Run,Start Debugging` to run a debug session. The Run and Debug window is the way you will most often run a Python program.

From here on you can learn about Visual Studio Code and slowly customize it to make your work easier.

Index

292

Related Titles by Mike James

Programmer's Python:
Everything is an Object, Second Edition
ISBN: 978-1871962741

This book, the first in the "Something Completely Different series, sets out to explain the deeper logic in the approach that Python 3 takes to classes and objects. The subject is roughly speaking everything to do with the way Python implements objects. That is, in order of sophistication: metaclass, class, object, attribute, and all the other facilities such as functions, methods and "magic methods" that Python uses to make it all work.

Programmer's Python: Everything is Data
Something Completely Different
ISBN: 978-1871962598

Following the same philosophy, this book approaches data in a distinctly Pythonic way. What we have in Python are data objects that are very usable and very extensible. From the unlimited precision integers, referred to as bignums, through the choice of a list to play the role of the array, to the availability of the dictionary as a built-in data type, Python has powerful special features. Complete chapters are devoted on Boolean logic, dates and times, regular expressions, bit manipulation, files, pickle and using ctypes.

Both these books are fairly advanced in the sense that you are expected to know basic Python. However, the ideas are explained using the simplest examples possible so as long as you can write a Python program, and you have an idea what object-oriented programming is about, it should all be straightforward.

Other books by Mike James

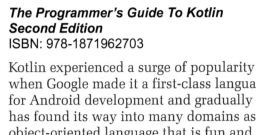

The Programmer's Guide To Kotlin
Second Edition
ISBN: 978-1871962703

Kotlin experienced a surge of popularity when Google made it a first-class language for Android development and gradually it has found its way into many domains as an object-oriented language that is fun and flexible in its approach. It is an interesting language because it is 100% runtime compatible with Java while being easier to use. Using Kotlin will make programming simpler and your programs better, and this is why you need to learn Kotlin.

Deep C#: Dive Into Modern C#
ISBN: 978-1871962710

Over two decades C# has achieved the status of a modern, general-purpose, cross-platform language that still has an edge when it comes to Windows programming. This book provides a "deep dive" into various topics that are important or central to the language at a level that will suit the majority of C# programmers. Not everything will be new to any given reader, but the intention is, by being to be thought-provoking, to give developers confidence to exploit C#'s wide range of features.

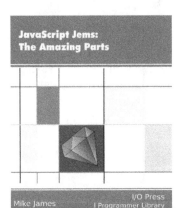

JavaScript Jems: The Amazing Parts
ISBN: 978-1871962420

This book is a "meditation" on the features that make JavaScript stand apart from other languages and make it special in terms of having admirable qualities. Each of the twenty short chapters is intended to be an enjoyable read for any JavaScript programmer by showing the language in a new light.

The Programmer's Guide To Theory:
Great ideas explained
ISBN: 978-1871962437

Computer science, specifically the theory of computation, deserves to be better known even among non-computer scientists. This book is targeted at a wide audience, It is full of profound thoughts and ideas, and contains some paradoxes that reveal the limits of human knowledge. It provides ways to reason about information and randomness that are understandable without the need to resort to abstract math.

This is not an academic textbook but could be the precursor to reading an academic textbook.

The Trick Of The Mind:
Programming and Computational Thought
ISBN: 978-1871962727

Programmers think differently from non-programmers, they see and solve problems in a way that the rest of the world doesn't. This book takes programming concepts and explains what the skill involves and how a programmer goes about it. In each case it looks at how we convert a dynamic process into a static text that can be understood by other programmers and put into action by a computer. If you're a programmer, this book will give you a clearer understanding of what you do so you value it even more.

Written to be easily understood and to introduce and explain the jargon of programming rather than intimidate, this book is for both non-programmers and programmers. Knowing even a bit about programming makes you view the world in a different, and better, way and having read this book you will appreciate the deeper ideas that underpin what programmers do.

Mike James has also co-authored books on using Python to program the Raspberry Pi and Pico

Raspberry Pi IoT in Python With GPIO Zero
ISBN: 978-1871962666

Python is an excellent language to learn about the IoT or physical computing. It might not be as fast as C, but it is much easier to use for complex data processing. The GPIO Zero library is the official way to use Python with the GPIO and other devices. This book looks at how to use it to interface the Raspberry Pi 4 and Raspberry Pi Zero to IoT devices and at how it works so that you can extend it to custom devices. Studying GPIO Zero is also a great way to improve your Python.

Raspberry Pi IoT in Python With Linux Drivers
ISBN: 978-1871962659

If you opt to use Linux drivers to connect the Raspberry Pi to external devices then Python becomes a good choice, as speed of execution is no longer a big issue. This book explains how to use Python to connect to and control external devices with the Raspberry Pi 4 and Raspberry Pi Zero using the standard Linux drivers.

Programming The Raspberry Pi Pico in Python
ISBN: 978-1871962697

This book explains the many reasons for wanting to use MicroPython with the Raspberry Pi Pico, not least of which is the fact that it is simpler and easier to use. This makes it ideal for prototyping and education. It is slower than using C and programs use more memory, but sometimes this is a worthwhile trade off to get the sophistication of a higher-level language. What is surprising is how much you can do with Python plus I2C, SPI, PWM and PIO.

Also in the I Programmer Library

JavaScript Async: Events, Callbacks, Promises and Async Await
ISBN: 978-1871962567

Asynchronous programming is essential to the modern web and at last JavaScript programmers have the tools to do the job – the Promise object and the async and await commands. These are so elegant in their design that you need to know about them if only to be impressed. While async and await make asynchronous code as easy to use as synchronous code there are a lot of subtle things going on and to really master the situation you need to know about Promises and you need to know how the JavaScript dispatch queue works.

Working with async can be confusing and disorienting, but by combining code examples and lucid explanations Ian Elliot presents a coherent explanation. If you want to work with JavaScript async read this book first.

Applying C For The IoT With Linux
ISBN: 978-1871962611

If you do any coding in C that interacts with hardware, this book brings together low-level, hardware-oriented and often hardware-specific information. It starts by looking at how programs work with user-mode Linux. When working with hardware, arithmetic cannot be ignored, so separate chapters are devoted to integer, fixed-point and floating-point arithmetic. It goes on to the pseudo file system, memory-mapped files and sockets as a general-purpose way of communicating over networks and similar infrastructure and continues by looking at multitasking, locking, using mutex and condition variables, and scheduling. Later chapters cover managing cores and C11's atomics, memory models and barriers and it rounds out with a short look at how to mix assembler with C.

Fundamental C: Getting Closer To The Machine
ISBN: 978-1871962604

At an introductory level, this book explores C from the point of view of low-level programming and keeps close to the hardware. It covers addresses, pointers, and how things are represented using binary and emphasizes the important idea is that everything is a bit pattern. It covers installing an IDE and GCC before writing a Hello World program and then presents the building blocks of any program - variables, assignment and expressions, flow of control using conditionals and loops.

When programming in C you need to think about the way data is represented, and this book emphasizes the idea of modifying how a bit pattern is treated using type punning and unions and tackles the topic of undefined behavior, which is ignored in many books on C. A particular feature of the book is the way C code is illustrated by the assembly language it generates. This helps you understand why C is the way it is. And the way it was always intended to be written - close to the metal.

Raspberry Pi IoT in C, Second Edition
ISBN: 978-1871962635

In Raspberry Pi IoT in C you will find a practical approach to understanding electronic circuits and datasheets and translating this to code, specifically using the C programming language. The main reason for choosing C is speed, a crucial factor when you are writing programs to communicate with the outside world. If you are familiar with another programming language, C shouldn't be hard to pick up. This second edition focuses mainly on the Pi 4 and the Pi Zero.

The main idea in this book is to not simply install a driver, but to work directly with the hardware using the Raspberry Pi's GPIO (General Purpose Input Output) to connect with off-the-shelf sensors. It explains how to use its standard output with custom protocols, including an in-depth exposition of the one-wire bus. You will also discover how to put the Internet into the IoT using sockets.

www.ingramcontent.com/pod-product-compliance
Lightning Source LLC
LaVergne TN
LVHW062308060326
832902LV00013B/2096